Heiman, J. D.
MTV's now what?! : a
guide to jobs, money, an
c1996.
3330500 53345
ji   01/24/08

D0400314

MTV's NOW WHAT?!

MUSIC TELEVISION®

A GUIDE TO JOBS, MONEY, AND THE REAL WORLD

By J. D. Heiman

MTV BOOKS

SANTA CLARA COUNTY LIBRARY

3 3305 00753 8345

This publication contains the opinions and ideas of its author and is designed to provide useful advice in regard to the subject matter covered. It is sold with the understanding that the author and publisher are not engaged in rendering legal or other professional services in this publication. Laws vary from state to state, and if the reader requires expert assistance or legal advice, a competent professional should be consulted.

In addition, statements made by the author regarding certain products, services and organizations are based on the author's research, and do not constitute an endorsement of any product, service or organization by the author, publisher or MTV, each of whom specifically disclaim any responsibility for any liability, loss or risk, personal or otherwise, which is incurred as a consequence, directly or indirectly, of the use and application of any of the contents of this book or any of the products, services or organizations mentioned herein.

Rankings from PLACES RATED ALMANAC, Rev. Edn. by David Savageau and Richard Boyer. Copyright © 1993 by Simon & Schuster Inc. Copyright © 1989. Used by permission of MacMillan General Reference USA, a Division of Simon & Schuster Inc.

An *Original* Publication of MTV Books/Pocket Books

POCKET BOOKS, a division of Simon & Schuster Inc.
1230 Avenue of the Americas, New York, NY 10020

Copyright © 1996 by MTV Networks. All rights reserved. MTV: Music Television and all related titles, logos, and characters are trademarks of MTV Networks, a division of Viacom International Inc.

Thanks at Pocket Books to: Lynda Castillo, Gina Centrello, Amy Einhorn, Joann Foster, Leslie Jones, Greer Kessel, Donna O'Neill, Donna Ruvituso, Kathleen Stahl, Kara Welsh and Irene Yuss.

And at MTV to: Eric Blazak, Juli Davidson, Pete Demas, Gwen Lipsky, Elizabeth Mahaffey, Robin Silverman, Donald Silvey and Van Toffler.

And special thanks to Deb Schuler and Carol Bobolts and everyone at Red Herring, and Jefferson Spady.

All rights reserved, including the right to reproduce this book or portions thereof in any form whatsoever. For information address Pocket Books, 1230 Avenue of the Americas, New York, NY 10020

ISBN: 0-671-00202-3

First MTV Books/Pocket Books trade paperback printing June 1996

10 9 8 7 6 5 4 3 2 1

POCKET and colophon are registered trademarks of Simon & Schuster Inc.

Design: Red Herring Design

Printed in U.S.A.

The sale of this book without its cover is unauthorized. If you purchased this book without a cover, you should be aware that it was reported to the publisher as "unsold and destroyed." Neither the author nor the publisher has received payment for the sale of this "stripped book."

CONTENTS

INTRODUCTION

Somehow, it happened.

Yesterday you were riding a Big Wheel, today you are supposed to know what you want to do with the rest of your life. Just like that? You don't even know where to begin. Better to crawl back in bed, sleep until three in the afternoon, then finish off the day eating Cap'n Crunch out of a dirty bowl watching *Geraldo.*

Hey, not a bad way to kill a week, but eventually it gets a wee bit stale. When it does, you're going to have to sort out exactly what your parents have been doing all these years while you've been cutting class.

Okay, you haven't been *that* out of it. There's plenty about life after school you may have sorted out already. Like the fact that it's good to iron a shirt before you go to an interview, for instance. Gold star for you.

But the little things, the scads of tiny details that go into landing a job, going to work every day, paying taxes, budgeting your income, and finding a place to live—well, nobody bothered to explain it all. And just thinking about getting started on deciphering a whole new set of rules is sometimes more than just a little nauseating. In fact, it can be pretty terrifying.

No argument here.

This book will help you nail all those little details, and then some. Here's what it won't do. It's *not* going to say that the transition from grabbing your diploma to being a solid citizen is a fabulous, spiritual Zen Odyssey. It won't list twelve guaranteed steps to a good job, financial independence, and your own infomercial. And relax. we aren't going to haul out loads of depressing examples of young people who made their first billion, started their own human rights organization, and directed their first feature film all by the age of 21.

We figure you've seen books like those around, and they pretty much made you want to pursue the *Geraldo*/Cap'n Crunch method of life planning.

One thing is certain. You have every right to feel stressed out. Getting a life after you grab your diploma is demanding *work*.

And what makes it even harder is that your preparation for your first steps into the job market has probably been spotty at best. You may come straight from the hallowed halls of your alma mater loaded down with debt, up to your temples in anxiety, and feeling absolutely, positively clueless. You may be biting your nails, throwing back a sea of black coffee, frantically searching for answers that don't seem to come.

Now take a deep breath, grasshopper. Here's the most important advice anybody can give you at this point:

You will get through this.

Sure, you'll make mistakes, and call up your mother and cry about the fact that you have no direction, that water is pouring straight down from the apartment upstairs into your bed, and your credit card company has called a hit man out on you.

But just the same, you'll spit out all the grit that's crept into your salad days and find your way. And you'll have *fun*, too.

This book is designed to help you accomplish both these objectives. We did our research and spoke to the so-called experts— career counselors, educators, employers, various and sundry gurus of this and that. But more important, this book is filled with advice from young people who have just crossed the divide between school and work, or are muddling their way through it.

The tips that follow will help dispel some of the bigger clouds of confusion swirling around your poor noggin and make entering a new phase of your life a bit less intimidating. It *isn't* exhaustive—there are sure to be important issues you'll face that we've missed. And we don't claim to be the last word on the subjects covered. There are no silver bullets, no hard and fast rules that you couldn't find exceptions to. Talk to six people about what it takes to make it and you'll get six different answers.

One thing is certain, though. When you're ready to roll out of bed and conquer the real world, you will. Think of all the jokers that came before you. If they can do it, you can too.

AIMLESS? AS IF!—SNIFFING OUT YOUR FIRST JOB

"Looking for a job can be a soul-destroying experience. You hit a lot of rejection. But you have to get through it. You have to work."

—Thea, 25, coffee-shop manager

We subscribe to a myth in America. Let's call it the Legend of Mary Richards. You pack up your car, drive to a new city with nothing more than a Pepsodent smile, great legs, and a high school diploma, waltz into your future boss's office, and convince him to give you a fabulous job where you work with loads of fun, interesting people. Wham, slam, bam, you make it after all. ● ● ● ● ● ● ● ● ● ● ● ● ● ● ● ● ●

"I feel confident about the job market. There's always someone that needs something done. If you're the one who says yes to doing it often enough—you'll get the job."

—Shawn, 23, truck driver

.....▶ Yeah, right.

If you are taking your first steps into the job market, you are waking up to the ugly truth. Some of the nasty news you've heard about the economy is true. You may have been fairly insulated from it as a student, but now you are on the front lines in the job wars. Guess what—it sucks.

America's industrial Big Mamas—the IBMs and Boeings, the GTEs, Westinghouses and General Motors—college-educated job seekers will pour onto the job market to compete for 1.05 million entry-level jobs that require a bachelor's degree. That means 330,000 individuals who sat through four years of college will have to take jobs that require a high school diploma or less. So it's no surprise that despite the fact that the recession of the early 1990s has been officially declared over and national unemployment is dropping,

"when i started looking for work i thought i'd be unemployed for the rest of my life. i realize now that the harder you work and the longer you keep at it, the better you get at finding a job."
—Amy, 24, advertising copywriter

"A lot of young people today are far more negative about their opportunities than the actual number of good entry-level jobs out there warrants."
—Denise Ward, Director, Macalester College Career Development Center

are getting more Kate Moss–like as we speak. Big companies that kept many of our parents and grandparents in wood-paneled station wagons and suburban dream houses are spewing out pink slips like so many Krakatoas.

It's an ugly little economic trend called "downsizing." Only there's nothing little about it. And it's happening at a time when more and more Americans are graduating from college than ever before—and finding that their degrees, once cherished tickets into the middle class, are now often worth about two Iraqi dinars to most employers.

A Bureau of Labor Statistics study projects that between 1992 and 2005, an estimated 1.38 million young Americans remain highly pessimistic about their career prospects. However, most experts say many people are far too pessimistic and unnecessarily so.

The economy is growing after all. About 8 million jobs have been created over the past three years (though they often demand highly skilled workers or are low-skill service jobs). But those more experienced workers who lost their jobs in corporate layoffs are often competing for them, too.

When you are lucky enough to land your first job, the odds of hanging on to it until retirement are pretty slim. A Department of Labor survey found that young Americans went through an average of seven or more jobs by the time their twenties were over.

Does all this mean finding a job is impossible? *No way.* True, we are wading through a period of profound economic change. There's no point in sugar-coating it. In many ways you have to be a bionic job hunter—better, stronger, faster than people who have gone before you. There are assumptions people once made about launching a career that simply no longer hold water—college is no longer an automatic ticket to prosperity and you cannot expect some big benevolent company to keep you fed and housed for your entire working life.

But you have an unprecedented array of weapons to help you get a job—tools your parents couldn't have conceived of when they were plunking their resumes out on a Smith-Corona. Not only that, the very instability of working life today has ironically given you an unprece-dented license to hop around trying on different careers. Many older people would have killed for that kind of freedom, even if it doesn't feel very liberating to you now. The multitude of choices before you is simply enormous, but fear not—the best way to find out what's right for you is to start trying things on for size.

REMEMBER THIS:
every year,
thousands of
angst-ridden,
frightened and
bewildered young
people still manage
to stumble their
way into good
entry-level
positions in
fields they are
interested in.

Not merely jobs
that help them
make the rent,
but the beginnings
of fulfilling
careers.

Honest.

Some of them are probably people you know. And some of them are a whole lot less brilliant, talented and altogether fabulous than yourself. They needed a good deal of time, perseverance and a healthy toleration of having doors slammed in their faces, but they made it. So will you.

If someone tells you setting off in search of your first career-oriented job is an exciting, fabulous opportunity to get in touch with your inner child, don't believe them. It is an often frightening, grueling and highly challenging job in itself—one of the toughest you'll ever have. The hours are hell, and the pay is worse. Being held at gunpoint by Shining Path guerrillas can be more of a fiesta. That's why it's especially important to be committed to the process before jumping into the abyss. If you aren't ready, motivated and completely focused, you aren't going to be prepared for the bruising you can get.

It may seem safer to try and hide from the job market by spending your days watching *Full House* reruns. In a perfect world, employers would beg us to work for them and send chauffeur-driven limousines to take us to the corner office of our dreams. Let the fantasies go, and you can truly get down to business.

Popular Jobs—Young Americans Speak

According to an MTV survey of 800 16-to-29-year-olds, these jobs were rated to have "quite a bit" or a great deal of appeal by those polled:

1. Small Business owner: 59 percent
2. Corporate Executive: 38 percent
3. Computer Programmer: 36 percent
4. School Teacher: 33 percent
5. Government Worker: 28 percent
6. Lawyer: 14 percent
7. Construction Worker: 14 percent

1. TAKING THE PLUNGE

"When I was in school it seemed like I knew exactly what I wanted. Now I have no idea what I want to do and it feels like there's nothing on the horizon. It's the most oppressive feeling. It actually drives me to the television set. At least then I can put it out of my mind."

—Harriet, 24

"I have just as much, if not more, respect for the kid who's waited tables, traveled, or done an assortment of odd jobs while they try and figure out what it is they want to do as I do for a kid who was recruited out of college to work in an investment bank."

—L. Michelle Tullier, Ph.D., director of Career 101 Associates, an employment counseling service that specializes in young people

Here's rule number one of career-finding:

You have to know what it is you're after if you ever expect to get it.

Not necessarily what you want to do for the *rest of your days*, or what is your life's driving passion. People spend their entire lives trying to work those things out. We're talking here about simply a focus, a target, a place to start.

Here's a question that you've probably become quite adept at avoiding until now: "What are you going to do when you grow up?" (Still a bit of a stomach turner, isn't it?) This society drowns us with options. Turn on the television and there are seventy-something channels from which to choose, your mailbox is stuffed to overflowing with consumer catalogs, a trip to the Cineplex or food court at the mall can prompt a minor nervous break-down. We are trained to think that all this variety is wonderful, and if it's takeout food you're after, it is. But when it comes to figuring out what we want to do for a living, all the possible avenues can be overwhelming.

The reaction many of us have to the dilemma of choosing a career is what one counselor calls "The Scarlett O'Hara Response." That is, when faced with something huge, like picking a college major, figuring out what career we want to pursue or the burning of Atlanta, like

Miss Scarlett we declare, "I'll think about that tomorrow."

That works for a while, but the closer you get to being shoved out of the nest, the more anxiety you feel. Suddenly it's back-against-the-wall time, and you feel paralyzed. The more hopeless your case, the more frantic you get — welcome to the tar pit of angst known as job panic.

It can cause you to flail about in all sorts of fruitless directions, and the more you flail, the faster you sink into the depths of despair. We've acknowledged that looking for a job is scary—but don't let fear freeze you. Inactivity only breeds more inactivity. There are some positive steps you can take, no matter how confused you are.

STEP #1: Remember, This Is Not a Race

"Young people sometimes forget that there's often at least nine months' worth of float time in finding a first job. Some people do their exploring while they're in school, others do it afterward. We all start the process at different points."
—Barbara Reinhold, director, Smith College Career Development Office

"I'll think about that tomorrow."

It really isn't a race. No one is going to be awarded a gold medal for most glamorous job, best apartment, quickest trajectory from classroom to executive suite. Your mother probably said this first. But deep down you

11

didn't believe her. After all, Mozart and Brandy had already reached the heights of greatness when they were younger than you. And it may seem that every friend you have seems to have known what they wanted to do since they were *in utero*.

Intellectually, you know that this is balderdash, that some of your peers with great jobs, apartments, cars and love lives are just as conflicted as you are. Emotionally you just want them to . . . well, die. This is not healthy. So, before we go any further, let's rehash some age-old wisdom:

Try to resist comparing yourself to others. It's a non-starter.

THERE WILL ALWAYS BE PEOPLE WHO ARE CUTER, SMARTER, MORE DIRECTED AND SUCCESSFUL THAN YOU ARE. GET THIS STRAIGHT—YOU ARE ENTERING A COMPETITIVE WORLD, YOU HAVE TO BE SHARP AND WORK HARD, NOT TO BEAT YOUR CLASSMATES TO A SIX-FIGURE INCOME, BUT TO GET WHAT IT IS YOU WANT OUT OF LIFE. Raymond Chandler was in his forties before he started writing mystery novels that made him famous around the world. Joe Pesci struggled until middle age before becoming a famous actor. Okay, maybe Joe Pesci isn't your role model. But the point is there simply is no use beating yourself up if you haven't made your fortune by the time you are 21.

Take a look around you. Chances are you know more than your share of successful people who went through several lines of work before settling on a career they liked.

Fast-Growing Job Categories

According to the Bureau of Labor Statistics, these occupations are estimated to be the fastest growing between 1994 and 2005, *by percentage.*

1. Personal- and Home Care Aides
2. Home Health Aides
3. Systems Analyst
4. Computer Engineers
5. Physical and Corrective Therapy Assistants and Aides

These fields will have the most *total* job openings:

1. Cashiers
2. Janitors and Cleaners
3. Salespeople (retail)
4. Waiters and Waitresses
5. Registered Nurses

By the time you are beginning your job search, you've probably run into at least one person—a counselor, parent, or veteran of the job wars—who's told you that you can really never begin one soon enough. This is true, but if your student days were consumed with things other than going to resume-writing workshops, garnering great internships, or making the right connections before commencement, you've far from mortally wounded your career prospects. Expect that someone who has done those things may get off to a quicker start. Wish them well, and take your own time getting to the finish line.

STEP #2: Start by Asking Yourself Questions

So how do you identify what it is you want to do for a living when you feel hopelessly overwhelmed and confused? Begin by recognizing that you know yourself better than anyone. You know what it is you like to do, what you hate, and you probably know a few jobs that you could never in a million years see yourself doing. What careers seem to link up with your interests? What do you see as your strengths and weaknesses?

13

Make Lists. This is the dinosaur of personal exploration methods but it really does work. Get a legal pad and write down everything you like to do; write down what you really hate. Be frank with yourself. If you break out in cold sweats at the very idea of chemistry, now might be the time to say *adios* to your fantasy of being a doctor.

Think critically about jobs beyond titles and salaries. Anyone who's seen *Wall Street* knows investment bankers can make a sick amount of money. But beyond that, what does the job require—do you have the stamina for grueling hours, can you adapt to a highly conservative business environment, do you know what training is generally required for various entry-level positions in finance?

Beyond nuts and bolts issues like what you are good at and what you like, there's the question of your **values**. That's a word that gets tossed around a lot today. People (especially politicians) have used it so much that, like the word "nice," it's been drained of a lot of its meaning. But it's still important when it comes to finding something you want to do. What's important to you? Material comfort, changing society for the better, being your own boss?

Separate that from what's important to or expected from the people around you. Your father has always wanted you to be a tax attorney and you dream of being a park ranger; your mother is going to throw herself off a bridge if you pursue a career as a disc jockey instead of managing a restaurant; your uncle, the organic farmer, will throw up if you pursue a business career; your friends will look at you funny if you decide that police work is what you really like, not dentistry.

There's tremendous pressure on everyone to get the "right" job or a "real" job—as if all the experiences

you've had before have somehow been phony. Guess what, it's your life:

You're the one who's got to face getting up in the morning to pull molars, nobody else. You have to find something that makes *you* happy—that doesn't give you license to sit around like a wart on a toad for the rest of your days until you find it, though. You have to go for test drives.

STEP #3:
Talk About It

Once you've begun thinking seriously about what you want, start talking about it with other people. Not just your friends, but older people you respect and trust. You know quite a lot of people who've been through this before you. Your parents, their friends, older siblings and relatives, teachers, coaches, professors, the woman who gave you a job filing documents in her office one summer. Sometimes, just stating a plan of action to another person helps it become more concrete, and gives you impetus to go forward.

"People often spend 18 years finding ways to not talk to their parents." says one counselor. "Talk to your parents. Ask them if they have friends in the profession you are interested in that you can meet." By finding those people you can start your first round of *informational interviews*—discussions aimed at not getting a job, but making connections and finding out what you might be getting yourself into. (More on that later.)

CAREER COUNSELING

Job searches are big complicated ventures. It's nice to get some advice from people who are old hands.

Friends and relatives who've gone before you are an invaluable resource. They can share their experiences of their first job search, talk about the mistakes they made in their interviews and offer great advice on how to cope.

But the job market is a dynamic thing. Times have changed since your uncle Ted started out at a filling station and worked his way up to president of an oil company. And a lot of the conventions of job hunting have changed. What was common practice a few years ago, like sending in your resume with a photograph, may be considered totally inappropriate today. "Parents are better cheerleaders than technical advisors," says one counselor. "You need their support, of course. But their experience of looking for a job was quite different from what you face."

Believe it or not, there are people who make a living telling other people what they could be doing for a living. They are called "career counselors," and they spend their days critiquing resumes, holding anxious job seekers' hands, and giving people advice on how to interview better, among other things.

As in any profession there are many sterling career counselors who are genuinely committed to helping their clients and a few creeps out to rip you off. Private career counselors are probably going to be out of your price range. They can be very expensive— especially in large cities, where they charge upward of $100 an hour. Outside the city, their rates can be about half that amount — cheaper but still beyond the means of many people just starting out. If you've found a private career counselor who works wonders and you can afford him, more power to you. But there are other options.

Most colleges and universities offer some career counseling services. You *definitely* should take advantage of them. (If you are a high school graduate with no college credits, you may want to skip ahead. However, if you are interested in any professional job and went to college for at least a few weeks, you may be considered one of the alumni of an institution that does not allow members of the public to walk in. Many vocational schools also offer career services.) For one thing, they usually don't charge you a dime. The quality of career centers obviously varies from institution to institution, but many offer the following:

- workshops on interviewing, resumes, and other job-getting skills
- general career counseling
- libraries of career books
- alumni job contacts
- information about jobs and internships
- standardized testing

Though most campus centers are only for students and alumni, some are open to the public at large. If you don't have access to a campus career center, find out if you can use one at an institution near you. Any fee they charge is likely to be nominal compared to those of a career counselor in private practice.

Career centers offer you a wealth of information when you are trying to figure out what it is you want to do. Many of the resources at these centers will be discussed later. But if you're having trouble finding out what your career path ought to be, they're a good place to start. You can arrange an appointment to talk with a counselor about your dilemma, use their library, and take a *standardized test* designed to help you get a bead on your job interests.

STANDARDIZED TESTING

You know the drill with standardized tests. Bring a number-2 pencil and fill in the little circles without going outside the lines. The most common multiple-choice tests offered by career centers are the **Myers-Briggs Personality Type Indicator** and what are known in the career biz as **standardized interest inventories**. The Myers-Briggs test has been around for ages and is meant to help you figure out what sort of personality you have. That in turn can be helpful in determining what careers you might be suited to. Interest inventory tests match your likes and dislikes against a whole range of career possibilities. Your answers to an inventory test might indicate a love of nature and the outdoors, for example—from these a list of suggested job possibilities are generated, say, park ranger, forester and wilderness outfitter. Hardly earth-shattering stuff, but it can be very helpful when you are totally in the dark.

You may find standardized testing an effective method of getting some answers you were unable to decipher on your own. Or you may find the results less than satisfying. Testing alone may not isolate what is the absolute, perfect thing you ought to be doing with yourself, but it can be helpful if you are confused. Ask yourself enough questions, and you're on your way to finding answers that will help you find a job that fits with who you are.

Aimless? As if.

Despite being stereotyped as a generation of shiftless, apathetic cappuccino-sipping slackers, an MTV poll of young Americans found **three out of four** *had chosen a career by the tender age of 22.*

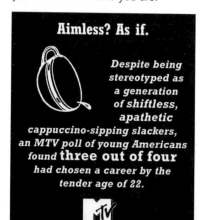

"When i went to college, i had no direction, and i didn't know what i wanted to do. A relative helped me find a job with my company, and i don't regret the decision to drop out. My education level hasn't hurt me at all in moving up."
—Melony, Title Insurance Coordinator

"Remember that scene in the movie cocktail, where Tom Cruise has great interviews but can't get a job because he didn't go to college? College is a way in, a foot in the door. if you don't have it, doors close."
—Carina Quintian, Associate Director, Career Advisement, John Jay College of Criminal Justice

Not everybody should go to college, and it's certainly true that a great many graduates of expensive institutions use their degrees pouring coffee and flipping burgers. But it's also true that if you want to find a well-paying job in this country, your chances are greatly improved with at least *some* post-secondary education. We know, the reason you didn't go to college is that you didn't want more school. But community colleges and adult education programs can help tremendously. Again, the more training you have, the better off you'll be. No value judgment intended. It's just a fact. (Though of course for every generalization there are a million exceptions—look around at the top executives at many corporations and you'll find non-college-educated people.)

Many of the fastest-growing jobs in the economy do not require high school (see inset), but usually they aren't as high paying as work available

16

to college graduates. And the most high paying among them demand special skills. So go out and get them as soon as you can.

College Required?

An MTV poll found that **two out of three** *people surveyed felt the value of a college degree was in the credibility the diploma conferred, not in the actual education.* **Only one in three** *people felt their job was directly related to what they learned in college and* **three out of four** *felt that by working hard, one could get ahead without a degree.*

MTV
MUSIC TELEVISION®

The first thing you should do if you are still in high school is talk to your guidance counselor if you have one, even if you haven't seen her since your first year. She can steer you toward resources that will be of help. Ideally, you want to enroll in a school-to-work or specialized job training program. Apprenticeships, where you start out as a helper and earn certification after you pay your dues, are another way to get good training. Plumbers and electricians are the most common examples of this route. If you are interested in office work, a **Temp Agency** may be able to help place you. (More about them later.)

that leaves you both in the hole and jobless. There are rip-off artists out there. Check with your Better Business Bureau and State Department of Education before you put money down.

You might also try a **state employment agency**. These are funded by your state's labor department, and their aim is to hook you up with jobs. They may be able to help with counseling and information about your areas of interest, apprenticeship programs and vocational programs. And lastly, there's always Uncle Sam—the military is one way into job training, good health benefits and knowing exactly

17

"i always knew i wanted to be in video—school just wasn't for me. i took a video course at a broadcasting school, went straight into an internship and got my job."

—Jason, 22, video producer

When looking into independent vocational schools and other job training programs, shop around. You want to find out how many of the students graduated into jobs and what the quality of the classes, facilities and staff are like. This is critical stuff—you can't afford to enroll in a fly-by-night-operation

what to wear to work every morning. (Though of course there are certain drawbacks—like the possibility of being killed or owing years of your life in service to the government.)

Sheepskin Optional

Many of the fastest-growing jobs in this country do not require four years of college. But they often require some additional training after high school.

The Bureau of Labor Statistics projects that these occupations will generate both large numbers of openings and offer above-average earnings (more than $457 a week). None requires a bachelor's degree, but many require advanced training or an associate's degree.

- Registered Nurses
- Electrical and Electronic Technicians
- Real Estate Agents
- Drafters
- Police Officers
- Industrial Machinery Mechanics
- Electricians
- Firefighters
- Postal Mail Carriers
- Instructors and Coaches— Sports and Physical Training
- Sheet Metal Workers and Duct Installers
- Truck Drivers
- Painters and Paper Hangers
- Corrections Officers
- Maintenance Repairers and General Utility
- Flight Attendants
- Paralegals

As the Baby Boomers age, the health-care area will boom, fueling demand for registered and practical nurses, health aides, medical assistants and medical technicians. Another big growth area is the legal field — court reporters, clerks and paralegals. Again, the more specialized your skills, the better you are likely to be paid.

STEP #4:
If You Are Still Confused,

One thing is certain. If you leap into the job market too soon, without thinking through what it is you are looking for, you may have a fairly ugly time of it. That isn't to say you shouldn't take a job if you need one. In this economy, most often you'll find yourself taking a job simply to pay the rent. If you aren't in school and are trying to figure out what you want to do, you are probably working at some job until you sort things out— maybe it's valet parking, delivering pizzas, bussing tables, or temping in an office. Don't be a job snob *ever*— it's work that puts a roof over your head and feeds you.

Maybe this work makes you feel cruddy, unappreciated, and undervalued. Remember this isn't the last chapter in your life story. If you knew exactly what you wanted, chances are you wouldn't leap into it right away anyway. You'd still have to find a way to keep yourself in cheeseburgers or vegetarian lasagna while you were looking for that dream job.

You are allowed float time in life, especially if you are still wet behind the ears. If you are able to afford it, you might consider spending your float time taking summer classes at a university or hiking the Pacific Crest Trail or backpacking through Thailand. If you can't, you might be living at home, waiting tables, volunteering at a homeless shelter, and renting every Orson Welles film ever made.

Float time does not mean sticking your head in the sand, and it should not drag on indefinitely. It's time you take for yourself, to get geared up for the stress and hard work of a job search. Everybody needs time out. But set some goals and keep yourself on a schedule.

Allow Yourself Some Float Time

The break between school and working life is a natural one for an adventure. If you have the bucks, you could consider doing *Outward Bound*, an expensive way to get in touch with the wilderness and yourself. Outward Bound is renowned for its character- and confidence-building expeditions into wild areas. Climbing sheer cliffs or learning to sail off a lonely coast can be just the ticket if you are feeling unsure of yourself. For a list of their junkets contact:

OUTWARD BOUND NATIONAL OFFICE
Route 9D R2 Box 280
Garrison, NY 10524

The Council on International Educational Exchange (CIEE) provides information about foreign travel and volunteer opportunities at home and abroad (see inset for address), but you don't need to go ice climbing on Mount Kilimanjaro or travel to Prague to have a ripping good float. You can save a lot of money by floating at home — and all the while be laying the groundwork for a good job search.

The most important thing to keep in mind during this whole process is that it's okay if you don't know what you ultimately want to do with your life — remember the key is it's all up to you.

International Work Opportunities

If you've ever dreamed of living and working abroad, this is the perfect time to do it. The experience of collecting a paycheck in another country gives you an opportunity to experience a culture in a totally different way than as a tourist or student. Teaching English—particularly in Asia, Eastern Europe, and Latin America, is a huge avenue of opportunity to pick up valuable language skills, and quite often no background in education is required. Young college graduates generally pick up on teaching opportunities through word of mouth or by contacting overseas private schools directly. Naturally any language ability you have is going to be a plus. Places to start—campus career offices, nonprofit organizations in your country of interest, study abroad offices. Unfortunately, many of the opportunities listed below are open only to college graduates.

British Universities North America Club (BUNAC)

BUNAC USA, PO Box 49, South Britain, CT 06487
(203) 264-0901

BUNAC is the great-granddaddy of overseas work programs. College students and recent graduates—you have six months to take advantage of the program after graduation—are eligible to work in the United Kingdom under their auspices. Canadians, as members of the British Commonwealth, may work there for two years.

Most BUNAC students work in restaurants, pubs and bed-and-breakfasts, but some land career-oriented jobs at everything from record companies to merchant banks. The program books you accommodations for your first few nights in the country and provides an orientation, a London resource center, and a handbook listing previous employers of BUNAC students. All that and good beer, too.

BUNAC takes a very dim view of students who try to stay longer, which many invariably do. Realize if you take the chance you risk deportation, which can get very nasty and prevent you from ever returning. The study abroad or career offices of your college should have information and applications, or you can contact their U.S. offices for more general information. The cost of the program is about $200.

Council on International Educational Exchange (CIEE)

205 East 42nd Street, New York, NY 10017
(212) 661-1414
(800) INTL-JOB
(for information on work abroad programs)
(800) 358-5971 (to order Student Travels Magazine)

Affiliated with BUNAC, CIEE offers many overseas work programs for college students and recent graduates. Host countries include Ireland, France, Canada, Germany, and Jamaica. Participants can usually work legally for three months.

In addition, CIEE offers a host of volunteer programs in the USA and overseas, open to any self-motivated young person over the age of 18. Information on CIEE programs is available from many college study-abroad offices as well as at branches of Council Travel, a student travel agency with 45 offices nationwide. CIEE also publishes *Student Travels Magazine*, a treasure trove of student travel bargains.

Japan Exchange and Teaching Program (JET)

Embassy of Japan, JET Office
2520 Massachusetts Avenue, NW
Washington, DC 20008
(202) 939-6772 or 6773
(or contact your nearest Japanese consulate)

College graduates under 35 are contracted to teach English in Japan for one year under this program. Under certain circumstances, JET participants can renew their contracts and work legally in Japan for up to three years. Airfare is paid by the Japanese government and participants can earn close to $30,000 a year.

World Teach

Harvard Institute for International Development
One Elliot Street
Cambridge, MA 02138
(617) 495-5527 or (800) 4-TEACH-0

World Teach recruits college graduates to serve as English teachers in developing countries. Year-long programs exist in Costa Rica, Ecuador, Namibia, Thailand, Poland, and South Africa. There is also a summer project open to college students in Shanghai, China. Although volunteers receive room, board and a stipend while in their host country, they must pay around $3,800 on average to participate in the program.

Search Associates International Schools Internship Program (SAISIP)

PO Box 636, Dallas, PA 18612
(717) 696-5400

SAISIP places college graduates with strong academic records in one-year teaching posts at English-language private schools around the world. Transportation costs, a stipend, and room and board are included. Applicants should send a cover letter, resume and self-addressed stamped envelope to the address above, or call for recorded information about the application process.

Volunteering

Obviously any community service work you can do not only brings meaning to your days while you figure out your career picture but does some good, too. There are a myriad of opportunities in this area. from volunteering at your local homeless shelter to reading to elderly people in their homes. The great thing about community service is that it's so easy to find—you don't have to wander far at all for opportunities to help people. Local charities, churches and synagogues, colleges and community centers are all good starting points. Here are just a few avenues for getting involved; to list all your options would take a whole new book.

The Peace Corps
1990 K Street, NW, Washington DC 20526
(800) 424-8580

Here it is, the big kahuna of them all. It certainly ain't a picnic. The Peace Corps selects Americans to serve in developing countries around the world. Those who are accepted after a very competitive review process are given an intensive training in the local language and culture and then work for two years on education and development projects. The Peace Corps covers all participants' major expenses. Applicants must be college graduates, those with strong science backgrounds and language skills are favored.

Americorps National Service
1201 New York Avenue NW, Washington DC 20526
(800) 424-8867

As of this writing, these government-sponsored volunteer initiatives have a precarious hold on their funding—VISTA, the oldest among them, will probably survive the congressional budget-cutting cleaver, but the two Clinton administration Americorps projects have dicey futures indeed. Information about all three can be had from the address and number above.

Americorps VISTA (Volunteers In Service To America)
A one-year program aimed at improving the lives of low-income Americans. Volunteers are assigned to nonprofit organizations in communities across the country. Among their jobs—teaching sign language to the deaf, AIDS education, public health work and community organizing. College is not required, but you must be at least 17 years or older and at least be working toward a high school diploma. Participants can earn a living allowance of about $700 a month, plus a child-care and health-care stipend if needed. You can also earn up to $4,125 toward college tuition for each full year of service.

Americorps
Unlike VISTA, Americorps volunteers apply directly to individual nonprofit organizations and work with one group for a year. A database of participating organizations is maintained by Americorps in Washington—call their 800 number for more information. As with VISTA, living costs and help toward college tuition are provided. The program is funded until September 1996—after that, it may be deader than New Wave.

Americorps National Civilian Community Corps (NCCC)
Members of the NCCC are assigned to defunct military bases and work in teams on disaster relief, urban revitalization and conservation projects. In terms of benefits and requirements, NCCC is similar to VISTA and Americorps, but volunteering takes place in a work-camp setting. This, too, is a highly endangered program.

Teach for America
PO Box 5114, New York, NY 10185
(800) 832-1230

Open to college graduates with a 2.5 GPA or higher. The TFA corps members go through a summer of training and are then placed for two years as teachers in public schools in inner cities and rural areas.

Inner-City Teaching Corps
2648 West Pershing Road, Chicago, IL 60632
(510) 579-0150

Recruits college graduates to teach in inner-city Catholic elementary schools in Chicago for a period of two years. There are no GPA or major requirements. Participants live in group house arrangements and receive a stipend. There is a summer orientation, plus ongoing teacher training.

Habitat for Humanity
121 Habitat Street, Americus, GA 31709
(912) 924-6935

Habitat for Humanity volunteers build homes for people in need at sites across the nation. There are more than 1,200 local affiliates of the organizations, and all you need to become a volunteer is time and enthusiasm.

Amigos de las Americas
5618 Star Lane, Houston, TX 77057
(800) 231-7796
Web Page: http://www.amigoslink.org.html

Participants work on public health projects in seven Latin American countries. Open to both high school and college students, a semester of Spanish is required before taking part in the summer-long program. Room and board are provided, but volunteers pay between $2,800 and $3,200 in order to take part.

Literacy Volunteers of America
5795 Widewaters Parkway, Syracuse, NY 13214
(315) 445-8000

Volunteers teach basic reading and writing skills to adult pupils in one-on-one settings. The number of lessons given each week is arranged between tutor and student. There are 423 local branches of the organization—a call to the national office can put you in touch with the one nearest you. There are no education or age requirements, but all participants must go through an 18-hour tutor training.

2. JOB SCAMMING STRATEGIES— THE GOOD, THE BAD, AND THE HORRIBLE

You've hemmed and hawed, you've floated a bit, you've written down lists, you've done preliminary research and talked to some people in the know. Now you're ready to begin your job hunt. This is serious. You are truly committed, right? This is not like a New Year's resolution to attend an aerobic step-class every morning; this is the first stage in launching a career. You've signed on for the long haul.

So let's **start** with your **most important** resource— **TIME.**

"Young people are often terribly unrealistic when it comes to the time they spend job-hunting. It's not something you can do for just two hours a week. Looking for a job is a job in itself. If you put things off or try to do it in your spare time, you are going to be terribly unhappy with the results."

—Samuel M. Hall, Jr., Director, Career Services, Howard University

You need to impose a structure on your jobless days that keeps you on track and not lolling around on the couch, which, frankly, would be a nice way to spend the day if you could get someone to subsidize it. High school counselors in polyester Sansabelt trousers bored many of us to tears with speeches about *setting goals*. Well, they had a point. You need to keep your eyes on the prize—the job of your choice—and devise strategies to get it. You won't get there if you don't commit a set amount of time every day to achieving that goal. This is critically important if you really want to find a good job. (Now hit the showers.)

Develop a schedule and try to stick to it. If you are in school, conducting a job search can be exhausting. Try and set aside time each day to concentrate solely on your hunt, even if it's just thinking time. If you are unemployed and looking for a job, do not exhaust yourself by trying to launch a 24-hour campaign. Organize your day around different tasks related to finding a job.

Try to keep regular hours—commit yourself to a 9-to-5 job of getting a job. But don't be exceedingly rigid. If you need to break your schedule, do it. The point of putting yourself on a schedule is simply to keep your search from becoming a black hole. Don't retreat from having a social life. Depression is not an employment asset. Looking for another job while working is especially tough— you'll need to budget your time *and* be discreet. (More on that later.)

DOING YOUR HOMEWORK AND NETWORKING

Talk to personnel people across the land and they'll tell you that one of the major problems they have with young applicants is this: while many of them are eager as all get-out to work for them, they don't know any-thing about their company. *Nada.* What did these kids expect, to waltz straight into a job with no clue at all about a potential employer? Apparently, yes.

This is really important. If you've decided that you really want to work in the auto industry, you need to learn everything you can about it if you want a job in it. You need to know more than just who makes which cars; you must know who the major players are at each company, what last year's profits were, what are the major issues they face as we enter the 21st century. *Everything.* Don't worry, there are lots of tools to help you do this.

You should think about your research as a two-tier process. Your first tier of research starts at the beginning of your job search. It consists of a more generalized effort aimed at getting the scoop on what entry-level positions exist for people in particular fields, what a career path of an editor or an architect or a pharmacist looks like, what skills you need to have at the out-set, and what qualities are important for the job. This information will help you decide on a course of action that will beef you up for the main event— an interview with someone in that field. At that point you should do even more research, finding out as much as you can about the particular employer before you talk to them.

Think of your research as mapping out the first stage in an expedition to a foreign country. You are an anthropologist, and you come from one culture, the wear-dirty-T-shirts-and-pierce-your-lip culture, if you will. That is to say, you've been a student. You are investigating different business and work cultures. You have an idea about them, of course, from books and movies and television. But some of the differences are subtle, and you need to pick up on those, too. The aim is to get somebody to hire your beautiful self.

Here are some general resources to help you start your investigation:

- Career centers and public libraries
- Informational interviews
- Electronic databases

If you were studying the Hutu and Tutsi of Rwanda, you'd go to the library and read up on them. You'd track down experts in their culture. And, of course, you'd seek out the Hutu and Tutsi themselves, asking them the meaning of particular practices and rituals. The same holds true for taxidermists and fashion models.

Almanac, Job Hunter's Sourcebook and *Dun and Bradstreet's Career Guide*. Even local branches of the public library are often linked to electronic databases that can speed you on your quest for information about particular jobs and companies. (More on that later.)

Hopefully, when you were thrashing about a while back in Chapter 1, you made contact with a career center. They often have great libraries of their own, and they come with people who are storehouses of information on where you can find actual, real,

Libraries are an invaluable tool in helping you get a job.

They can clue you in on the location of major firms, professional associations that cater to people in a particular field, and the state of the industry. They can hook you up with trade and industry journals that frequently list job openings and tell you what the issues are in a particular field.

There are wonderful reference tools like the **Encyclopedia of Associations**, which can steer you toward industry societies and clubs, **Standard & Poor's Register of Corporations, Directors, and Executives**, the **Thomas Register** and the **Standard Directory of Advertisers**, which give in-depth information about particular companies and their products. The last three are also available on CD-ROM. Among the myriad other resources about job finding are the **Adams Jobs**

live people in a business to talk to who are alumni of your school. That can be useful in setting up **informational interviews**.

INFORMATIONAL INTERVIEWS

Before you plop down money on a used Pinto, you talk to somebody who knows something about Pintos. It's a big investment, and you certainly want to know what you are getting into. The same holds true for jobs. You'd be crazy to say you wanted to work in publishing if you just loved reading but had never met anyone who actually worked in the industry.

Let's say you were incredibly lucky and managed to find a job. You'd still have no idea what you were getting into. Which is where informational interviews come in. They are a low-risk way to get your feet wet, find out about a business, and make **connections**, which you'll need. A phenomenal number of people never take advantage of this opportunity, and they work twice as hard to get to the same place as people who do.

Some of us are lucky. If your father's best friend is an X-ray technician, and your dream job is to be an X-ray technician, you call him up and ask him what his job is like. But if not, you are going to have to find a way to track down some nice X-ray technicians to talk to. **Not get you a job**, mind you, just talk. By conducting an informational interview, you can find out all sorts of wonderful things about an industry and gain a contact in it—someone you can keep in touch with who may be able to put you in touch with someone who is hiring.

You may find out from informational interviewing that a career you had your sights set on just isn't for you. Or you may really click with someone and reaffirm your choice of a particular field. That's why it's important to do more than one. You should treat an informational interview as a dress rehearsal for the real thing. The rules are much the same as in a job interview. (More on that later.)

In short, you need to be professional. That means taking a shower, dressing nice, sending a thank-you note **immediately** afterward. If you do the interview over the phone, you should still send a thank-you. A person is taking time out of her busy day to tell you all about what she does. Show her some respect. Before you ring to ask for a good time to set up an interview, think about when might be a good time to call in the first place. First thing Monday morning is most definitely not a good time for most people who work in offices. Try calling in the middle of the week, in the afternoon. For the interview, be prepared with lots of good questions. Here are a few you can try on for size:

- How did you get your start?
- What advice would you give someone just starting out?
- What kind of background do I need to get an entry-level position?
- What kinds of opportunities are there for people in my position?
- What do you like and dislike about your job?
- What does the future look like in this industry?
- Do you know of anyone else in this industry I can talk to? And can I use your name and say you referred me to them?

In general, people love talking to a young whippersnapper about what they do for a living, and you never know what it might lead to.

NETWORKING IN GENERAL

Networking is a word that may conjure up an image of some sleazy guy in a shiny suit handing out his cheesy business card and offering to "do lunch" with everybody. It isn't. You're not running for Homecoming King. You're looking for work. And most career experts agree that networking is one of the most effective tools in your arsenal.

Start talking to everyone you can in an industry. You'll not only know the territory, you'll be building a network of contacts that will serve you in good stead.

The people who meet with you aren't stupid. They know that you are calling up trying to scam jobs. They did it themselves when they were in your shoes. That said, networking isn't easy for a lot of people. You may be shy and nervous about calling up a stranger to talk about finding a job. You have to get over it. This is, after all, just a conversation—there are no icky issues like hiring you or paying you a decent salary involved. If you are a wreck about it now, you'll fall apart for the main event.

"Our most important job contacts are our alumni." Go to any small liberal arts college and private university in the country and you are likely to hear that refrain.

So use your fellow alumni.

Alumni contacts are the first critical links in many young college graduate's network. They're going to be the most receptive informational interviewees out there.

If you've started looking in college, you can most likely find contact

numbers for them at the career center. Another resource for many graduates are *alumni clubs*, which often hold informational sessions about job finding and other activities for new members. Graduates of many private high schools may have a powerful second alumni network to tap into.

All that information is grand if you are a graduate of a college with a strong alumni network and a good career center. If not, you aren't at a critical disadvantage. You simply need to create much of your own network from scratch. Start by talking to friends and family — do they know anyone in the field you are interested in? Here's an old trick that career counselors have been pulling out of their hats for ages—talk to a doctor, lawyer, priest, minister, rabbi or accountant, if you know one. They come across people from all walks of life in the course of doing their jobs.

If you're a student at a large public university, you may need to work harder to make yourself known in a class and at a campus career office— invest in the effort and it will pay off. "Professors can be key leads on large campuses," says one college career counselor. "They can often be a critical help to a favorite student."

Professional organizations and associations are another useful starting point for many people. There are hordes of these, and requirements for membership usually don't preclude you. Join up. Go to meetings and conventions. If you join the Public Relations Society of America, you can't help but meet PR people. You'll get newsletters and trade magazines. You'll learn the language of the industry you are interested in, and you'll be on your way. No need to feel creepy about this. Networking and using an association's membership for contacts are a large part of the reason these associations exist.

"i think the most important thing to say about job searches is do whatever it takes. i found a few great jobs simply by going through the yellow pages and calling up companies i wanted to work for. you never know what can come up."

—Alex, 29, realtor

CLASSIFIED ADVERTISEMENTS, COLD CALLS AND MASS MAILINGS

Playing the lottery is not a bad thing. The chances of you winning may not be great, but you never know. Depending on who you talk to in the career world, the above strategies are a total waste of time, or just one more thing you can do to increase your odds of getting a job.

Answering the classifieds is a big gamble when you have few skills, because so many people see the advertisement when you do. Many employers will not place an ad in the classifieds for just that reason— they get bombarded with resumes. People do get their jobs from the classifieds every day, though. And there is no sense in not working the newspaper as a *part* of a larger job strategy.

If you are a smooth operator, you can make cold-calls—ringing people you have absolutely no connection to—and get a lot out of them. You can call to set up an **informational interview** for a later time, or the person you have contacted might just be willing to speak about their business right then and there. You can't come out and say you want a job if you cold-call—it will immediately alienate the person on the other end of the line. But you can build leads this way, which could very well turn

into a job. That's if the person wants to talk with you: if you're polite and well spoken, they will probably melt. Never try to call unprepared, though. It can be a disaster. Know something about the company or field about which you're inquiring.

Mass mailings are usually not very effective (we'll discuss why in the resume section). For now, know that if you do decide to do a mass mailing, it must be tightly targeted to be in any way useful to you. A few unsolicited resumes never hurt anybody, and could help—it's the postage stamp lottery, and you might get lucky.

27

Job Search Strategies

An MTV survey of young workers found that they employed these methods in their job searches:

- **Used friends to find jobs: 85 percent**

- **Looked at classified advertisements: 66 percent**

- **Went door-to-door and filled out applications: 64 percent**

- **Used their parents' friends: 56 percent**

- **Sent out resumes: 47 percent**

- **Went to temp/placement agencies: 36 percent**

- **Had internships: 25 percent**

- **Went to a job counselor: 25 percent**

"I used a headhunter to get my job. I would highly recommend it to anyone. We clicked, and he set me up with a company that I enjoy working for and see a future with."

—Tony, 24, telecommunications sales

HEADHUNTERS AND EMPLOYMENT AGENCIES

Headhunters, or executive search firms, are not for everybody. In fact, they are almost never, ever, for young people just starting out. If you're changing jobs later in your career, a headhunter can be useful, but when you have nothing to offer in the way of skills, you may have a difficult time finding one who can help you. Headhunters are paid by corporations to seek out qualified people to fill specific jobs.

If you happen to send your resume to a headhunter, it's strictly "don't call us, we'll call you." When your skills fill the headhunter's particular needs, he'll call. Remember, they work for employers, not you.

Employment agencies are a different kind of creature. Your state employment agency handles a wide variety of people and may be able to place you with an employer. Very generally speaking, state employment agencies are better at placing people in low-skill jobs, but they are free resources, so check them out even if it seems like a long shot. Some also have computerized job-bank terminals. Usually, private employment agencies are for white-collar office work. The employment agency gets a fee from the employer, so in most cases, you pay nothing. Agencies often specialize by profession, and that can be a boon for you. There are agencies that specialize in banking, advertising, publishing, sales and insurance, to name just a few industries.

Temporary Work

is one of the fastest growing segments of the American economy. According to the National Association of Temporary and Staffing Services, the number of people employed by temp agencies tripled in the last decade, and more than two million people go to work as temps every day.

A few employment agencies are rip-off artists. Steer clear of anybody who charges you fees up front. Another good thing to look for is if the agency is a member of the National Association of Personnel Consultants (NAPC).

Whether you decide to go to a temp agency or not, it's important that you use a variety of resources in your quest for employment—never put all your eggs in one basket. By going down a number of different avenues, you can make the whole hellish process a lot shorter.

There are, of course, also **temp agencies**. Temp work can get your foot in the door and, if you play things right, lead to permanent work. **Never be a snob about it.** While you're floating, it's a good way to pick up office skills and work experience that can reassure employers in any industry. Most people don't exactly love their temp jobs, but they can be useful and you shouldn't think you are wasting your time doing them.

Is This What Employers Want?

An MTV poll on young workers asked respondents to decide which of these factors were important to an employer filling a job:

- related experience: **75 percent**
- computer literacy: **74 percent**
- college education: **70 percent**
- appearance: **62 percent**
- willingness to work overtime: **57 percent**
- technical or vocational training: **55 percent**
- willingness to relocate: **26 percent**
- age: **22 percent**
- race: **13 percent**

3. JOB SURFING ON THE INFOBAHN

Online job-hunting is increasingly popular, and for good reason. You can now get loads of useful job-search information on your computer that your aunt Clara only dreamed about. With the tap of a few keys you are able to link up with discussion groups focused on the career you are interested in pursuing, do research about a field or community you would like to move to, gather information about a particular company, and even post an electronic version of your resume. The networking and research possibilities are nearly endless.

If your personal computer is online, then getting started may be as simple as typing a few key words into your web searcher. If you are not, a great many public libraries, universities and student career centers offer access to these services. One great place to start is the NOW WHAT?! page at MTV Online (http://www.mtv.com/index.html), which is chock-full of info on employment, career counseling, packaging yourself, and how to be a success on the job (starting as of September, 1996). Here are just a few other resources available via the worldwide web. Some serve as springboards to other job sites; others feature listings posted by employers:

The Monster Board
http://www.monster.com/home.html/

America's Job Bank
http://www.ajb.dni.us/

Career Mosaic
http://www.careermosaic.com/

Adams JobBank Online
http://www.adamsonline.com/

JobHunt
http://rescomp.stanford.edu/jobs/

web dog's Job Hunt
http://csueb.sfsu.edu/jobs/bestjobs

College Grad Job Hunter
http://www.execpc.com/~insider/

The Internet's Online Career Center
http://www.occ.com/occ/

JobWeb
http://www.jobweb.com/

CareerWEB
http://www.cweb.com/

JobTrak
http://www.jobtrak.com/

Employment Opportunities and Job Resources on the Internet
http://www.wpi.edu/%7Emfriley/job guide.html

Federal Job Openings
http://www.jobweb.org.fedjobsr.html

Fedworld job listings
ftp://fwux.fedworld.gov/pub/jobs/jobs.html

This is just the tip of the cyberspace job-hunting iceberg. Many college and university career centers have web pages, which not only serve as fonts of useful information in themselves, but also link up with larger databases. Career centers and state employment agencies are also frequently connected to electronic job-listings databases.

In addition to these and other Internet resources, there are specialized business databases that can be invaluable research tools for job seekers. The best place to find them is at college and university libraries. Among the most well-known of these databases are **Dun's Electronic Business Directory**, **Moody's Corporate News**, the electronic version of **Standard and Poor's** and the **Thomas Registry**. **Nexis-Lexis**, a database that stores thousands of newspaper and magazine articles, can also be tremendously useful before interviews, because it allows you to scan through a zillion relevant articles about the company you are interested in working for.

Most of these special databases are far too expensive to use on your home computer. A single search can cost you hundreds of dollars, so if you are hooked into any of them via a student computer account, use them like there's no tomorrow. Many public and university libraries will let you search them for free, or will search for you for a fee. If you are going to get charged, be very thrifty and narrow your search at the outset.

Online service providers such as America Online, Prodigy, and CompuServe feature job bulletin boards and places to post your resume. There are also quite a few specialized services that will store your electronic resume for a fee. More and more people are actually posting their resumes online—the jury is still out on how effective this method is. But as with a hard copy, an effective electronic resume must be focused on the opportunity at hand. Whether you send a resume via e-mail or not, computers have invaded the world of work in earnest. When you send a resume to a large corporation, there is a good chance it will be scanned into a resume-reading database—so an effective resume is a computer-friendly one. (We'll touch on electronic resumes in greater detail later.)

Hunting for jobs online is no magic ticket to employment. A job-listings site may be seen by hundreds of people every day—it's simply an electronic want-ads page. And time is literally money if you are relying heavily on your home computer to pound the pavement for you. You can charge up a hefty bill on your service if you aren't careful. No matter how many contacts you make or how much great research you dig up, in the end you'll have to get your job the old-fashioned way—a human being has to hire you. That said, you can open up a whole new front in the job war if you know your way around the information superhighway, and that's a good thing.

4. EARNING YOUR STRIPES— PLAYING THE INTERNSHIP GAME

Ah, irony of ironies. You are green, so nobody wants to take a risk on hiring you. But you can't get experience if no one gives you a shot. Welcome to the world of internships.

Don't tell us you never heard of them before. They are practically mandatory nowadays. Employers are looking for some sign of commitment from you. They want to know you are serious, that you've invested time in figuring out that this is the career for you. And quite simply, internships are the best way to do that.

It didn't used to be that way. Let's take a newspaper reporter's job. In your grandfather's day, a smart lad straight out of high school often went to the big-city paper and asked to be a copy boy. He ran about the office doing menial clerical tasks, and if he hung around long enough and pushed hard enough he got promoted to reporter. Or maybe he came straight from college (this is your grandfather's day, a she need not apply. . .) and got that reporter's job with just an English BA. Times, unfortunately, have changed. There are very few firms willing to take on inexperienced young people as full-time employees, giving them a chance to prove their mettle, which is a bummer. But then again, the internship market has exploded. Just a few years ago, there were only a handful of companies offering young people a chance to gain professional experience by giving them a chance to work for them (albeit for little or no money).

The sooner you start interning, the better. For one thing, it will help you get the office skills you need to get a good job; for another you'll get critical on-the-job experience, and third, you may develop useful contacts in your hunt for work. Having an internship and dealing with your course load at school can be hard, but being able to carry it off is doubly impressive to employers. And there are internships in virtually every area one cares to name—from jobs at dance companies and museums to large corporations to wildlife refuges. And you never know, your internship could lead to a permanent position.

College internships are the most common, but some are open to students still in high school. Think of interning as an opportunity to try on a few hats. If you always wanted to work for a nonprofit that aims to protect the environment, interning at one gives you a chance to see what it's like. Some internships may even lead to jobs—and in any event you have your foot in the door. What's more, applying and interviewing for them is a relatively low-stress way to practice for the main event. Some internships even gain you course credit.

The main problem most people have with interning is that they say they can't afford it. The truth is, you can't afford not to. It's true, if you are dying for a career in politics and a summer internship at your dream political think tank in Washington pays nothing, you have a serious dilemma. But it's in your best interest to figure out a way to make it work. Frequently, unpaid internships require you only work a few hours a week to allow you to have an outside job that does pay. For instance you could intern two days a week from 9–5, or Monday to Friday for three hours in the morning, and then go off to waitress and pull in the dough.

There's no arguing that it's unfair few internships pay a living wage. But they provide invaluable experience. Working two jobs isn't appetizing, but if you really want to work at that think tank, it's worth considering. If the summer internship you want is in a distant city, check into the summer rates to stay in local college and university housing, or find a friend or relative willing to let you crash on their couch for a couple of months for free or low rent. You might want to consider internships close to home, where you can save on rent money.

If for whatever reason you haven't done any internships by the time your search for full-time work rolls around, don't despair. Career centers and libraries are usually well stocked with books listing them. And, of course, if there's a company you'd especially like to work for, there's no reason you can't simply ring them up and ask if they have an internship program, or you can try to arrange one yourself. Most people are thrilled at the chance to have a young energetic person helping them out, even on a limited basis.

5. CRAFTING A KILLER RESUME

Whether you are looking for an internship or a full-time job, you'll need a resume. Think of it as your calling card. But don't be lulled into relying too heavily on it— yes, your resume is important, but too many young job hunters allow it to become a crutch.

THE MEGA MAILING— DON'T DO IT

Sending out a resume is one of the easiest ways to apply for a job. You don't have to do anything but throw together an appropriate cover letter, attach it to your resume, and toss them in the mail. You don't have to risk the humiliation of calling someone up or meeting someone and risk having them turn you down. By putting a safe distance between you

and potential employers it handily neutralizes the whole rejection-anxiety thing and gets you interviews, right? **Wrong**. Nearly every employment counselor and personnel director in the land can tell you a version of this story.

There once was a young man who really, really wanted to work for an environmental organization. He was a nice guy, who liked organic food and earth shoes and fleecy outdoor wear. He had a great personality and terrific grades and won an honors prize in biology. Not only that, he'd spent three summers working for a county parks department as a nature guide. In college, he'd chaired the student recycling committee, organized a petition to protect some local land as a wildlife refuge, and wrote an environment column for the campus paper. All in all, he was a regular green dreamboat, a real catch for any environmental organization looking to fill an entry-level position.

Our friend, let's call him Leif, set to work finding a job. He heated up the computer, cranked out a general resume detailing his stupendous employment and educational experiences, then drafted a cover letter. He knew he wanted a job with an environmental group and he knew that competition would be tight. There were hundreds of organizations out there—how could he reach them? He was able to find the names of about a hundred managers and personnel people at environmental organizations around the country from books in the career center at his school. He called their employers to check their titles and addresses, then changed his cover letter slightly to fit each organization.

Leif then printed out 200 slightly different cover letters with 100 resumes, and blanketed the USA with semi-articulate pleas for work. Weeks passed, then months. Poor Leif was reduced to selling used friendship bracelets on the sidewalk

Leif Grubeater III
1 Biosphere Curve
Roadless, Nev. 88888

OBJECTIVE To obtain a challenging and demanding job where my communication skills, organizational strengths and leadership ability would be put into play, allowing for maximum personal and professional growth

EDUCATION **John Muir College**, Scraggy Butte, NV
Bachelor of Science, Organic Studies, May 1996
Grade Point Average: 3.75
Marty Stouffer Award, April 22, 1995

Experience **BABY HUEY'S PIZZA TIME PLAY HOUSE**, Scraggy Butte, Nevada   1994 to Present
Assistant Manager
Assistant Manager at a busy fast food restaurant. Worked five days a week.

Fullerton County Parks Department   May 1-August 31, 1994
Guide   June 1-August 31, 1995
    May 5-September 1, 1996

Spent last three summers leading groups of tourists through the natural wonders of Musty Mesa County Park, in Fullerton county. Lead nature talks for tourists. Lead overnight camping trips to Three Needle Valley, in Musty Mesa County Park.

Penny Haig Diet Centers   Summer, 1992
Receptionist
I answered telephones and set up appointments at a health and fitness centre, filing, meeting with clients, and answering the telephone. When clients came into the diet center, I greeted them, gave them some forms to fill out and, often had to answer the telephone as well.

ACTIVITIES Chairperson, NAUSEA, 1996
Member, John Muir University Greenpeace, 1994-1996
secretary, student environmental caucus
Varsity Curling Club, 1994-1996
Tenor Sax, John Muir Bighorns Marching Band, 1994-1996
Thurgood Marshall Scholarship, 1994
Homecoming King, 1995
Pledgemaster, Sigma Sigma Sigma fraternity, 1996
Arrested six times in 1995 for disorderly conduct at protests against the clear-cutting of virgin forests in the Sierra Nevada Mountains
Voted "Best Looking in Senior Class" at Mason Valley High School, 1992
organized pettition to preserve Limpopo swamp as a national wildlife refuge, 1996

SKILLS A little Spanish, ASL, word processing

INTERESTS Reading, writing, nature, my friends and taking long walks on romantic summer evenings.

The Unholy Resume of Leif Grubeater III

Poor Leif, he never learns. Not only does he send out 200 resumes, he doesn't even bother to proofread them. Don't be as careless. In order to display some of the more common resume mistakes, we've cooked up a real monstrosity here—just one of these errors would be fatal enough, so this resume is beyond terminal. Hopefully no one would be this out of it—even the address is wrong (there's no phone number, and look at the abbreviation for Nevada). Remember, even the smallest spelling or punctuation error can hurl an otherwise respectable resume straight into the reject pile.

The objective is badly phrased and generic, and Leif's Marty Stouffer prize is not sufficiently explained, and farther down he's used the acronym for his most important student activity "NAUSEA" (National Association of United Student Environmental Activists) as if the reader will know instantly what he's talking about. His formatting and spelling are a nightmare. In resume land you must be consistent—especially when it comes to dates and section headings.

Take a look at three experiences highlighted on his resume—only the second one seems relevant to the job at hand, and the descriptions are poorly worded and riddled with mistakes (including use of the word "I" and the flogging of the word "lead" in his second job description). Several of Leif's significant environmental achievements are buried in his activities section, which is much too long and filled with information that is questionable (an arrest record, even for a noble cause, stays off a resume). His skills section is written in a way that points to his lack of language and computer ability rather than his strengths, and his interests are either too bland or too intimate. As you read through the rules in this section, keep poor Leif in mind— he broke most of them.

to make ends meet. Finally he got two letters back, politely thanking him for his interest, and that was it.

What did he do wrong? Well, everything, actually. Statistically, Leif's chances of becoming the next Dalai Lama were probably greater than getting a job through this method. Yet year in and year out, hordes of inexperienced job-seekers send out mega mass mailings in the hopes of finding employment. Why? Because it's just about the lowest-risk method there is of going about looking for work—only it's not really looking for work at all, it's simply another way to *avoid* looking for work in a serious fashion. Before you rush off to drown personnel departments with query letters, ask yourself this: who do I know that got a job this way? Chances are, nobody.

As we said before, if you want to do a mass mailing, make it a **targeted** one. That is, cut down on the volume and tune your letters to each specific employer. You never know, you could get lucky for the price of a stamp. But don't count on it.

THE ESSENCE OF A RESUME

Put a resume in its place. It is quite simply a summary of your skills, education, and experience. It is not the cruise missile in your job hunt, but a critically important weapon in your arsenal. No resume, no matter how gleaming with fantastic internships and prestigious academic honors, can take the place of pounding the pavement. The purpose of a resume is to convince an employer to give

Leif Gustav Theobald Beowulf Grubeater III 1 Biosphere Curve • Roadless, NV • (888) 888-8888

September 30, 1996

Human Resources Director
The Free Willie Foundation
22 Greenmarket Square
Portland, OR 33333

Dear Sir:

I recently graduated from John Muir University with a bachelor's degree in Organic Studies and am interested in pursuing a career with an environmental organization. Your organization is the kind I would like to work for, because it doesn't just sit back and let the polluters of this world get away with their dirty politics, underhanded tricks and brutal rape of our natural resources. I would be an invaluable addition to your team.

Since I was eight years old, I have dreamed of working for your foundation. In both high school and college, I was president of the National Association of United Students for Environmental Action (NAUSEA). Particularly in college, but also high school, I juggled a very full schedule as a student and got good grades, except during my sophomore year, when I was captain of the varsity curling squad and bit off a bit more than I could chew. I consider myself to be a well-rounded, dynamic, and intelligent person. The kind of person that would be right at home in the Sierra Club.

I look forward to hearing from you. Please contact me at your earliest possible convenience. We can then discuss how I can help your foundation in greater detail. I can be reached at the number above. It must be beautiful in Oregon this time of year—we here in Nevada could use some of that rain!!

I hope to hear from you very soon.

Cheers,

Leif Gustav Theobald Beowulf Grubeater III

The Noxious Cover Letter of Leif Grubeater III

If his resume weren't putrid enough, Leif's cover letter would be a nail in anyone's coffin. He hasn't bothered to find out the name of the human resources director of the company he's writing to and then resorts to that dinosaur of an opener "Dear Sir" when for all he knows the person reading the letter may be female. We really start heading south fast in the first paragraph, with the repetition of the word "organization" and the rather alarming rape metaphor.

Paragraph two contains a one-two punch to Leif's chances with the jumbled sentence about his student activities and needless reference to his poor academic performance during one of his sophomore years (it's not clear if it's high school or college). Even worse, his careless editing delivers the killer blow in the last sentence. You see, the previous letter he wrote on his computer was to the Sierra Club, and like a ninny, he forgot to change the sentence to match a different employer. If you crank out multiple letters on your computer, be forewarned—this kind of blooper is quite common.

Then there's the closer, complete with yet another remark that implies Leif is doing a favor to the Free Willie people by deigning to write to them, a completely inappropriate remark about the weather, and the informal "Cheers" sign-off. One last thing—if you feel compelled to include your middle name, stop at one. Leif's unwieldy moniker would be just fine on a graduation or wedding announcement, but here it looks pretentious and silly.

you an interview, not hire you. It is, as one counselor puts it, "an entree to a handshake."

But if your resume in and of itself won't get you a job, you probably won't get a job with a lousy resume either. A good resume is short, snappy and filled with useful information about its author. The information it provides should leap right off the page. And it should contain nothing, and we mean **nothing**, that might prevent you from being hired.

Think about it—you are recruiting people for an entry-level job at a large company. You probably have no more than a few minutes to scan over an Empire State Building–size heap of resumes. You're tired, you want to go to lunch and you can only pick three people to interview. Basically, you are looking for anything that can give you an excuse to disqualify someone. Why, here's Leif's resume. Gosh it looks generic. It doesn't even seem like he took the time to write a resume designed for this particular opening. Hey, look, he even misspelled a word. How careless. How unprofessional. Next. "Think of someone with three piles on their desk, one labeled

Yes, one labeled *Maybe*, and one labeled *No*," says an employment counselor. "Your job is to make it into that *Yes* pile."

Resume writing is one of those things that people seem to especially dread. And if you've never done one before, competing in a triathlon seems easier. The whole process has taken on the aura of an arcane discipline, known and understood by only a few, whose rules are so complicated that the uninitiated can easily trip up on and forever doom themselves to a lifetime of odd jobs.

There are some ground rules to follow, and they've changed a bit from when your parents were looking for work. But once you've mastered them and become comfortable with the resume format, you'll realize there's no mystery to it.

Still, most people find sitting down to the computer to reduce their life experiences to a few short sentences about as enjoyable as getting teeth pulled with no Novocain. Because of that, there are scads of people out there who will write your resume for you—

for a fee. These operations range from expensive consultants and resume preparation companies to your local copy shop. The temptation to have someone else write your resume for you is a natural one—*avoid it.* You should always try and write at least the initial draft of your resume on your own. It can help you narrow your job search and figure out where your particular strengths lie. It is also invaluable preparation for any interviews you land.

"But I've got nothing to put on my resume!" you howl. That's a fear many people have. But in fact you do. What activities you pursued would be useful in the work world? Clubs, extracurricular activities and academic honors are all fantastic resume boosters. People are often reluctant to talk about experiences in school that might help them on the job, but school's been your job for most of your life. Say you were in an advanced senior history seminar where you gathered an enormous amount of primary resources together, worked in a team to put together a presentation and then put together a group report for every member of the class. All of that says volumes about what kind of employee you could be.

Then there's summer employment, internships and any specialized skills, such as computer knowledge and foreign languages, that you might have. And what if you look at our new resume and find that you still lack something absolutely required for the job you want? Your resume has helped you identify where the hole is. Now you can go about filling it.

RESUME BASICS

First, a big old disclaimer. People get passionate about resumes. They have strong opinions and get mad when you cross them. A few might disagree—vehemently—with some of the advice here. There are several good books out there devoted

exclusively to resume building by people who have spent their whole lives mastering the craft. If you want a second opinion, check one out.

For now, these rules will help you construct a crisp, professional and inoffensive resume. Tinker around with it all you want. Reject a few of our ideas down the line if they seem too starchy. It's your resume and your life, so you make the call.

Now, on to business. Not long ago it was possible to get by with one generic version of your resume. It sure saved time for other things, like love-ins, be-ins, and sit-ins. Unfortunately, the times, they have-a-changed, moonflower. The most effective resumes are tailored to the position that's available. And now that computers are a fact of most people's working lives, you haven't got any excuses not to change your resume each time you look for a job. Even if you don't personally own a computer, you still need to create a general resume and modify it as you target different jobs you want. Remember our poor friend Leif.

COSMETIC ESSENTIALS

A resume for a student or recent graduate should never be more than one page. If you've never written a resume before, your first few drafts may break this rule. You'll feel conflicted about what's important and what should be left out. Weeding through your resume is an important part of the process, and a continual one. Think of your resume always as a work-in-progress. If you find, after intensive and rigorous weeding, that your resume is still running long, then you obviously can toy with the font, margin and point settings on your computer. But be careful, the people who read resumes for a living were not born yesterday. Any obvious fudging will work against you. Printing your resume in 4 pt. pica won't win you any friends.

Your final copy of any resume should be printed on standard 8 1/2 " x 11" paper. The paper itself should be "resume quality," a heavier bond than the flimsy paper usually used in schools and offices. You can find resume paper at any stationery store. Or you can have your resume printed onto quality paper at most copy shops. There is nothing cheesier than a resume on cheap paper—it says you don't really care enough about the position being offered to go out and spend a few bucks on something nicer. This is one area where you don't want to cut costs.

One of the first things you'll notice about resume paper is that it comes in all sorts of dazzling shades. The best for resumes are of the plain old white and off-white variety. They are marketed under chi-chi names like Silken Ivory Enchantment or Baronial Classic Shangri-La Surprise, but you'll know them on sight. Now that computers allow us a myriad of fonts to write in, you should also be similarly conservative in that department. Palatino and Times fonts are acceptable. Unless you are applying for a job with Emile Guttenberg, Gothic type is not.

Now there are many areas in life where we want to demonstrate our flair for the outrageous and our QUiRKY iNDiViDUALiTY. Sadly, our resume is not one of them. You have to be slightly subversive when it comes to resume writing—

you want to play by the rules, and yet let just enough of yourself shine so that you stand out in a positive way. In these uncertain economic times, there's one thing you can be sure of: the world of resume readers is inhabited by some real humorless types, even in pretty creative professions.

Outrageous resume colors like purple and hot pink, as well as resumes packaged in bizarre ways (like the applicant for a job at a record company who sent in a music-video version of why the firm should hire him), risk getting you exactly the wrong kind of attention. Who knows, you might get lucky, and your wild and crazy resume will find itself in front of someone who is really tickled by what you've done. But do you really want to take that gamble so early on in the process? Chances are you don't want to be remembered as that girl who sent in the fuchsia resume any more than you'd want to be known as the girl who came dressed for her interview in the fuchsia-colored rubber pantsuit.

Just in case you have managed to make it to the dawn of a new century without realizing it, typing a resume is the kiss of death. "The days of the typed resume on onion skin paper are over," says one employment counselor. If you don't own a computer, you'll need to use one to create a final version of your resume.

You have a few options: take your rough draft to a resume preparation service, enter in the changes yourself on someone else's computer, or go to a copy center that lets you use one of its computers for a fee.

Most copy centers charge by the amount of time you've spent sitting in front of one of their word processors. It adds up if you are trying to generate a resume from scratch—an hour's work, plus the cost of laser printing and copying your resume, will cost you plenty. If you end up using the computers at copy centers, come prepared. Have your rough draft in hand and budget your time.

The best option is a campus computing center, where you are usually free to take as much time as you want and the price of printing and copies is minimal. Even if you do have a computer of your own, you'll need to print your resumes on a laser or letter-quality printer. Daisy Wheel, Dot Matrix, and Near Letter Quality (NLQ) printers are not up to snuff. Anything else but the sharpest type is not acceptable. Excessive copying of your resumes will muddy that sharpness, so whenever possible, avoid copying a copy of your resume.

Desktop publishing has its advantages—you can create a sharp resume on your own in a matter of hours and won't have to keep starting over every time you mess up. You can save your original version on a disc until the next ice age, and always work from it. You can choose from a variety of fonts and squish things in a little to make them fit. Imagine how much time that would have saved your mom. The downside is that employers have very high standards for how resumes look. Take the time to make yours gleam. Everyone else will.

Now. Let's recap. Here are some rudimentary facts about how your resume should look. It should not exceed one page of standard-size paper, it should be laser-printed on resume stock paper in a conservative shade, and the typeface you choose should also be a conservative, professional one. In short, resumes are curt, crisp and businesslike.

Think of your resume as Daria Morgendorffer from Beavis and Butthead. Daria is a smart, sensible gal in glasses and a nice brown skirt. She's not a deranged menace to society like the cartoon's stars, nor is she wimpy and wishy-washy like Stewart Stevenson or Mr. Van Driessen. Daria is someone you can take seriously, the sort of person you could trust to feed and care for your pet hamster. There's nothing too flashy or erratic about her. She's the consummate professional.

Oh, and if you're going to highlight your computer skills, don't plunge your reader into a swamp of geeky language. It's fine to refer to computer programs without defining them, especially if you are applying for a technical job. It's just better to keep things simple, so the human resources person who first sees your resume can make sense of it. Remember, the best resumes are filled with pithy, easily intelligible sentences. And, of course, remember not to abbreviate words.

Before digging deeper into the world of resumes, you should be aware of one of its cardinal rules:

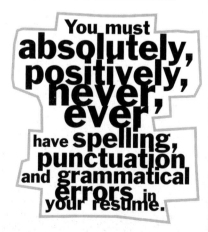

You must absolutely, positively, never, ever, have spelling, punctuation and grammatical errors in your resume.

Electronic Resumes

Nowadays, if you send your resume to a big corporation, you can lay odds that the first person to read it won't be a person at all, but a computer. More than half of all medium-size and larger employers now employ resume-scanning software that sucks all the data off your resume and stores it in a database with those of other applicants. That means your resume must be computer-friendly in order to be effective. The same is true if you send a resume to an employer over the Internet. We'll touch on more specific resume-building tools in a minute—for now, here's some advice to follow before you send your resume trucking down the information superhighway.

• Use industry buzzwords. When a computer is in charge of keeping track of your resume, it will file and retrieve it by searching for certain key words specific to the industry you are looking for work in. Know the key words that people in the industry are after—if you are applying for a computer operator's job, for example, be sure you list all the programs you know (one would hope you would do this anyway). Keep your eyes peeled for words when reading journals and want ads describing the skills and qualifications that prospective employers are looking for. If an ad asks for someone who is comfortable in a Unix environment, for example, you had better mention that you are.

• Put buzzwords high up in your resume. If a computer is searching its memory banks for "Systems Analysts," by putting that title high up in your resume, say in a job objective, you maximize your chances of getting picked for an interview. Don't over-load your resume with buzzwords though—use them strategically—and in context.

• Nouns that emphasize specific talents work better on computer-friendly resumes than the fancy "action words" that are used to beef up traditional resumes. In other words, saying that you have a BA in engineering is more effective in a computer-friendly resume for an engineer's job than wasting your breath digging around for just the right verb to characterize your leadership of the college engineering club. A computer isn't going to do back flips if you use words like "oversaw," "coordinated," or "spearheaded."

• *Using italics (like these)*, bold fonts, underlining, fancy graphics and layouts can confuse a computer scanner and scramble your resume. Stick with simple fonts like Times, Palatino and Courier. Stick with white or light paper shades and use standard-size type—never go smaller than a point size of 10.

• Include your e-mail address on a resume sent via the Internet, but leave off your address and phone number—too many people can get it. On any computer-friendly resume, your name should come first. If you use a fancy resume style that puts your address higher up on the page the computer tracking system may think "Elm Street" is your name.

41

• Be extra careful about spelling. Any spelling error in a resume is a huge no-no, but a computer-friendly resume must be absolutely flawless. Misspelled words will confuse the computer.

• Send your resume in flat, in a 9 x 12 envelope. Never fold, staple or fax a resume destined for a computer scanner—if it's all creased up, it will have trouble being read by the machine. Faxes can be hard for computers to read.

• Don't apply for a multitude of jobs at the same company. Computers can keep far better track of how many resumes you've sent in than a human can. If you send in three different resumes and cover letters saying that you are perfect for three different jobs, you are going to get busted by the human resources department—and you'll look like a phony.

• **Resume Databases**
For a fee, some companies will store your resume in an electronic database that is sold to employers. The word is not yet out on how effective this approach is, but it's one more front in the job wars, and that can't hurt. Some services charge around $20 for your resume, others hit you up for nearly $100. Shop around for the service that best fits your needs, and don't expect miracles.

How shatteringly obvious, you say. But employment specialists and recruiters are nearly unanimous in voicing this as a problem rampant not just among young job seekers, but also with sixty-two-year-old corporation CEOs and everyone in between. "We had one job offer actually rescinded because the applicant had spelling errors," recalls Susan Gordon, president of the Lynn Palmer Agency, which places young people in publishing jobs. "The person with final hiring authority found the mistakes after the initial offer had been made, and because this was an editorial assistant's position, felt it wasn't appropriate to hire someone who couldn't even edit her own resume."

Such horror stories abound, and if you've been rushing to get a resume to an employer quickly, it's easy to see how errors get past you. It's a hassle to go back and correct your resume for the millionth time, but it's more than worth it. Do not rely on a computer spell checker to find all your errors—if you've misspelled "to" as "too," the computer is not going to catch it. Proofread your finished resume extremely carefully after printing it out, then have someone else read it. Then proofread it again. You simply cannot afford to slack off on these details.

THE TWO BASIC RESUME TYPES AND WHICH ONE YOU SHOULD USE

When first you plunge into the thorny thickets of resume writing, it can seem that there are innumerable varieties of the beast out there. There are really just two basic types. The most common is that old war horse called the **chronological resume**, which details your experiences in reverse order, from your most recent educational experience and employment back. The chronological resume

has a rarer, funkier sister in the **functional resume**, which highlights an individual's skills but does not list education and job experience in reverse order. In fact, the functional resume often leaves out dates altogether. Some experts also identify a mutant third kind of resume, called the **combination**, which is just that— a fusion of the two resume styles.

Functional resumes sure sound appealing. Say you want that job in the insurance industry, but just out of school, you've got no real experience in business or insurance to put down on a resume. Why not simply highlight the skills you bring to the table, and forget about niggling details like dates of employment and when you graduated from school?

Because many employers will immediately suspect you are trying to hide something from them, that's why. Remember the three stacks of resumes mentioned early in this chapter? A resume that raises questions in the mind of the employer— questions like **What did she do at school that she doesn't want me to know about?** and **Why didn't he put any dates on his resume?**—is a zillion times more likely to get tossed in the No or Maybe piles than a resume that doesn't.

Functional resumes are most often employed by people reentering the workforce after a long hiatus, such as women who've stayed home to raise children, or those changing careers in the middle of their working lives. They are generally not considered appropriate for recent graduates. But in certain cases they can be a good idea, if you want to take a risk and play up skills over job titles.

A combination resume is sometimes considered a better alternative for recent graduates, because it provides solid data about your employment history. It is also used by professionals who are switching jobs. (Some critics contend that this brand of resume is a huge space waster, often demanding two pages. That makes it off limits to most young job seekers. If you still feel compelled to use a resume format other than the standard chronological when just starting out, realize you are taking a risk.)

Now some people look at the dinosaur, the chronological resume, as a straitjacket. Actually, the format is rather elastic, a good pair of sweats, with just enough set rules to keep you from feeling like you're flailing about struggling to sum yourself up in a pithy way. Most important, the chronological resume is still the form that most employers are comfortable with and understand. For one thing, they know they can find things, like the dates of your previous employment. Because this book is not devoted exclusively to resume writing, most of the advice you'll find here is geared to creating a ubiquitous old chronological, which most people use. Libraries and bookstores are stuffed to overflowing with volumes pitching endless improvements and variations on the traditional resume format.

Dates are critical on resumes, but what they look like is largely up to you. If you've glided from one job experience to another without a single break, you can write out the exact dates of when you started at each and when you left. Most people haven't done that, especially when they are looking for their first few jobs. You can feel safe writing just the month and year, like so: May, 1995–September, 1995 (or 4/95–9/95). If you have participated in an activity or worked at a job that spans more than a year, you can drop the month altogether, like this: 1995–1997. Whether you write or spell them is a function of your personal taste and space, but if you adopt one style, **be consistent** throughout your resume.

Generally, a chronological resume includes these elements:

1. Your name, address and phone number
2. An employment objective
3. Your education, with your most recent academic accomplishment first
4. Academic honors and special awards
5. Any specialized courses you've taken that are relevant to the position you are applying for
6. Your work experience, including internships (whether paid or unpaid), with your most recent job first
7. Activities you have taken part in, such as sports teams and community service
8. A line or so detailing any special technical skills you have, such as computer programs you know
9. A brief section that details a few of your personal hobbies and interests
10. A line that reads: **References available upon request**

Not everything listed above goes in every resume. Resumes are like arguments for why you should be considered for a job — pick the items that best make your particular case. There's quite a bit of wiggle room to shape the data you provide to your best advantage.

1. Obviously, you need to put your name on the resume if you

43

expect to get called in for an interview.

It should appear on the resume in the same form you'd use to introduce yourself. Charles Windsor would be Charles Windsor on his resume—not Charles Philip Arthur George Windsor. Unless you are known as Melissa Sue or Betty Lou, we suggest leaving off middle names. Likewise your middle initial. And only the likes of P.J. Harvey and J.D. Salinger can get away with using only their initials on their resumes. It's not a major issue, but these things can be confusing.

If you are called John Jr. or Richard III, it's really up to you whether you include that information on your resume. The same holds true for nicknames. But keep in mind you are after a job, not a spot atop a Rose Bowl Parade float. The fact is that Corkie, Bucky, Bitsy, and Kippy sound a bit more trivial than Caroline, William, Elizabeth, and Christopher. Fluffy may be a heck of a nice gal, but do you want her to work for you? Your name is the first thing a potential interviewer is going to see—you can always tell her what you prefer to be called when you meet.

Ethnic names that an interviewer may not be familiar with and gender neutral names can also pose a problem. If your name is Chin Suei, but your friends know you as Carrie, you might consider using your Westernized nickname. You may not want to use Chin Suei "Carrie" Chung, though, because it fuzzes the issue of what to call you rather than clarifies it, (though some experts disagree). Again, go with what feels most comfortable.

It's also perfectly legitimate to refer to yourself as Ms. Chin Suei Chung on your resume. You can follow the same rule if you have an ambisexual name like Mr. Blair Underwood or Ms. Cameron Diaz. Whether you feel it necessary to make your gender known is a delicate subject and totally up to you, but you may want to spare the interviewer any potential embarrassment. In all other cases leave off titles like Mr., Ms. and The Artist Formerly Known As. . . .

Your address and telephone number are integral parts of any resume. Your address should look like this:

Jan Brady
4222 Clinton Avenue
Westdale, CA 99999
(777) 555-3333

If you are looking for a job while living in a dorm or other temporary situation, remember to include **both** your current and permanent addresses and telephone numbers. You don't want to miss out on a job because someone couldn't reach you. Be sure to identify which one is your present place of residence and which is your home.

Aside from the name of your state, which should be shortened to its standard postal abbreviation (such as TX for Texas), never shorten words in your address. "Street" should be spelled out, not written as "St." If you are absolutely up against the wall and writing out "Apartment" is going to turn your resume into a two-pager, make sure you abbreviate consistently. In other words, 225 Flaming Spear Street, Apartment 12 would become 225 Flaming Spear St., Apt. 12.

2. Up to this point what you put on your resume has been very clear-cut, but here's where the waters get a tad muddy.

A great many people, especially those taking their first baby steps into the job market, put **objective statements** at the top of their resumes. An objective spells out just what job you want and often mentions a few of the strengths and skills you bring to the table. Some folks adore objectives, while others think they are cheesy chunks of nonsense-speak. Here are just a smattering of the opinions wafting around out there on the subject.

"I use a job objective on my resume because i think it helps target it to the particular job i want. it narrows the sweep of a resume."

—Kat, 27, nonprofit administrator

"i can't imagine using an objective on my resume. They are unbelievably cheesy, for one thing. when you are first starting out, you have no idea what you want. what a pain if you are applying for jobs in different industries."

—Jeff, 23, editorial assistant

"when i first graduated from college, i used several different, very general objectives on my resume, depending on what job i was applying for. Now that i've been working a while, i don't use them. my resume speaks for itself, and my objective is usually pretty explicit in my cover letter."

—Amy, 24, advertising copywriter

"i think objectives are essential for all new grads. They come right out and say what it is you want."

—Alan Hoon, Human Resources Director, Fujitsu Corporation

Few nooks of the resume world are more controversial. And the annoying thing is, both sides in the great objective debate make some very good points. The pro-objective camp is right—a specific job objective, right at the top of your resume, can give it added direction and oomph. And now that computers are scanning resumes and storing them in databases in many companies, it helps to have your desired position right up there at the top of the document, so that it can be easily filed and retrieved. So if you know exactly what you want, an objective like the one below can be useful:

Objective: To obtain an entry-level position as a computer programmer

But here's where the anti-objective camp scores a few points. That kind of statement only works if you are tightly focused in your job search. When your objective statement is too narrow, you may not be considered for other jobs available in the same company. Say you send an unsolicited resume to a publishing company and write "editorial assistant" as your job objective. The human resources department will file you with all the would-be editors. If a great job opens up in the marketing department, you probably won't be considered. To keep your name in circulation, a few counselors recommend writing very generalized objectives, like the following:

Objective: A challenging position in the publishing industry, offering an opportunity for personal and professional growth

That's a stinker of an objective. Empty expressions like "personal and professional growth" have been pummeled into the ground by legions of eager beavers before you. Does anybody seriously want an unchallenging, dead-end job in publishing? Not bloody likely. You might as well write, "Objective: To get a job and be happy." The statement also commits another cardinal sin of resume writing—it focuses too much on what an employer can do for you, rather than on what you offer the employer. If your aim is to set yourself apart, rest assured a bland, generic-sounding objective won't do it. "I tend to discourage general job objectives," says resume guru Tim Haft, author of the book *Trashproof Resumes*. "They tend to be fluffy and a waste of lines on your resume."

The key to any good resume, objective or no, is

The more you can tailor your document to a particular employer or opening, the better off you will be. The fuzzier you are about what you want, the weaker your package. Before you ever send a company a resume, you must have some objective in mind as you craft your resume and cover letter.

Whether you choose to write it as an objective statement is largely up to you. If you do choose to use one, get right to the point. An objective that goes for more than two lines is way too long. Avoid flowery language, and if you don't know exactly what position it is you are after, narrow it down to a corporate department or an area within a given industry—saying you desire a fund-raising position, for example, is better than an objective that says you are interested in working for a nonprofit company.

You can mention a few special skills you have in an objective statement, but they should be ***specific***. Mentioning "strong communication skills," for example, does nothing for your resume. But if you were applying for a position as a systems analyst and mentioned a few complex computer languages you knew straight off the bat in an objective, rather than leaving them for the ***skills*** portion of your resume, you've made a smart move.

For example:

Objective: To obtain a position as a systems analyst utilizing my knowledge of X, Y, and Z programs

is better than

Objective: To work with computers

3. If you decide to include an objective or not, your education should come right after it.

If you are just out of school, this is going to be more important to who is hiring you than where you've worked. Once you've been out in the working world awhile, you can flip your education and experience sections, so that your last job comes first. Like everything else on your resume, your most recent achievement in your education section comes first. If you are still in school, put down the month and year you expect to receive your degree.

> "I really got nervous about my resume because my grades were not so hot in college. I really thought that they would keep me from getting the job I wanted. Now I realize how silly that was."
>
> —Michael, 23, broker

The education portion of your resume may cause you a lot of stress. Many people think that if they haven't graduated Summa Cum Wonderful from Ivy U., they will *never* get hired. Now, there are undoubtedly some firms that insist on knowing a young person's grade-point average as part of their hiring process—large corporations and financial institutions that recruit on college campuses often do. But in most cases, you can get away with not putting it on. If you have a GPA of 3.5 or above put it down. If you went to college, but didn't graduate, you should still list the institution and the dates you attended it on your resume before your high school. Do not explain your reasons for leaving on the resume—you can discuss this during the interview. Under no circumstances should you say you've received a degree if you haven't. And no matter how wonderful they were, keep your SAT scores off your resume.

Don't fret about whether or not you made the honor roll. GPAs don't mean what they used to—grade inflation is a nationwide phenomenon. Remember rule number one of resume writing—never put down anything that weakens your case. Again, you can address the issue of your grades with candor should the question arise in an interview. This is not the same thing as *lying*.

Lying about anything on your resume, or inflating anything that is verifiable—like your GPA—is a big no-no. Don't be stupid—even if you get the job, your lie may cause you to **lose** it later.

4. If you've received a prestigious scholarship or award, you should definitely put it on your resume.

But remember to spell out why what you've received is special. "Young people make too many assumptions in their resumes," says one resume consultant. "They'll put down a scholarship which the interviewer has never heard of and think he knows why it's important." For example, if you've received the Idalis Scholarship, let the reader know that it is awarded for an outstanding student in music broadcasting, for example. Making the Dean's List obviously needs no explanation.

5. If you've gone on to college, the choice to put your high school on your resume is up

to you. In most cases you'll be adding nothing by putting it on and saving space by leaving it off. You may want to mention a particularly significant high school honor if it strengthens your case, such as a prestigious academic award, or if you are demonstrating a long commitment to a particular interest that spans both high school and college. An example might be an applicant for a job in broadcasting who has been working at campus radio stations since she was 16.

If you attended a prestigious high school and want to mention it on your resume, know your audience. The fact that you went to Miss Snottingham's School may have a different effect on the director of a food bank than the vice president of an investment bank. (If the director of the food bank is an alumna of the school, put it on.)

6. After education comes the heart and soul of any resume— the experience section. It should come smack dab in the middle of the page. Describe your past experience in hard terms—don't get all squishy and ethereal. What did you do? What did you accomplish? Avoid wordiness. List the organization you worked for, its location and a brief description of your job. **Think about experience in a broad way—not just as simply paying jobs.** Here's an example: Amy has just graduated from Standard University. She's looking for a job with a non-profit that deals with child welfare.

She's done some marvelous things— volunteering at a homeless shelter, interning at a halfway house for troubled youths, writing a senior paper on Victorian orphanages and joining her college community service group. She didn't get paid for any of these things. She did have paying jobs, though. To support herself while at school she worked in an athletic shoe store and delivered pizzas.

Now there are many important, valuable skills she gained from her "real" jobs, but the fact is that her volunteer and student activities are far more relevant and interesting experiences. What if much of her "relevant experience" came *before* other jobs? Split the experience section in two parts, and create a new heading called "Related Experience" or the like. Now you can put your more important experiences first, in the same reverse chronological format. You want the person who is picking out qualified applicants to see them first. There's a saying in resume-land that a prospective employer only looks at a resume for 30 seconds. This means you have to convince that person *quickly* that you're qualified for the job. Don't make them try and figure out why you have the experience for the job—make it obvious.

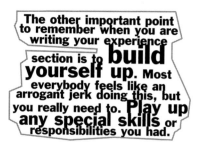

The other important point to remember when you are writing your experience section is to build yourself up. Most everybody feels like an arrogant jerk doing this, but you really need to. **Play up any special skills or responsibilities you had.**

Here are two descriptions of Amy's halfway house job:

Student Intern
Hope House, Happy Valley, TN
1994–1995
I worked as an intern at a nonprofit center for abused and abandoned children, filing documents, typing the weekly program schedule, and

answering phones. I also served as a peer counselor for three residents of the house, and wrote up rules for a new game called Tell Me A Story, which was designed to help young people share their experiences in a non-threatening way.

Okay, this blows. Why? Aside from not mastering the basic language of resume writing—never write "I" in your resume (it's all about you, after all)—this is a plodding, wordy description that manages to make poor Amy sound like a drudge at a not very interesting or demanding job. The most interesting facts about her internship come dead last, and all the stuff at the top is material from universal intern hell. Amy counseled troubled young people, and even created a new method for them to work out their problems. Yet it appears she'd rather talk about answering the telephone. Here's one way she might rewrite it:

Peer Counselor 1992–1993
Hope House, Happy Valley, TN
Counseled young people at a nationally recognized shelter for runaways aged 13–18.
Created *Tell Me A Story*, a game designed to help troubled children talk about their experiences.
Assisted in the daily administration of a 25-bed halfway house.

There's no question which description does a better job of building Amy

Action Verbs

No standard resume is complete without a heaping helping of action verbs that describe your accomplishments in a zingy way. Action verbs make you look productive, effective and take-charge when describing past experiences. Invest in a good thesaurus, and stay away from stale, dull-as-dishwater phrases like "responsibilities included" or "duties included." In a resume, how you performed a task is just as important as your title. A good resume sentence is short, snappy and emphasizes RESULTS. Quantify your accomplishments—if you served 300 customers, say it, don't write "waited tables." Here are some rock 'em sock 'em action verbs that liven up a resume:

Achieved	Coordinated	Fostered	Mastered	Regulated
Acquainted	Counseled	Founded	Mentored	Reorganized
Acquired	Decreased	Fulfilled	Moderated	Reported
Activated	Defined	Gained	Modified	Researched
Adapted	Demonstrated	Gathered	Monitored	Restored
Administered	Designed	Generated	Motivated	Restructured
Advised	Developed	Guided	Negotiated	Revamped
Aided	Devised	Handled	Obtained	Revised
Allocated	Directed	Helped	Operated	Revitalized
Analyzed	Discovered	Hired	Organized	Saved
Assessed	Distributed	Identified	Originated	Scheduled
Assisted	Documented	Implemented	Overhauled	Selected
Attained	Drafted	Improved	Oversaw	Served
Authored	Earned	Increased	Performed	Shaped
Boosted	Edited	Informed	Pinpointed	Spearheaded
Broadened	Effected	Initiated	Pioneered	Sponsored
Budgeted	Eliminated	Innovated	Planned	Staged
Built	Encouraged	Inspired	Prepared	Strengthened
Calculated	Enhanced	Instigated	Presented	Streamlined
Cataloged	Enlarged	Instilled	Presided	Structured
Centralized	Enlisted	Introduced	Produced	Supervised
Challenged	Established	Instituted	Promoted	Supported
Collaborated	Evaluated	Instructed	Proposed	Surpassed
Composed	Executed	Invented	Provided	Taught
Conceived	Expedited	Investigated	Published	Tested
Conceptualized	Facilitated	Launched	Recorded	Trained
Conducted	Financed	Lectured	Recruited	Translated
Consolidated	Forged	Led	Redesigned	Tutored
Consulted	Formed	Located	Redeveloped	Upgraded
Contributed	Formulated	Maintained	Reduced	Utilized
Converted	Fortified	Managed	Refined	Wrote
		Marketed		

up. The sentences are short and to the point. She used words like *created, counseled,* and *assisted*—career gurus call them action words (see preceding list)—that make her look like a dynamic, take-charge kinda gal. She gives little hard factoids about the number of children in the shelter, and how old they were.

The most interesting, creative and demanding aspects of her internship come first; answering telephones comes last. She didn't dither over the mundane little details of her office work; she will be asked to go into all her administrative duties in her interview.

Notice she did not unreasonably inflate her duties or lie about her job. If Amy said she was a member of the paid staff of the center, or executive vice president in charge of fund raising, she'd be lying *and* potentially dipping herself into an Olympic-sized pool of hot water. She simply chose a snazzier way of characterizing her actual job.

By the way, it's not written in stone somewhere that you have to put "intern" as your job title. You can make your title sound a little less crummy if you want, as long as it describes your actual duties accurately. Most people who read resumes can spot an internship a mile away, anyway. Point is, it's a minor fudge, not really a lie. If you were to answer dishonestly when you were asked about your internship, well *that* would be a big fat one, and big trouble.

Because space on your resume is so limited, you'll probably only have room for two or three of your most important experiences. That's why taking the time to shape your resume to fit different jobs is important. An executive looking for an administrative assistant at a high-tech company and a museum administrator looking for a go-fer in his fund-raising department are both looking for people with strong office skills. Beyond that, they want someone who shows an interest in their particular line of work. The person who shifts his resume about a bit to play up his computer knowledge for one position and his interest in art for another is in a better position than the person who plunks down the same resume for both.

7. After your experience section comes the gutter of your resume. It's like a little catch basin that collects interesting bits of errata about yourself.

Believe it or not, student activities are the thorniest cranny of the gutter. You should put them down, because they make you look well-rounded and involved. There are heaps of student activities that employers seem to love. "Team sports are great because they show the individual's ability to work as part of a group," says Deborah Rothstein, Director of Columbia University's Career Counseling Center. Student government, tutoring, academic clubs and community service work are also nice, apple-cheeked kinds of student activities, real Brandon Walshes. You can proudly declare your membership in the model UN.

But what about activities that make a true-blue pin-striped member of the establishment blanch, such as your arrest for protesting the construction of a nuclear power plant? "You are looking for a job, not a date," says one job counselor. "Realize that you are entering a business culture, and that that culture is a conservative one. Some things may just not be appropriate to mention." Wait a minute. You didn't get arrested at that power plant just to hide it the minute you went to look for work.

You may be poor, desperate and unemployed, but you're no SELL-OUT, right?

The counselor has a point. But so do you. Chances are, if you've been a committed activist in school, there are jobs you simply aren't going to be interested in for ideological and moral reasons.

An animal rights advocate won't be working for a furrier anytime soon. It's also doubtful that most former members of a campus Gay and Lesbian alliance are hoping to make careers at fundamentalist religious organizations. But those are the easy scenarios—there's the vast gray middle out there. Do you leave something off your resume you've been committed to, something you've gained a host of great organizational and people skills doing, because it might offend the person reading it? The choice of whether to include

set out to work for in advance, you should be able to gauge whether including such activities could in any way harm your chances.

Fraternity and sorority membership used to be real pluses on resumes, sometime around the time when Charles Blutarsky first pledged Animal House. Unless you're sending a resume to a person or company with strong ties to your society, many counselors advise leaving them off. However, like leadership roles in political organizations, your presidency of and community service work for Alpha Beta Theta can show your potential, so you make the call. Greek-letter honor societies are another matter entirely. Your Phi Beta Kappa key is always an asset.

"i think the answer to whether or not you put political causes down on a resume is it depends. if you are going to work for a political organization that shares your views, then fine. But where i work, it would be totally inappropriate."
—**Amanda, 24, investment banker**

"i wouldn't leave off the abortion rights campaigning i've done, partly because i've never looked for jobs where it would be a problem, and partly because it's a huge part of who i am."
—**Isabel, 25, nurse**

potentially controversial information is yours. If you feel like eliminating the information would be a personal betrayal, then don't. Chances are that a boss that finds your views on gun control or school prayer extremely offensive is not the person you should be working for. If you've done your homework about the industry you've

Finally, remember to spell out the names of clubs you participated in. If you were a member of OLAS, don't expect people to automatically know that it stands for Organization of Latin American Students. "Young people expect us to know what all these initials stand for," says one human resources manager, "but we don't."

Whatever student activities you decide to put on your resume, be selective. No employer wants to read a laundry list of 20 student activities. Try and limit yourself to no more than three or four, like your high school data, student activities information gets old fast. It should probably not be hanging around your resume several years into your working life.

8. Usually people include a section called SKILLS. You have skills, just by virtue of your age, that older people would kill for. Knowledge of computer programs such as Wordperfect, Microsoft Word and Pagemaker count as skills, as do foreign languages. These things will be viewed as strengths on any resume—no matter what the job. This is also a good place to mention any special training or knowledge you have for the job at hand.

9. If you have space, a short section on your personal interests often ends an entry-level resume. This is supposed to give the reader a personal snapshot of who you are, though it seldom does a very good job of it. Stay away from gut-wrenchingly intimate information, of course, but don't make the mistake of being too general. Reading, watching television, and going to movies, for example are how millions of people spend their free time. Those sort of interests are too flabby, generic and boring to be worth putting down. Reading spy novels, cross-country skiing and seeing Mel Brooks films are interests that give you a wee bit of depth. Coming as it does at the very bottom of your resume, the interest portion is often the first casualty of trimming for space. Nobody's going to care if you don't include it.

10. The same can be said of that old line: *References Available upon Request* which appears at the very bottom of the page. Of course they are. They'd better be. If you want to be absolutely orthodox about resume writing, including a line that says you have references readily available is not simply a nice little flourish, but a way of saying, *I stand behind everything I say on this piece of paper, check it out if you don't believe me.* But if you haven't got any room, don't lose sleep over not including it.

The Three Faces of Jan Brady

Okay, here's the resume of somebody you may know. She's a college senior, with a strong interest in women's issues and politics. She's been interning at a local women's center (but decided not to write "intern" in her job description), and highlighted some relevant classes she's taken to compensate for her lack of career experience. Her extensive education section also highlights her junior year abroad experience, always impressive to employers.

There are infinite ways to craft a resume and we do not pretend to present you with the gold medal standard. Use the information you've gained from this section to build one that best highlights your particular skills and abilities. Try not to copy the examples in this book—your resume should read like your own individual calling card, and nobody else's (certainly not Jan Brady's).

Jan Brady

education

4222 Clinton Avenue, Westdale, CA 99999 (777) 555-3333

Westdale University, Westdale, CA
Bachelor of Arts, Women's Studies, expected May 1997

University of Benghazi, Libya
Junior Year Abroad 1994–1995

Minor: Ceramics
GPA: 3.5
Honors: Clark Tyson Essay Prize, "What America Means To Me"
Dean's List, 1995–1996

Relevant Courses   Senior Seminar: Women, Race and Class in Society
Women, Violence and the Media
American Civil Rights Movements

experience

1995–Present   **Westdale Women's Center** Westdale, CA
Youth Education Assistant

Direct afternoon program for girls stressing leadership and self-esteem
Build links between center and local schools
Provide administrative support to Youth Program Manager

1994–Present   **Westdale University** Westdale, CA
Assistant Manager, Campus Dining Services

Coordinate 25 student workers in college dining hall
Contribute to planning monthly menu
Assist in serving 300 student diners three times a week

Summer 1994   **Haskell's Ice Cream Parlor** Westdale, CA
Sales Associate

Revamped food display and artwork in busy retail environment
Launched intensive promotion of low-fat dairy desserts

activities

Westdale Women's Collective—organized voter registration drive;
developed Women's History Month Westdale celebration

Westdale Whackers field hockey team—captain

Westdale Silver Platters—four-year member of college singing group

skills

Languages: Fluent in Arabic
Programs: Microsoft Word, Excel, Wordperfect 5.1, Aldus Pagemaker

interests

Tap dancing, stamp trading, collecting antique gold lockets

Here is a modified chronological resume by a slightly different Jan Brady. She's still interested in women's issues, but let's say she's heard about an opening in the fund-raising department of a local feminist organization. She's decided to include a specific job objective, and splits her experience section into two parts to play up a relevant extracurricular activity. She's also moved her skills section up the resume, above student activities. The point is you can manipulate information pretty freely on your resume to strengthen your case.

JAN BRADY

Permanent Address
4222 Clinton Avenue,
Westdale, CA 99999
(777) 555-3333

Current Address
5 Partridge Street
Cassidy Hall
Westdale, CA 99998
(310) 555-9532

OBJECTIVE
Seeking a fund-raising position with a women's rights organization

EDUCATION
Westdale University, Westdale, CA
Bachelor of Arts, Expected May 1997
Major: Women's Studies; GPA: 3.5

HONORS
Clark Tyson Essay Prize, "What America Means To Me"
Dean's List, 1995–1996

RELATED EXPERIENCE

Youth Education Assistant
Westdale Women's Center Westdale, CA   1995–Present

Direct afternoon program for elementary school girls
Build links between center and local schools
Provide administrative support to Youth Program Manager

Events Coordinator
Westdale University Women's Collective, Westdale, CA   1994–1995

Coordinated all organization fund-raising activities
Planned university-wide concerts, seminars, and lectures
Organized Fall 1995 campus voter registration drive

OTHER EXPERIENCE

Assistant Manager
Westdale University Dining Services, Westdale, CA

Oversee 25 student workers in college dining hall

SKILLS
Conversant in French
Familiar with Microsoft Word, Excel, Wordperfect 5.1

ACTIVITIES
Westdale Whackers field hockey team, varsity squad captain

Westdale Silver Platters Gregorian Chant Society, member

INTERESTS
Collecting antique gold lockets, macrame, and cycling

Our Jan's still gunning for that fund-raising position, so she's decided to take a risk and construct a **functional**, or skills-centered resume. As we said at the outset, in most cases, a functional resume is not a good idea because it will raise the hackles of some employers. Here, Jan decided to play up her various fund-raising experiences and other skills rather than focus on her actual job titles. The effect is provocative—and sometimes it works. The substance of what she's done makes a strong impression. Still, it's a gamble, especially because she doesn't use dates except in her employment section.

Jan Brady
4222 Clinton Avenue
Westdale, CA 99999
555-3333

EDUCATION

Bachelor of Arts, Women's Studies, May 1996
Westdale University, Westdale, CA 99999
GPA: 3.5

Activities

- Westdale Women's Collective, Events Coordinator
- Whackers field hockey team, captain
- Silver Platters Gregorian Chant Society, member

FUND-RAISING SKILLS

- Organized fund-raising events, including a faculty/administration talent show, a Banana Splits concert and an all-campus Hustle-A-Thon, which raised a total of $2,000 for the campus women's group.
- Canvassed door-to-door for the Alice Nelson Domestic Workers Retirement Fund
- Sold pet rocks to raise money for new team uniforms

LEADERSHIP

- Advised and tutored elementary school girls from disadvantaged backgrounds
- Built links between local schools and a community women's center by making classroom presentations about after-school programs
- Managed 25 student workers in a college dining hall serving 300 patrons daily
- Elected captain of Whackers field hockey team for two consecutive years

ORGANIZATIONAL SKILLS

- Coordinated fall 1995 campus voter registration drive, enrolling 50 new voters
- Contacted universities throughout California to arrange field hockey matches
- Selected and ordered team uniforms for three successive seasons
- Contributed to planning monthly menu for campus dining hall
- Planned schedules, compiled electronic database and managed official documents for women's center Youth Program Director

EMPLOYMENT

1995–Present   Youth Education Assistant, Westdale Women's Center
1994–Present   Assistant Manager, Westdale University Dining Services
Summer 1994   Sales Associate, Haskell's Ice Cream Parlor

55

Again, there are endless variations on resume formats—you can try to use a skills-centered resume with dates, thereby combining chronological and functional, flip your sections up, down and around; use objectives or drop them, and experiment with loads of funky fonts. This book is not designed to give you an endless supply of resume prototypes from which to choose. There are several excellent volumes out there that do just that. Hopefully, our examples give you some idea of just some of the possibilities so you can now go out there and craft a masterpiece.

WHAT SHOULD NEVER GO INTO A RESUME

If you can craft a good resume using the above ingredients, what follows is a list of resume poison. Put this stuff in and opportunities curl up and die.

Lies and distortions

Some of these items have been touched on before. If you've made it through this chapter without understanding that you shouldn't lie on your resume, you've got the morals of a slug. Everyone understands the pressures of trying to find work today, but misrepresenting who you are causes more harm than good. No one should have to lie their way into a good job.

A generic label on your resume that says "resume" or "c.v."

Don't put a label on your resume. Your name is all you need on the top of the page. Writing RESUME is redundant, FACT SHEET is corny and stupid, and CURRICULUM VITAE is pretentious in this country unless you are writing a specialized academic resume.

Information about your personal life and physical descriptions

Personal information about yourself, outside of what is acceptable in the INTERESTS portion of your resume, is a very bad idea. Do not volunteer drippy anecdotes about how you won the sixth-grade spelling bee, conquered your fear of shyness, or were crowned Homecoming Queen. **Never give your height, weight, eye or hair color in a resume. Your marital status, sex, sexual orientation, national origin, religion and race are also strictly your business.**

Photographs

"We still see mug shots. The other day I got a resume from someone with two photographs attached. One was him in a business suit. The other was apparently his casual look. It was pretty ridiculous. You think people would learn."

—Sherri, employment agency president

Forty years ago it was common for people to send a photograph of themselves with a resume. Unless you are trying out for a commercial, leave your snaps in your wallet.

Unflattering information that weakens your resume

Likewise if you were kicked out of school, arrested, or are the product of a bizarre genetic experiment— remember to leave off any information that makes you look unreliable, unsavory, or points to your lack of qualification on a resume. If you tell a potential employer every reason in the world not to interview or hire you, you'll be successful.

Graphics or Illustrations

Resumes are not hip. There is no such thing as a hip resume. Dressing your resume up with eye-popping graphics, charts, graphs or cute little cartoons will only underscore how woefully unhip it is. It's like forcing Mother Teresa to wear a sequined micro miniskirt. Naturally, a resume for a graphic artist's job is going to be less conservative than one for a position in a law firm. We've all endured stories of that sassy, plucky kid who took a big risk and got noticed. In almost any situation this is not the way to do it.

Testimonials

Personal references are important in the job interview process—but they don't belong on your resume—leave off turgid testimonials that hawk your filing ability as if you were a bag of Fritos. If your interviewer asks for references, you should be able to produce them.

Salary demands, reasons for leaving and availability to work

Never mention what you want to be paid in a resume, or what you've been paid in the past. Even if the person evaluating your resume isn't immediately repulsed by your crassness, you may be cutting yourself out of the race by aiming too high. Your reasons for leaving a particular job and availability to fill a new one are space wasters that can also take you out of play too early; they are subjects discussed in an interview and written on employment applications.

6. GOING UNDER COVER

A resume without a cover letter is like Regis without Kathie Lee, Hootie sans Blowfish, Ed Lover severed from Dr. Dre, Mary Kate without Ashley Olsen, Homer Simpson without Marge. In short, it ain't working, babe. Whenever you send your resume out, it _must_ be accompanied by its little pal, the cover letter. Otherwise, you stand a very good chance of having it thrown straight into the rubbish. We hate old Mr. Cover Letter, poor blighter. There's probably no single element in a job search that's more loathed. Why? Because unlike a resume, which despite all the sound and fury is really just a modified list of qualifications and experiences, a cover letter demands we be truly expressive. We have to put together a punchy little pitch that enhances the information on a resume and sells an employer on the advantages of working with us. That's not easy, even for people who are truly gifted scribes. And there's the added pressure of knowing that if a cover letter is shoddy, a resume may never get read.

57

Having given the cover letter that huge, scary buildup, you should know that there are plenty of human resource people out there who **don't even look at cover letters**, or merely skim them. "I only look at a cover letter after I look at a resume," says one. "It fleshes out material if I'm interested in a person." The rise of resume databases at many companies is also bad news for cover letters. Your resume is going to get scanned into the computer, and the letter you slaved over most likely gets trashed.

Great, you say. I can get away without writing one.

Don't even think about it.

Until some time in the distant future when the cover letter is officially declared extinct as a form of business correspondence, you are making a big mistake not including one with every mailed resume. Once you get in the habit of drafting cover letters, they'll come fairly easily to you. A fantastic cover letter is still a powerful tool in any job search, and the basic recipe for one is easy to master.

COVER LETTER ESSENTIALS

First, the basics. Appearance is as important on a cover letter as a resume. That means no grammatical or spelling errors, cheapo printing jobs, shabby paper, grease stains, lies, or sickening frou-frou artwork. As with resumes, don't copy the same cover letter over and over again. Print out each new letter, otherwise your type will lose its sharpness.

Use the same kind of paper for your cover letter as your resume, and keep it to a single page; around three paragraphs long is ideal. The best cover letters cut to the chase quickly. They introduce the writer, highlight the strongest points of her presentation, and slide to home plate with a zinger close.

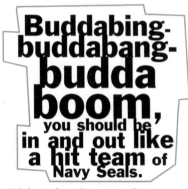

Buddabing-buddabang-budda boom, you should be in and out like a hit team of Navy Seals.

"Make it short," says one human resources officer, and "you'll have less chance of saying something stupid."

Generally, cover letters follow this format:

- An opening—tells why you are writing
- The meat—your sales pitch, which gives specific examples of why you are perfect for the job
- The kicker—a snappy closing that may detail how you'll follow up

Try and write your first cover letter without looking at examples. Go crazy. Break all the rules in that draft. Worry only about conveying your enthusiasm and talent. A cover letter is a **personalized** piece of business mail—your style has to shine through.

As you labor on succeeding versions, start to rein yourself in a bit. You can take far more creative risks in cover letters than in resumes. Stuffy firms prefer stuffy cover letters, of course, but if you are responding to a wittily written advertisement, there's no reason you can't be witty yourself. Nothing ventured, nothing gained. If you don't feel confident about being snarky, keep a serious tone. The last thing you want is a letter that sounds forced, false and not very funny.

Perhaps the most important element in any cover letter comes before the main body of your letter. It is the name of the person you are writing to. Never send a cover letter to "Attention Personnel," "Dear

Sir/Madame" or "To whom it may concern." Nor should you address your letter to a title with no name attached to it—for example, "Attention: Fashion Editor." **It will never get read.** You have to work harder than that. (The only possible exception might be a response to an ad in which only a post-office box number is given.)

You want your letter and resume to go to a person in the organization who has the capacity to hire you. If you're sending an unsolicited resume, you are going to have to dig around and **find out** who that person is. If you are writing to a large company, it's a good idea to send your resume to **both** the human resources department and the head of the department that you are interested in working in.

Never rely exclusively on the human resources department, particularly in large bureaucratic companies. Unless they are trying to fill a specific position and your resume happens to pop in at the right moment, you are going to be "put on file" and that means you are headed into a great big resume limbo, perhaps forever.

The manager who actually does the hiring, on the other hand, will have your resume close by in the event of an opening. Where do you get their names? From your research, you knucklehead. You might get the name from contacts you've made in the industry, find it in a trade magazine or employment directory. Always call up the company to see if that person is still working there, double-check the spelling of their name and ask what their official title is. It may have changed.

If you have no name to begin with, simply ring up and ask for the head of department X's name and its spelling. **Do not ask "Where can I send my resume?" unless you want the name of a personnel or human**

resources person, which is probably the information you are going to get if you immediately blurt out that you are looking for work.

Once you know whom to write to, you can work on your opening. Set the stage by explaining why you are writing. If you are responding to a specific opening, explain where you heard about it.

Dear Mr. Hasselhoff:

I am writing to apply for the position of Baywatch Babe, which you advertised through Sunshine Surf Academy's Career Development Center. I will be receiving a degree in Body Sculpting this coming May.

or

I am applying for the position of Baywatch Babe, which was advertised in the November 29th issue of *Cosmopolitan*. I am currently enrolled at Sunshine Surf Academy, and will graduate with a degree in Body Sculpting this May.

Here's a cardinal rule for cover letters—

 **DROP NAMES.**

If someone referred you to the person you are writing, don't be shy about it. It will move your resume to the top of any pile. "Most of our new hires are employee referrals," says one personnel director. "Someone comes in and says 'my next-door neighbor's kid is looking for work and he's really good'." Like it or not, connections matter. They distinguish you from some stranger who has no track record. Someone is vouching for you.

Dear Mr. Hasselhoff:

I'm writing at the suggestion of your colleague, Pamela Anderson Lee, who informed me that you are looking for a new member of the *Baywatch* cast. I have just graduated from Sunshine Surf Academy with a degree in Body Sculpting and have two years' work experience as a swimwear model.

or, if you previously met the person you are writing:

Dear Mr. Hasselhoff:

I enjoyed meeting you last Monday at the Sunshine Surf Academy job fair. You may recall from our discussion that I am graduating this May with a degree in Body Sculpting and have worked for two years as a swimwear model.

Having the name of a contact to drop into the first paragraph of your opening is the best case scenario. You will almost definitely get some kind of response.

Of course, it's always easiest to write a cover letter tailored to a particular job opening. Your chances of actually landing a job by sending out unsolicited letters is slim, **but there is nothing wrong with pursuing this option as one of many job-search strategies**. "Cold" cover letters and resumes may immediately get sent to a personnel department for "Filing," but if they are crafted skillfully, they can lead you to good contacts, if not jobs. Again, you must have the name of a contact person before writing. It's the postage stamp lottery—

who knows, you might get lucky, and you are only out the price of mailing a letter.

Think about direct mail offers. Gargantuan volumes of junk advertising are headed your way as you read this. The vast majority of it will end up in the garbage. But not all of it. There'll be that CD-of-the-month club you can't pass by, or a subscription offer to a magazine you like. Every once

in a while, you'll bite and order something. You certainly aren't doing yourself any harm by sending out letters, particularly if you have targeted the industry you want to work in and have a good deal of relevant skills. Just don't expect more than a tiny number of responses for all your efforts.

One method that may improve your results is to take a little of the desperation element out of cold letters. Instead of writing a stranger for a job, request an *informational interview*. Don't mention working for the company or scheduling a job interview—simply ask if you can meet to talk generally about opportunities in the industry. You may get a better response if the person doesn't feel pressure to give you a job or kick your resume down to the personnel department.

Your opening should be very brief, around two or three sentences long. Then it's on to the meaty portion of your cover letter, which goes into greater detail about your experiences and explains why you would be a good match for the job. Avoid simply regurgitating information that's on your resume. You want to go into detail about a couple of your key experiences—say, organizing a student film festival or chairing a voter registration drive—that not only demonstrate your interest in a particular field but illustrate positive qualities like leadership, organizational skills and the ability to work as part of a team. Don't just write, "I am a good leader, organizer and work well as part of a team," you ninny. It won't do.

When every strength you mention can be hand-tailored to the position at hand, your sales pitch will be strong and convincing. As in your resume, *do not point out any lack of experience or*

weaknesses you may have. Think about what the employer is looking for in a candidate and what strengths you have that match those needs. If you are sending out something cold, know what entry-level opportunities there are in a given industry, and what people in those jobs actually do before you go off half-cocked and write a letter.

Once again, research research, research.

After one or two paragraphs pitching yourself, close with a brief statement thanking the reader for her consideration and time. You can also reaffirm your interest in the position in the closing if you choose—by saying something along the lines of "I would welcome an opportunity to discuss how my skills might best contribute to the success of Virgin Airlines," or the like.

Many employment counselors advise closing with a specific time period in which you call to follow up on your letter, say a week. Don't be squeamish. A simple statement, such as "I will contact you next week to discuss this opportunity" is fine. It's the kind of an ending that makes you sound forthright and committed to a job in a given field. If you are writing to an out-of-town employer and are going to be in his neck of the woods sometime in the future, mention it, and ask if you can schedule a meeting then.

Here's a sample cover letter, for that coveted

Baywatch job. The masterpiece before you is only intended as a general sample, but it should give you a good sense of a cover letter's groove. Notice how it sticks to the form we outlined in this section—the first part of the letter identifies the speaker and explains why she is writing, the middle paragraphs illustrate why she is a strong candidate by mentioning just two key experiences, and the short closing paragraph mentions her intention to follow up. Cowabunga. We think Tiffany Amber's got a hammer-lock on that job.

TIFFANY-AMBER SOLEIL   777 Sunstroke Lane, Apartment 10 • Malibu, CA 90000 • (333) 333-3333

June 29, 1996

Mr. David Hasselhoff
Executive Producer
Baywatch Productions
70 Bayview Terrace
Playa de las Chicas, CA 99999

Dear Mr. Hasselhoff:

I am applying for the position of Baywatch Babe advertised in the June 1st issue of the *Chronicle of Higher Education*. I received an Associate's Degree in Body Sculpting from the Sunshine Surf Academy this May, and have spent the past month interning as a television spokesmodel.

Since graduation, I have worked in the Fashions Department of Home Shopping Network, where I model sportswear, perform in one-act plays, and appear in five-minute advertising spots viewed by more than 3,000 viewers in the greater Tarzana area. Previously I acquired extensive acting and life-saving experience as captain of the Sunshine Surf Aqua Tumblers. As a member of this precision water ballet squad, I toured 52 cities in the United States and Canada. In my senior year, I acted before a worldwide television audience as Cinderella in an underwater version of the fairy tale performed at the 1995 Goodwill Games in Ougadougou, Burkina Faso.

Physical fitness and search-and-rescue work are the twin passions of my life, and I would welcome any opportunity to put my skills to work on the set of *Baywatch*. I hope to have the opportunity to discuss my experience and qualifications with you at greater length.

Thank you for your time and consideration. I will contact you next week to discuss this opportunity.

Sincerely,

Tiffany-Amber Soleil

In the interest of equal time, let's bring back that budding Gloria Steinem, Jan Brady, and a cover letter she might write for that fund-raising job at the women's group.

5 Partridge Street
Cassidy Hall
Westdale, CA 99998

April 30, 1996

Ms. Athena Friedan
Director
The Blue Stocking Fund
444 Fourth Avenue
New York, NY 10000

Dear Ms. Friedan:

I heard about the Fund Raising Associate opening at your organization through Dean Gaea Mitford at Westdale University, where I am a senior. I will receive a Bachelor of Arts degree in Women's Studies this May, and after hearing Dean Mitford describe the requirements for the associate's job, I feel my skills and experiences would be a perfect fit.

For the past year, I have interned at the Westdale Women's Center, where I coordinate *I Am Somebody!*, an afternoon program for underprivileged girls designed to promote leadership and self-esteem. As Youth Education Assistant, I work as a peer counselor, design elements of the curriculum and act as special liaison between the center and local elementary schools. For four semesters, I also served as an officer in the Westdale University Women's Collective, raising over $2,000 for the campus women's group through concerts and other special events—a club record.

While at Westdale, I have taken part in a number of activities that have both deepened my commitment to feminism and broadened my organizational abilities. I would welcome any opportunity to meet with you to discuss my background and qualifications in greater detail, and am eager for a chance to contribute to the continued success of the Blue Stocking Fund.

Thank you for your consideration.

Sincerely,

Jan Brady

63

Once you've finished your cover letter, you just have to get the entire kit and kaboodle into the loving arms of some lucky employer out there. How to send it? *QUICKLY*.

7. TAKING YOUR SHOW ON THE ROAD

If you are sending out a flock of letters, regular mail is still the most cost-effective method. For a few cents, your letters will arrive in reasonably short order, unless you are applying for a position in Kinshasa. But for specific openings, the mails may not be fast enough.

If you are responding to a job opening you would take a hit out on your father for, consider sending your resume and cover letter via an express courier service. An overnight letter will cost you a few spondoolicks, but it will be worth it. Employers want to fill job openings ASAP. If you are eager enough to send in your material in a high-priority fashion, it can only reflect well on you.

Of course the fastest method of all is by that futuristic wonder, the fax, and it's cheaper than couriers. Increasing numbers of people are relying on faxes to transmit their resumes, but if you choose this method remember to *ALWAYS* send along  a hard copy in the mail. Faxes can be devilishly hard to read, and you don't want a blurred resume on slippery paper to be the only copy an organization has for its files. Imagine the horrible photocopies. Before you head for your modem, check ahead to see if sending in a faxed resume is appropriate. The last thing you want to do is get someone's back up over a niggling little thing like that.

Another approach is to **hand deliver** your material if the company is nearby. If the person doing the hiring can see you do this, it can be impressive. Don't linger or ask to speak with her. This is not your interview. Just courteously drop off your package, and be gone. It will also give you a chance to check things out in advance.

Whatever method you choose to send your resume, make sure your package looks crisp and professional. Try to use envelopes that match your resume paper. You may use standard business-size envelopes or large 9" x 12" envelopes. Larger envelopes have the added advantage of keeping everything flat. If you have a fancy printer that allows you to print out addresses with little hassle, great. If not, a neatly handwritten address is fine, and adds a personal touch. Always include your return address. Wait about a week, then give a ring to see if your masterpiece has arrived. **Never wait for an employer to call you— chances are they won't.**

Follow-up calls can be nerve-wracking, but don't put them off. You want to make your call when your resume and letter are still fresh in the mind of the person you sent it to. Before picking up the telephone, think through what it is you are going to say. Come up with a simple introduction, like  "Hello, I'm Stephen Urkel. I was calling to see if you received the information I sent you. I hope I'm not calling at a bad time" or the like. The last thing you want is to stutter nervously through your spiel. Don't read off a script though, because you'll sound robotic.

Whenever somebody refers you to a contact, that person's name gets thrown into your greeting—

"Bill Gates suggested I call" is going to open doors.

If you sent your resume in response to a specific job opening, or at the suggestion of a friend of the employer, you may have an easier time hooking up with the person you are trying to reach. When you send an unsolicited resume, you will have to work a little harder. Remember, requests for informational interviews always work better than pleas for work. At larger companies, unsolicited resumes are often immediately kicked straight into that black hole known as human resources or personnel. You want to connect with the person who has hiring authority, not the department in charge of screening out riffraff.

When you contact the person and find she has forwarded your resume to the human resources department, try telling her you are not applying for a specific position, but were looking for advice and wanted a few minutes to chat about opportunities in her industry. "I sent you my material because I wondered if you had a few minutes to share some information with me about advertising" may work.

Be unfailingly polite and highly conscious of your contact's precious _TIME._

You never want to come off as if you are demanding something from her— "I want a job" is far too threatening a message to send. Asking for the wisdom of an old hand, on the other hand, is flattering and appealing.

 65

When you speak to your contact, ask for a meeting of fifteen or twenty minutes, either over the telephone or in person—whatever is best for them. Call prepared with a few thoughtful questions—the person may want to have the meeting right then and there over the phone. If she refers you to someone else, thank her and move on to the new contact. In the very best-case scenario, this kind of call after an unsolicited resume can lead to an actual job interview. Who knows—a job may have opened up that day. But even if that isn't the case, you just might come away with a plethora of new contacts.

Whether you send a resume in response to a specific opening or not, often when following up you'll run straight into a **gatekeeper**—the assistant in charge of keeping nuisances like you from bothering Ms. Bigshot. Getting around a gatekeeper can be next to impossible if you sound unfocused or unsure of yourself, but it's important to try and speak with your contact person. Leave the "ums" and "ahs" out of your speech and strive to sound businesslike. A forthright "Luscious Jackson, please" often gets you ushered right in.

But if the assistant is good, he's going to ask you a few questions before he lets you fly past. Tricky questions like **"may I ask what this is regarding?"** Never say "I'm looking for work and I wanted to set up an interview," or "I just sent him my resume and I wanted to discuss it with him." Then the gatekeeper will **never** let you talk to his boss—the mere mention of the word **resume** is

going to grind everything to a dead halt. "I wanted to check and see if she received the information I sent her a few days ago" is the best response—it sometimes works, but assistants weren't born yesterday. Ask for a convenient time to call back. If you get a "don't call us, we'll call you" response, politely leave your name and number. Again, when leaving a message, don't mention annoyances like interviews or resumes.

Never get stroppy or rude with an assistant—it can ruin your chances of ever talking to his boss. Your aim is to make that person your ally, so be nice. And if a gatekeeper goes out of his way for you, he gets a thank-you note.

When you call to check if your package has been received, remember your call is not an interview or a chance to campaign heavily for the job. You want to make sure it arrived and **delicately** find out when the employer may be getting back to you. In this case, the person you speak with will usually be able to tell you when you can expect to hear back. If you don't hear back within that period, call back and try something like "I was wondering when I might get the chance to discuss the position with you. I'm very interested in this opportunity and wondered what your time frame might be."

Just how many times you should call an employer is a matter of some debate. But generally, after four calls or so, you may have to write an opportunity off. **Never badger**; space your calls out—twice a week is too much. And, as always, be polite throughout. After you've followed up, you are ready for the next phase of your job search—interviews.

8. GOING TO AUDITIONS— THE INS AND OUTS OF INTERVIEWING

You've done it—your resume and cover letter gleam like the top of Michael Jordan's head, your thorough networking and research have paid off—lo and behold, you've landed a job interview. Now a large number of people view interviews as a kind of diabolic torture, designed to reduce them to a quivering, sweating—and still unemployed— mass of insecurity. Get a hold of yourself, sunshine. You've come this far, why panic now?

A FEW POINTERS

There have been thousands of pages written on how to conduct yourself in a job interview, and hundreds of seminars designed to help you conquer your fear of stuttering through that all-time favorite interviewing question: "Tell me about yourself?" But it seems no matter how much information is added to the Interviewing Skills canon, most knees still get wobbly at the idea of sitting down with a potential employer and talking. And **talking** is, after all, what many of us do best.

Before an interview, we are facts and figures on a resume, little itty bits of data that are easy to dismiss or throw in the rubbish. In an interview, we are fully fleshed-out carbon-based life forms, finally given a chance to really shine. Being "interviewed" implies a very passive sort of interaction—you are called to the 50th floor office of Mr. or Ms. Bigwig, and they fire all sorts of horrible questions at you until you crack and admit you are not cut out for the job. That's not the way it should go. Ideally, you are having a conversation with an employer, checking each other out, deciding if the job would be right for you. That means **both of you have an active role to play**, not just the guy signing paychecks.

Think about it this way. You are shopping for a pair of trousers. You did your homework, you got a sense of what styles you liked and what kind you wanted, and now you're taking the trip to the dressing room. Maybe those brown velour gauchos looked better on the rack, maybe the elephant bell-bottoms make you look fat. A job interview is a chance to see if the fit between you and a prospective employer would be a good one. Okay, that's a neat analogy, but it probably does little to dispel your nervousness. The fact is, interviews make most people nervous. That includes interviewers.

With the exception of a sadistic bully or two, **interviewers do not get off on finding fault with you.**

What follows are some tips to successful interviewing that will help you avoid some of the traps many inexperienced interviewees fall into. Remember, even the most polished among us have disastrous interviews— unlike other elements in your job search, it all boils down to human interaction, to the million little differences between people that either make us click with another individual or run screaming in the other direction. That's why so many employment counselors compare the whole experience to a blind date. You simply cannot predict if your interviewer is going to fall in love with you or not, no matter how well qualified you are. But if you come prepared and anticipate what the interviewer wants in a candidate, you'll go a long way toward clinching a job offer.

TIP #1:
How Do You Get to Carnegie Hall Again?

Practice, practice, practice. Okay, it's a joke that dates from the first ice age, but it really holds true for interviews. Very few people pop out of the womb with an amazing knack for convincing people to hire them. If you are looking for your first job,

your interview muscles are flabby and undeveloped. You need to pump them up. The best way to do this is to put yourself in interview situations. The more interviews you do, the better you'll become.

Different Types of Interviews

Believe it or not, in the course of your job search you may discover that there are different breeds of interview styles out there to contend with. Most people don't know their names, but you should be aware of the different formats you might encounter. Come prepared and relaxed, and you'll conquer any of them:

Directed and Nondirected Interviews are the most common kinds of interview styles. A *directed interview* usually implies a single interviewer working from a checklist or a set list of questions, and your responses are then compared with other candidates. A *nondirected interview* is more free form, with plenty of open-ended questions that allow you to be more expressive with your answers. Most people experience some combination of the two. If you find yourself in a straight directed interview, resist the temptation to give a one-word answer. Instead, illustrate your answers with good anecdotes that show off your particular skills. In a really unstructured, loosey-goosey interview, avoid rambling answers that don't do a good job of explaining what qualities you would bring to a particular job.

Stress Interviews might also be called Butthead Interviews, because only a butthead would put someone through one. The whole point is to shake you up, and see how you react under pressure, with extremely difficult or embarrassing questions. Stress interviews are most common in macho fields like investment banking. The best tactic—don't lose your cool or take offense. The whole point is to see how you'll respond.

Tests are given in many job interviews because you can't bluff your way through them, or so it's thought. You'll encounter examinations for civil service jobs and frequently in jobs demanding any kind of specialized skill. Jobs in journalism often require some kind of "tryout" where you work as a reporter for several hours to test your abilities. Writing and grammar tests are also common in that profession, as well as in some publishing jobs. Last, many entry-level office jobs still require some kind of *typing test*—so brush up on your typing speed now.

Board or Panel Interviews. Yikes. These are thankfully very rare for entry-level jobs. In this format a candidate is asked questions by a group of people in a single session. The questions can take any form—but you'll be addressing not one but several people. If you are so unblessed as to have to go through this, remember to remain focused on the person who asked you the question when you answer it. When someone else asks you a question, turn your attention to them. Maintain eye contact and don't get flustered.

Group Interviews are also rare. In this format, you are interviewed with a group of candidates. The interview might be structured as a problem-solving exercise or discussion. The point is to see what role you play and what qualities you exhibit within the group, sort of as if you were a chimpanzee being studied by an anthropologist. Remember the interviewer(s) are looking for character traits like leadership and the ability to work well with others, not simply the right answers to their questions. The best thing to do is to attempt to figure out what qualities they value, and behave accordingly.

Multiple Interviews are very common. If you are recruited from a college interview or job fair, expect to have at *least* one more interview at a company. Your initial interview may be very brief—maybe only about five minutes in which you offer your resume and have a brief chat. Based on that information, you may be asked to come in for a formal interview. At job fairs, the key is to not linger. Introduce yourself, hit the high points, listen to what the human resources person has to say, ask when you should call them, and when they signal the mini-interview is finished, move on. Recruiting interviews are usually full-fledged appointments that take place on campus.

The key to multiple interviews is *stamina*. If you are contacted for additional interviews, try to change your spiel a bit. If your first interview only allowed you to speak generally about one or two skills, broaden and deepen the discussion with each successive meeting. Once you get past the gatekeepers—the human resources people who'll conduct the initial interview(s) in an effort to screen out applicants— you'll meet with the manager who you will most likely be working under. This person has the authority to hire you. Your later interviews are very important, and should be the most detailed of all.

"i'd never make an interview with
an employer i really wanted to work for my
very first interview. i'd build up to it. even
if you have appointments with companies you aren't
that interested in working for, do the interviews
for the practice."

—Debra Engel, Vice President of Corporate Services, 3Com Corporation

If you are dying to work for Bubba's Chicken Niblets, do what you can **not** to make them your first interview. You don't want to dive in cold, get all flustered, lose it and start babbling on senselessly about poultry. So interview at McDonald's first, Wendy's second (grab a shake), and then go to Bubba's after you have some interview experience under your belt. If you are in college and other companies are coming to interview at your campus career office, sign up to see them, even if you aren't chomping at the bit to punch a clock for them. Treat these interviews seriously, though—just because they aren't the employer of your dreams doesn't give you license to appear disrespectful, unenthusiastic or bored.

Informational interviews, interviews for internships, and any "rehearsal" sessions you can put together with a friend or career counselor are also great practice for the main event. As you gain confidence in interview situations, you'll feel more relaxed by the time of your appointment with an employer you have your sights set on.

What else should you be doing? Your homework. You are ready to kick into a second round of intensive, in-depth research.

TIP #2:
Do Your
Homework TWICE

Once you've landed an interview, learn everything you can about your potential employer. If you were smart, you did a fair amount of preliminary investigating before you ever got called to come in. If not, you better bust your butt digging up material now. Don't even think about going to an interview with no information about the company you supposedly want to work for. "Really know the industry inside and out," says an executive at a California high-tech company. "Young applicants often come in and don't know a thing about the company. It makes a big impression."

Yeah, a terrible one. Just imagine, someone asks you the name of the company's CEO and you haven't a clue. How humiliating. But there's more to it than that—the more you know about where you are applying before you go, the less of a big scary mystery your interview process is going to be.

Head back to the library or electronic database and get cracking. Look for related newspaper and magazine articles about the company, check with your local **Better Business Bureau** to see if they keep any information about a potential employer. Get a hold of any company literature you can, such as brochures, booklets, the company's annual report. You can get a lot of this stuff simply by calling up a firm's public relations or human resources department and asking for it. College career centers often keep company information on file. You might try the local Chamber of Commerce as well. There is information to be had about even the smallest companies.

Read any trade publications about the industry. Tap everybody you know for the names of people who either work for the company or in the same field. If you can arrange an informational interview or two beforehand, you'll be loose as a goose when you need to be. Write down information about the company on 3" x 5" cards, and have someone quiz you.

If you've done any networking to get this far, check back with your contacts and give them the good news. Not only can they help prep you for the interview, but it's polite to keep them posted about your progress.

Research is going to acquaint you with the ins and outs of a particular company before you even walk in the door. You'll know not just the simple facts, such as what a company makes or what their quarterly profits were, but what new innovations they are planning in the field, what their subsidiary companies are, what the future holds for the industry. Research is also critical in helping you prepare for questions that will be asked in an

interview. Perhaps more importantly, you will be able to **ask** intelligent questions of your interviewer that demonstrate your depth of knowledge about the company and your commitment to working there.

TIP #3:
Gear Up
For
Questions
You May
Be Asked

"A lot of interview questions we ask are aimed at finding out how an individual works with others. Try and think of examples from your life—from school or athletic teams, for instance—where you took initiative or solved a big problem. It's really embarrassing when you interview someone and ask about a conflict they helped resolve and they say, 'oh, I've never had a conflict.' Give me a break."
—Allan Hoon, Director of Human Resources, Fujitsu Corporation USA

"When i first started going to interviews i memorized answers to all these questions out of career books—like 'What was your biggest achievement?' or "What was your worst mistake?' i would spend all night thinking up answers. What i found was that those questions rarely got asked of me. And now that i've been out in the working world a bit, they never get asked at all."

—Vanessa, 26, copywriter

You and your interviewer are engaged in an intricate little dance. You're trying to score points without being too obvious and ferret out information about a company that will help you decide if it's a place you'd like to work. She is trying to decide if you are the kind of candidate who'll fit into the company like a glove, or a possible ax murderer. She doesn't have too much to go on, and she has 35 people lined up after you to talk to about the same job. She'll look at your resume, of course, check out how you're dressed and note whatever annoying nervous tics you have. And, in a desperate attempt to get at who you are, she's going to ask dozens of questions—about your experiences, qualifications, goals, interests, and values.

Now some of those questions are going to be specific to the particular job you are interviewing for. You can anticipate many of them from your research. If you apply for a job as a mechanic for large passenger jets, you are obviously expected to know a thing or two about airplanes. Beyond that you are going to have to explain why you are drawn to a particular employer (don't say because they are the only one with an opening) and what makes you special among the hordes of others applying.

There will also be questions based on your resume. Almost certainly you'll be asked about where you went to school and your experiences there. Know what's on your resume like the back of your hand. You'll be expected to comment on information you gave there at length.

Whenever possible, write out questions you feel might be asked in advance. Ask a friend to do a dry-run interview with you. "If you have friends interviewing at the same company, ask them what questions were asked, and how the interview went in general, that can help prepare you," says one corporate recruiter.

However, you should never, ever memorize set answers to possible interview questions. It will backfire. You may waste your time rehearsing a speech you'll never give and draw a blank when your interviewer asks you something you didn't expect. Worse, some of those questions will get asked and you'll sound like a robot.

The vast majority of interviewers aren't thick—they can spot a pat or wooden answer a mile away. You want the whole exchange to be as relaxed and casual as possible. Sounding like a Miss America finalist with some saccharine, canned response to a tough question will hurt you.

If there are gaps in your resume—say the three years you spent in a Turkish prison—come prepared to explain them. This is where having thought through an answer can really pay off. Think through what you are going to explain that year in the clink. How will it sound? Will the interviewer roll her eyes or admire your candor and interest in other cultures? You want to sound polished and thoughtful. You don't want to appear surprised, caught off guard or embarrassed.

Other questions you will be asked won't necessarily be tied to the job offer. They are designed to get at what kind of person you are and what kind of employee you'll be.

Look them over. Try to answer them. It will help you prepare. But don't cling to it like a life raft. You can't possibly predict every query that will be posed to you. That's okay. It's far more important to step into the interviewer's shoes and ask, "What is this person after?" Then pitch your answers accordingly. What they are invariably after is a good employee, with the appropriate skills and experience, who has some quality or spark that sets them apart.

It's easy, believe it or not, to forget the purpose of an interview when you are in one. Somebody asks you what it was like to be captain of your synchronized swimming team. Next thing you know, you're prattling on for 20 minutes

Can you work well with others?
Will you thrive at my company?
Can you take initiative and come up with novel solutions to complex problems?
Or are you going to wind up a disgruntled, insubordinate twerp?
Are you a liar?
Are you a lazy, sloppy, irresponsible thief?

The interviewer knows if she asked you any of these questions flat-out you'd tell her what you think she'd want to hear. So she has to be a little sneaky and try to get you to reveal your true colors.

Most interviewers, and certainly all good interviewers, do not have a single, unvarying laundry list of questions that they always ask. The sidebar of sample interview questions featured here is far from an exhaustive list of what you can expect. Most of the questions on it are the sort many employers use with entry-level people to get a sense of their strengths and weaknesses.

about wearing nose plugs and waterproof makeup. Unless you are trying for a job at a company that supplies water ballerinas with spangly swimsuits, you are going to sink your chances. You've lost sight of what it is you want out of the conversation— a job offer and information about the company. Your interviewer is not your therapist, nor does she feel spasms of delight listening to your monologue about the joys of being Miss Aquatennial. She wants to know if you are up to snuff.

"when i first went interviewing, i thought great, i get to go someplace and just sit and talk about how wonderful i am. it seemed like the easiest thing ever. i forgot that there are two people in the room. i soon realized that just talking about yourself is no way to get a job." —Angus, 26, writer

Now don't get this wrong.

You want to be pleasant, charming and funny—all the things you naturally are.

And you want the interviewer to walk away thinking, "What a great person. I really loved talking with her." But this is still a professional exchange, not a tryout for the Daisy Chain. Steer a mile clear of your personal problems and inner child. Nobody, and we mean nobody, goes very far in a job interview talking about old girlfriends.

You are selling yourself in an interview—you want to demonstrate what a talented, skilled asset to the company you'd be. If you linger too long on past glories without providing some solid examples of how you took charge, kicked butt and bit the bullet, you aren't doing your job. As important as it is, your resume is not the script for your interview. Don't let it dictate how things go. If that happens, and talk never shifts to the present, and what you'd be doing on the job, you are probably not going to get an offer.

That doesn't mean you lunge across the desk, grab your interviewer by his lapels and beg him to hire you. Everyone knows that being shy is a bad idea in an interview—but being overly aggressive is also poison. Don't say, "I'm perfect for this job. I have all the right skills and experiences to make me a natural here." Okay, there may be people out there who would see that approach as ballsy and gutsy. Most people, however, would feel their lunch coming back up.

And don't throw around nonsense language you've heard from motivational speakers. If you are a "self-starter," explain what that

means. Give an anecdote that shows *how* you took initiative. Don't say, "I take initiative." In journalism, it's called "Show, don't tell."

Back to that water ballet experience—what makes it important? *Illustrate* the blips on your resume, don't restate them. Point out that floating around in a pool to Swan Lake is more than that. Show how you pulled together to win a national competition, how you outlined a plan of action, how you delegated responsibility, how you learned self-discipline and organized a T-shirt sale to raise money for a team trip to Greenland. It's all relevant.

Don't go overboard on a single experience, or close an anecdote with some tacky line straight out of America's Junior Miss, like "and that's why I want to be an electrical engineer." You've got to have a light touch. Stand behind everything you say. You make scads of claims in your resume and cover letter, and here you are, in person, to show that they aren't a bunch of hoo-hah.

Lying, here it is again, our favorite subject. Don't do it. What if you claim to speak Serbo-Croatian and your interviewer is from Belgrade? You're going down, sleaze-ball. Now, as in resumes, you don't want to dwell on your various flaws and weaknesses, ever. But misrepresenting yourself is not the answer. If an interviewer asks you about a job you

were fired from, don't lie, but don't wallow in the negative. Simply explain what happened briefly and honestly. And, **do not badmouth your former employer**, no matter how tempting it is. Try to spin your response so that it stresses what POSITIVE lessons you gained from the experience. You'll look mature, thoughtful, and professional.

If you get tripped up, fall off your train of thought or just go blank, take a deep breath. A pause for a good answer is much better than a mad rush to fill up the black hole of silence with a bad one. Again, most interviewers aren't looking for you to slip up. Many of them dread the experience as much as you do. This is frequently true of interviews with potential supervisors, as opposed to appointments in personnel departments. A woman who drills for crude oil all day is different from her colleagues in the human resources office. After all, she doesn't interview people for jobs for a living. She's got to figure out what to ask you, pick a candidate and tell all the others they didn't get the position. Not fun. She doesn't want you to be uncomfortable—she's already uncomfortable as hell.

Having said that, there are real beasts out there. We've all heard stories of interviewers who treat the process like a fraternity hell night. Maybe you'll get one of these characters, someone who thinks its cute to ask you to stand on your head or sing the national anthem, make you compute complex equations on the spot and ridicule your education (see the inset on interview styles).

Don't let them intimidate you or get you flustered. That's the game. Some sick people actually believe that by putting you under a white hot spotlight they'll reveal how you'll react under pressure, and thus see just what it is "you are made of." If the job is important to you, be calm and direct, then jump through only the hoops you choose to. You may not know the answer to a complex question. Say so. If it's a preposterous question, say so. The answers aren't as important as your response to them. Attempt to sound cool and confident, and try not to take it personally.

But if you feel someone is needlessly jerking your chain, or saying something completely inappropriate, remember **you can put the breaks on.** You can politely thank them and walk away, laugh it off or ignore it. It's your choice. **This should go without saying—sexual innuendo and harassment, racist jokes, gay jokes and insults of any kind simply do not have to be tolerated.** Frankly, some people are just bad news. Write them off. You certainly don't want to work with them no matter how badly you need a job. Life is too short.

Try and keep your answers to any questions pithy and to the point. Don't ramble on for ten minutes on a single subject. This is a dialogue, after all. The best interview questions are the **open-ended ones**, such as "Tell me about yourself." They give you plenty of room to take the ball and run, run, run.

Remember, you want the interviewer to get a sense of what makes you especially suited to the job. Hit your high points again. Avoid a string of monosyllabic answers. "Yes" and "No" aren't the kind of responses an interviewer is looking for. As you answer a question, watch your interviewer's reaction to it— you'll likely be able to spot whether you are giving her material she wants or are going off on a tangent.

Unless you really hit it off, or you can't shut yourself up, a first interview for most entry-level jobs is probably going to run around 30 to 45 minutes. A good interviewer is going to keep you blabbing a lot of that time, but it's important you get her to talk her fair share, too. That's where your questions come in.

Common Job Interview Questions

You will encounter variations on some of these questions in your interviews. Try to think of good answers to them. Have a friend ask you a few. But don't treat this like a cheat sheet for a final exam. You can never be certain of what will be asked in an interview. Rest assured there will be quite a few questions that aren't listed below.

- Tell me about yourself.
- What are your greatest strengths/weaknesses?
- What achievements are you most proud of? Why?
- What have you learned from your mistakes?
- (For college grads) Why did you go to college X? What was it like there?
- Why did you major in _____?
- (For high school grads) Why didn't you go to college?
- Which courses at school did you enjoy the most? And what ones did you hate?
- Which were your extracurricular activities?
- Tell me about your job at _____. Describe your responsibilities there.
- Why did you leave your last job?
- How did you become interested in this field?
- Where do you see yourself in five years' time?
- How do you like to spend your free time?
- Give me an example of a conflict you helped resolve. How did you resolve it?
- What was the toughest decision you ever had to make?
- What book are you currently reading? Who is your favorite author?
- Are you good at working under pressure, and under deadlines?
- What do you think it takes to be successful in our organization?
- Describe your ideal work environment.
- Will you relocate?
- How do you define professional success?
- What do you know about my organization?
- Why did you apply here?
- Why should I hire you?

TIP #4:
Come Prepared
with Good Questions

Asking questions—not just answering them—is critical in interviews. Nobody wants to hire a blob who shows no fire for the business or interest in the firm. Interviews are tougher than mere inquisitions—you want to ask intelligent questions because you are a highly desirable candidate shopping for the **RIGHT** job, not just begging for someone to put you out of your unemployed misery.

By interacting with the interviewer, not simply being passive and waiting for questions to answer, you are being conscientious and demonstrating your enthusiasm. Come up with several good questions you can ask in the interview—even if you know the answers to some of them. Write them down. You don't want to be caught empty-handed when the interviewer asks you if you have any questions—and she most definitely will.

What kind of questions can you ask? Say you are at your Bubba's Chicken Niblets interview. From your research you recall an article that mentioned Bubba was a pioneer in using a particular cooking method that rendered his chicken much less likely to clog your arteries with fatty goop. You ask about it, and mention how impressed you were by Bubba's leadership in the effort to make fast food more nutritious. It's one of the reasons you were attracted to the company. In fact, you wrote a paper on the nutritional value of fast food in biology. Will the cooking method be employed in every Bubba's franchise? Where does Bubba see the company headed in the next ten years? Are Bubba's competitors getting into the nutritious niblets? You read that one rival is about to announce his own newfangled niblet recipe. Suddenly you are having an interesting conversation with your

Inappropriate Interview Questions

Some questions are red flags—a strong sign that a job isn't for you, no matter how much you may think you want it. Certain kinds of questions suggest that the employer may discriminate against you based on your answer. For example, asking whether or not you are Jewish is technically not illegal, but discriminating against you because you are Jewish most certainly is. The majority of employers avoid trouble by steering a mile clear of questions like those listed below. If you do get asked one of these slimy questions, don't be shy about voicing your objections to them.

- *Are you gay?*
- *Are you married?*
- *Do you plan to get pregnant?*
- *Have you ever been on strike?*
- *Do you believe in unions?*
- *Have you ever been hospitalized?*
- *What political party do you belong to?*
- *Do you live with your girlfriend?*
- *Are you a practicing Christian?*
- *Have you ever been discriminated against for being Asian-American?*
- *Do you think a person who weighs as much as you can do this job?*
- *What's a nice girl like you doing applying for a job like this?*
- *Have you ever filed a worker's compensation claim?*
- *Are you busy this evening?*
- *Are you sexually active?*
- *Do you think it's appropriate to wear a skirt that short to an interview?*
- *Have you ever been in therapy?*
- *How could you afford such a nice suit?*

interviewer—you both have relaxed and are enjoying the chat. Bubba is going to be weeping for joy. Here's someone who really knows his niblets.

Now don't get silly here. If you are being interviewed by Bubba, who wrote the niblet recipe, you can ask fairly technical questions that a human resources person would not be able to answer. Never try and stump your interviewer, grill her with rapid-fire questions, or trip her up. You would hate that if she did that to you—and she'll surely hate you if you come off like a snotty little know-it-all.

Good interview questions *subtly* show off your expertise, your ability to solve problems, and the strengths you have as an employee. **They center on what the employer needs in a candidate, not on what you want from an employer.** Bubba has a hole he needs desperately to fill. Asking him what he can do for you is not going to make him want to fill it with you.

78

TIP #5:
People DO Judge Books by Their Covers

We've mentioned that your interviewer is trying to make a big decision with a few scraps of paper and a brief meeting. That's not a lot of evidence. What else can she do? Watch you like a hawk. If you are repulsive, stinky, abrasive and rude, she's going to use that information to make a decision. It really is not just what you say to her, but how you say it **and** what you are doing while you say it.

Undoubtedly, there are interviewers out there who have their own peculiar prejudices. They might just hate red-heads or people who wear brown or people from big cities. Nothing you can do about that. But you can brush up on **interview etiquette**—the rules and conventions that are pretty much universal. Ignore them at your peril.

Good Questions to Ask in an Interview

- **What qualities are you looking for in a candidate for this job?**
- **Can you tell me about your own experience with this company?**
- **How long do people generally stay in this particular position?**
- **What do you see as this company's greatest strengths?**
- **What do you think of your competition?**
- **Where do you see this industry heading?**
- **What happened to the person who was last in this job?**

. . . And Some Bad Ones

- **What would my starting salary be?**
- **How many vacation/sick days do I get?**
- **How many hours am I expected to work per week?**
- **When can I expect a raise?**
- **Why should I come to work for you?**
- **So, do I get the job?**

Never ask an interviewer "How much will I make?" or "What kinds of health benefits can I expect?" Yuck. Bringing up your potential salary in an interview is like throwing water on the Wicked Witch of the West. Sit back and watch your opportunity melt away.

For one thing, it's incredibly bad form. After all, you haven't even been offered a job yet (and most likely, you won't get an offer now). On the other hand, it's a good possibility that your interviewer will bring up the subject of money. If he does, listen attentively, smile and be generally agreeable. What if Bubba's offering a half of what McDonald's pays? Don't dispute the figure or tell him they pay twice as much down the road at company B. You can always discuss money in more detail at your next interview—just never during your first. (More on negotiating a salary later.)

If you've done your homework, you should have a pretty good idea of what the company pays its entry-level people in various jobs. Many companies take the time to give all interviewees information packets about their benefits programs. Try to read it over before your interview. Don't poison a perfectly nice person against you by asking how many sick days you get. "It's just so mercenary to ask about that stuff," says one personnel director. Not exactly a positive character trait.

BIG NEWS

TIP #6:
Mind Your Manners—And Your Body Language

Good manners are important in everyday life, but nowhere are they more important than in an interview. "Remember you are being interviewed from the moment you walk in the door," says one employment counselor. "Don't come late— get there two hours early and walk around the block until it's time for your interview if you have to, but be on time.

It's true rolling in late to an interview looks lousy—do anything in your power to prevent it from happening. Call and confirm your appointment a day or so ahead of time. Make sure you know the name of your interviewer, and the location of your meeting. Get very good directions. If you are unsure about how long it will take to get to your interview, do a test run the day before. Try to make the trip around the same time of day as your appointment to get a sense of what traffic conditions are like. If you are early, cool your jets somewhere until show time.

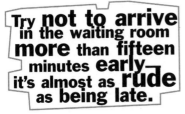

If you are early just tell the receptionist who you're there to see, but explain that you're early so you'll tell her when to notify them. Wait until a few minutes before your appointment to ask them to call.

Sometimes, unfortunately, even the best-laid plans blow up in our faces and we are unavoidably tardy. Don't run into an office, frantic, panting and disheveled. Apologize politely, and explain the reason for your lateness, then move on. If you know in advance that you have an unavoidable impasse in your path and you are going to be late, the best thing to do is to call your appointment and apologize then. Perhaps they can reschedule you.

It should go without saying that you are nice to **everyone** you meet at a job interview, but unfortunately some people fail to figure this out. First of all, you never know who may be called upon to help make a tough hiring decision. And second, it's just common courtesy. Be very polite to receptionists, administrative assistants, and anyone else you meet.

Don't schlep a bag full of dirty Kleenex, hair spray, stale chewing gum, smashed compacts, chewed pencils and crumbling cigarettes into an interview situation. If your interviewer asks for an extra copy of your resume you'll have to go rummaging through all that mess for several minutes to fish out a crumpled, stained piece of paper. You'll look like a neurotic old lady, and the last thing you want is to appear sloppy or crazy.

If you have a leather portfolio or nice-looking satchel or case to carry your papers in, bring it. Take along a pen and a pad of paper, a few extra copies of your resume and copies of any reference letters you might have. That, and a book to read while you wait, is more than enough baggage to carry.

When you meet your interviewer, don't **slap** him on the back, **punch** him on the shoulder, **call** him by his first name (unless he insists), kick your feet up on his desk, **tell him** a **vulgar joke** or play with the model airplane on his desk. **Being aggressively familiar is as bad as being hopelessly withdrawn.** And **don't flirt. Ever.**

Wait for him to offer you a chair. Don't plop down in your seat until he takes his. Of course, remember to look him in the eye and give him a firm handshake. Listen attentively to everything he says—even if you've heard all the information before. Never look at your watch. The meeting is over when the interviewer decides it is, and not a moment sooner.

Obviously, you should appear interested and enthusiastic at an interview. Even if a bomb dropped on your apartment the same morning, resist any urge you may have to be nasty, pessimistic or in any way negative. If your interviewer is prattling on about all the various odious tasks you'll have to do if hired, don't betray your disgust or fear. Make your interviewer believe you can handle anything they throw at you. Worry about whether you **want** to handle everything they throw at you after you get a job offer.

Don't confuse enthusiasm with syrupy buckets of cutesy-pie cheeriness or with desperation. Desperation is extremely off-putting. No matter how long you've been looking for work,

no matter how much of a loser you feel you are, don't act like a pathetic, whining schlump, begging for a job, any job.

That can be hard—sometimes you just want to fall on your knees and offer to scrape the grit out from underneath your interviewer's fingernails in exchange for work. It's a mistake. Employers are attracted to confident individuals who seem to have it on the ball—if they don't snap you up, someone else will. But never cross the line from confidence into arrogance. Cockiness and insolent behavior will never be rewarded.

You may be very nervous in an interview, and it's okay to have butterflies. Just make sure your butterflies don't manifest themselves in irritating ways. Many of us have **nervous tics** we simply never think about. We suck our fingers, blow our bangs out of our faces, kick the floor, twirl or constantly flip back our hair. Curb yourself.

If you are really worried about having an obnoxious habit, you might consider **videotaping** a mock interview situation with a friend or counselor. If that sounds a little creepy to you, you can cure yourself of any annoying tic simply by taking note of how you behave in conversations. Start catching yourself when you lapse into the ol' giggle/hair flip combination or whatever it is you are hooked on. If your mother has been needling you about your posture for ages, now is the time to listen. Body language is important— sit up straight, don't slouch around or stare at the floor. You are not in the principal's office. If you act like you are, people are going to think that's where you belong.

TIP #7:
Dvess
Appvopviately

"The worst part about my first interview was wearing panty hose. I just hate wearing panty hose. It's so uncomfortable. I dreaded getting dressed for interviews."

—Josephine, 26, newspaper reporter

At least once in your life, someone has probably told you that your skirt was too tight, your tie was too loud, your belly-button ring made their stomach turn, your pink hair was most definitely a fashion *don't*. Maybe it was your dowdy old great aunt Beryl, whose style you certainly did not want to emulate, or maybe it was someone equally out of it and stuffy. Nobody likes being told what to wear, and we like being told what *not* to wear even less. There's nothing more oppressive than reading a prim little magazine article about what one should and shouldn't be seen in. After all, we come in different shapes and sizes, and polyester hot pants definitely do not show everyone off to their best advantage.

Perhaps that's why we instinctively balk at advice about how to dress in the workplace. It seems a none-too-subtle way to get us to abandon whatever individuality we have and melt into the big charcoal-colored middle. *Yecch.* "Who are you to tell me how to dress?" you say. "If people do not accept me for who I am, well then screw them." That works fine, if you are Madonna. Swallow this ugly truth—you must dress appropriately for every job interview, no matter what the industry, if you expect to be taken seriously.

"If you look at your clothes and say 'This is a great date outfit,' it's probably a really lousy interview outfit."

—Susan Gordon, the Lynn Palmer Agency

Your interviewer doesn't have time to get to know the real you. She's got maybe 30 minutes to find something **wrong** with you. Don't let it be the fact that you showed up in a half shirt. Even if brilliant words are spilling out of your mouth, she's going to be staring at your navel.

Dressing appropriately means just that— **judging what clothing best fits the situation.** If you've done your homework about an industry beforehand, you should have a good sense of its dress code. "You should dress up in something that looks suitlike and noncontroversial," says one human resources director. "Beyond that, one way to get a sense of what to wear is to drive by the place you are interviewing around five or six in the afternoon, and see what people are wearing as they leave."

Some professions, such as banking and accounting. are still very much navy-blue suit territory. Many of these firms even have written dress codes for employees to follow. Others, like publishing and film, tend to be much more laid back. But even if you are applying for a position that requires you to wear grease-stained coveralls every day, **interview etiquette demands you dress in some form of serious business attire.**

"It sounds trite," says one human resources director, "but you really never get a second chance to make a first impression."

81

DO

DON'T

82

Here's a general rule of thumb to follow— dress as you would for a day on the job, only better. If you have a friend who works for the company you are interviewing with, and he tells you he comes to work every day in khakis and a polo shirt, you don't need to wear a suit to your interview but you should still wear a jacket and tie. After all, you don't work there yet. Once you do, you can relax your standards a bit. If you have any doubts about what to wear to an interview, it's far better to go conservative than casual.

For most industries, when you bear an X and Y chromosome, you should come to your interview in a suit. A nice, staid, conservative suit in a comfortably dull shade like blue or gray. The kind of suit you could wear to a funeral or a bar mitzvah. The kind of suit the president would wear to chair a Mideast peace conference. In other words, boring, boring, boring is best. Keep in mind these are the most conservative guidelines—it's perfectly acceptable in more relaxed environments for a student or recent graduate to come to an interview in the equally ho-hum navy-blue blazer and dress trousers combination.

Whatever the case, what you wear should not look like it's been hanging in a garment bag since 1972. Make sure it's nicely pressed. The same goes for your shirt. Don't wear one that's fire-engine red, burnt sienna or truck-stop peach. Try bland old white on for size. Top the whole thing off with a tie that compliments your suit but doesn't look like it might leap off your chest and throttle your interviewer at any moment. You are set.

Except for one thing. Two actually. Your feet. None of the above-mentioned wardrobe articles should cost you an arm and a leg. You don't need to get an Armani original for your first interview. In fact, it would probably be far too flashy. Resale and warehouse stores across the country offer quality suits and ties at reasonable prices. But good leather shoes are one item you should not skimp on. Invest in a good conservative pair you can wear for years. When you come to your interview, they should be polished and in good condition. People really do notice. Remember to wear matching socks. **And please, no Pee Wee Herman white socks, ever.**

Women have more options. This wasn't always so. When our mothers entered the white-collar workforce in large numbers, they made a bestseller out of a little handbook called *The Woman's Dress for Success Book*. Basically it told them to wear masculine-cut suits in navy blue, skirts at just the right below-the-knee length to make their legs look like Polish sausages and grim little bow-tie contraptions at their collars that flattered absolutely no one. It was a particularly gruesome chapter in our history, thankfully closed.

Women going to interviews today are free to wear suits, jackets and skirts or professional dresses in fairly somber colors. "Pants and pantsuits are not acceptable for interviews," says one employment agency owner. Egregiously sexist and stupid? Yep.

But many employment specialists agree with her. Again, sartorial rules vary from job to job—and region to region (what flies in Manhattan may not go over in Salt Lake City, for example). There are definitely plenty of places out there where a professional-looking trouser outfit is more than fine. If you absolutely can't bear wearing a skirt, try to find out if the place you are interviewing is one of them.

For the most part, hemlines are not the red-hot subject of controversy they once were. Skirts several inches above the knee are currently quite acceptable for most job interviews. However, anything too high on your thigh is not a good idea for a first

83

appointment, even in the hippest office. Droopy skirts that fall too far below the calf are *equally* unprofessional.

Whatever length your skirt, wear it with a conservative blouse and make sure your clothes are neatly ironed. Wear the dreaded pantyhose in a neutral hue, and check for any runs or snags. Like men, women should invest in a good pair of traditional shoes. They should have a low heel—don't teeter in on spikes or come clunking up in platforms. Avoid open-toed shoes, slingbacks, and clogs.

Pretty starchy rules, right? About as chic as a Baptist choir convention in Nowhere Gulch, Saskatchewan.

Ultimately you'll have to make the call about what you wear. Friends and contacts in the industry and career counselors are good resources. Many college career centers also run free workshops on dressing for work. You may hate your "interview suit" with a passion, but it's best to have at least one outfit in your closet that makes you look like a wholesome, dependable, crisp and utterly competent slice of American Pie. You can sleep easy knowing that it will pass muster in interviews at the most diverse array of employers, from investment banks to rabble-rousing political groups, from record companies to microchip manufacturers.

If telling you how to dress wasn't bad enough, you also need to think about how you smell. You may adore your *Throbbing Titan of Testosterone* cologne or your *Eau de Steamy Fantasy* perfume, but it's probably not what you want wafting around your interviewer's

head, inducing nausea. Avoid all fragrances—not only are they potentially vexatious, many people are allergic to them. Reducing a potential boss to a sneezing seizure with one whiff of your patchouli is not the first impression you want to leave.

Nor do you want him to remember your own home-made musk. In other words, take a shower, you old stink bug, and slop on some deodorant. The Red Hot Chili Peppers can get away with smelly. Smelly for you is interview cyanide. The thing is, some perfectly wonderful people out there can't really tell when they are getting a wee bit ripe. You may be one of them.

Scrub! And wear a clean shirt.

If your breath says "Welcome to Marlboro Country" or recalls the anchovy garlic pizza slice you ate for breakfast, you may have a very short interview. Be kind—brush your teeth and use mouthwash, suck mints, spray Binaca, sandblast the inside of your mouth if you have to. Nothing is more toxic than a putrid kisser. **Nothing.** Needless to say, coming into a business setting with alcohol breath is about as cool as extending an arm full of fresh needle marks. Kiss the job goodbye.

If you wear jewelry, keep it at a bare minimum—if your baubles tinkle every time you turn your head, it's distract-ing. Even if you are pierced six ways from Sunday, stop at a single pair of simple, small, nondangling earrings for job interviews at traditional firms.

There's no question that men are still held to a more conservative standard in this department.

Men who wear earrings, necklaces and bracelets should consider leaving them at home for interviews

at old-fashioned organizations— they are probably the last thing you want to have the interviewer focus on.

Women should use makeup very sparingly. Save the thick Tammy Faye foundation, thick eye shadow, and garish lipstick for your televangelism career. If your hair is sprayed big, beautiful and bouffant, subdue it. Hair should be brushed, out of your eyes and freshly washed. If you are a man with Fabio-fabulous long hair you'll never part with, make sure it's clean and pulled back from your face.

> "when i first went out looking for jobs after college i had shoulder-length hair. i knew this could be a problem for some employers, but i loved my hair. so i compensated for it by dressing as conservatively as i could in every other department. if my hair was considered a minus, i had to work extra hard at showing how professional the rest of me was."
>
> —Jack, 26, graduate student

Extreme hair is going to be a big minus in most job interviews. If you have made the decision to keep your locks spiky and puce for eternity, and feel that doing anything to mute them is selling out, stay true to yourself and gear up for a rockier road. Mustaches and beards should be trimmed, free of crumbs and otherwise neatly groomed.

Your fingernails should be clean, and if you're a gal who's naked without her polish, choose a very subtle shade and apply it neatly. As proud as you may be of your Catwoman-length claws, having super-long nails can play against you. Into body art? Tattoos are probably not an asset outside of *Outlaw Biker Magazine* and a few nightclubs. Play it safe and cover them up.

Great, you say. You've just turned me into Barbara Bush's more conservative younger sister. Again, nothing above is written in stone. You have to decide whether a particular job is worth ditching your Passion Purple eye shadow for. But even if you have spent your whole life ignoring admonitions about your grooming, now it's time to pay attention.

There may be plenty of people out there who don't give a damn what you look like, how you smell, or how gloriously high your hair is. They don't care if you show up in a black leather jumpsuit; it's your *ideas* that matter. The unfortunate thing is, in the world of job-getting, they are a minority.

Employers are under tremendous pressure to hire the right candidate for a job because *you cost money.* In a short interview, they have to determine, with very little information, whether you're the sort of person who is a good investment, or someone unreliable who'll end up being a big malodorous stain on the organization's good name.

If you are in human resources, your job depends on bringing in solid, dependable employees—you can't afford to take too many risks. Put it this way—you work in personnel for Ultramegacorporation Incorporated and must hire one of two candidates. One is smart, qualified and well groomed. One is smart, qualified and looks like road kill. Guess what? Road kill is out.

For the most part, assume you are dealing with fashion Klingons when you go to an interview. Feel sorry for them—they have no idea at all about what's hip, they may have horribly dated ideas about what passes for style. You can't change their stodgy opinions in half an hour, so don't even try. Even for jobs at fashion magazines, interview clothes should never be about the latest fad. The trick is to look presentable without drawing attention away from your words and toward an element in your wardrobe or a part of your anatomy. If you think your look is potentially frightening, disgusting or says "Hello, sailor" to someone more staid than yourself, you are going to have to decide how important it is to you. Because like it or not, it could cost you a job.

"ums" as punctuation, saying "he goes" instead of "he says" and ending every sentence with a question mark, you need to work on breaking yourself of those habits **NOW**.

Rachel, a 27-year-old editor at a New York magazine, calls our quirky generational speech pattern "uptalk." When every phrase you utter ends

Um . . . like, you know . . . watch the, um . . . uptalk?

It's true, we talk differently than our parents do, and they talk differently from their parents before them. Watch an old movie from the forties. It isn't simply that slang changes over the years or that many regional dialects have softened or faded. Throughout North America, educated people actually spoke differently—their intonation and pronunciation sound almost foreign to a contemporary ear. At one time Katharine Hepburn's accent wasn't as distinctive or old-fashioned as it is today.

You may have, simply by growing up in the late twentieth century, picked up some speech habits that a great many people find **grating**. For example, you are a brilliant Rhodes scholar, but when you get nervous you begin to babble out a stream of "likes" and "you knows" and "ums" in between your sentences. Start to listen critically to your speech. If you find yourself using a truckload of

on a high note, you come off sounding uneducated, insecure, immature and about as bright as a plank of plywood. "My mother used to tell me when I phrased every sentence as a question—I'm so glad she called me on it, because otherwise people would never take me seriously," she says. And she's right— once you've ditched your high school letter jacket and pom-poms, talking like Garth from *Wayne's World* or a cuddly little mall refugee from *Clueless* isn't endearing. It can be a real handicap—people will assume you are, like, totally stupid.

In an interview (and work) setting, you want to sound articulate, forthright and sure of your answers. You aren't seeking the interviewer's approval for your every thought—but that's what uptalk inflection implies. What if the president gave a special television address and said, "Like, um, I think we should send, um, troops, you know? To, like, Cuba." You'd be very, very afraid. This is not a person you want as Commander In Chief of anything—you wouldn't trust somebody who spoke like that to pick up your dry cleaning.

Some of us don't uptalk exactly—we speak in a kind of demented, slurred Surfer Drawl. You know what this sounds like. *Iwenttuhseetermunatur twulvelastnightitwasrullygud.* Instead of "I went to see Terminator Twelve last night, it was really good." Slow down and **enunciate**. Not only does mumbling mask all the wonderful things you are saying, but it drives many older people absolutely batty.

Imagine you are a forty-five-year-old, leather-necked, barrel-chested, hard-of-hearing, cholesterol-plagued supervisor. You have a snotty thirteen-year-old kid at home who's running you ragged. She mumbles everything she says. It positively enrages you. Some bright young thing walks into your office for a job interview, opens her mouth and out comes the same mealy-mouthed garble. AARGH! BASTA! YOUR HEART HURTS! GET HER OUTTA HERE!

Seriously, being able to communicate articulately in your working life is no joke. You wouldn't present a resume that was riddled with grammatical and spelling errors, or come to an interview with pit stains on your shirt. Your speech should be as polished as the rest of your presentation.

That doesn't mean you should rehearse your answers, put on a phony accent, or enroll in the Eliza Doolittle School of Elocution. *Just start paying attention to how you sound*—it's something that most people never do. Some experts even go so far as to recommend you record your voice to get a sense of the bad habits you might have picked up. That probably isn't necessary. If you slow down your rapid-fire delivery, really listen to yourself, and think of better words than "like" to pepper your sentences with, you'll have the situation licked.

TIP #8: Always Follow Up

This is so important, it hurts. You must be certain that your name sticks in the mind of the interviewer after you walk out the door. If you passively sit around by the phone waiting for someone to contact you for work, you'll never get anywhere. Before you leave an interview, ask when you can expect to hear any word about the job.

Asking when you will hear back is not rude or presumptuous. You have a legitimate right to know this information. You might politely say "When do you expect to reach a decision?" or "When can I expect to hear from you?" Don't settle for a fuzzy answer—try to subtly pin them down on a specific time frame, say a week. If you haven't heard from the company within that time frame—call to follow up.

Follow-up calls make many people very queasy. The last thing you want to do is start badgering someone about a position, calling them every week without fail. If you are worried about harassing someone, state in the interview that you'd like to call in a week or so, and ask what a good time would be. If the interviewer expressly tells you not to call, don't call. A couple of follow-up calls is enough. If several weeks pass and you still haven't heard anything, it's probably time to write off the job.

Before you ever get to the point of making a follow-up call, repeat this

Interview Stink Bombs

If you are serious about getting a job, *avoid* doing any of the following:

- Appear uninterested and unenthusiastic (a big complaint about young applicants).
- Forget the day or your appointment and miss your interview.
- Show up late.
- Smoke or chew gum in an interview.
- Be painfully shy.
- Be overly aggressive or arrogant.
- Be overly nervous or flustered.
- Forget to speak clearly and look the interviewer in the eye.
- Swear, use poor grammar, or make abusive or offensive comments.
- Lie to an interviewer or exaggerate your qualifications.
- Bring up the issue of salary or benefits too soon.
- Be poorly groomed, sloppy in habits and dress, or dressed inappropriately.
- Badmouth past bosses and jobs, have a bad attitude.
- Give one word answers to questions.
- Interrupt or ignore the interviewer.
- Seem desperate to land any job .

to yourself a thousand times—

I will never, no matter how tired I am, or how horribly my interview went, **forget to write a thank-you note** or follow-up letter to an **interviewer.**

This isn't simply civilized—it's crucial. Your interviewer may have seen 50 candidates. If only three take the time to follow-up, guess which three are likely to move to the top of the list.

Before you head out the door, ask the interviewer for her business card. If she doesn't have one, ask or call the receptionist for the correct spelling of her name. *Immediately.*

Try to do it within twenty-four hours—write a quick note or letter of thanks and reassert your interest in the position. Some people even fax them, or hand-deliver the note to the receptionist the next day. It need only be a few sentences long.

If you feel you gave an answer in your interview that needs clarification, or want to hit again at the few strengths that make you an ideal choice for the job, do so. But be brief—two or three short paragraphs are more than enough.

Some career counselors stress sending a professional-looking follow-up letter on resume stock paper, much like your cover letter, after a meeting. "It's a piece of business correspondence, after all," says one. Many others say a neatly done handwritten note on a plain card is fine. You'll have to gauge what you think is most appropriate for the business where you interviewed or the person you interviewed with.

Do not send a card with tacky gold-stenciled writing on it, flowery pictures or psychedelic designs. One hapless job applicant sent an interviewer a thank-you note on a card bought at a prominent museum. The card was decorated with a beautiful Renaissance painting of the Virgin Mary. The interview had gone very well. Unfortunately, after receiving the card the interviewer assumed the poor guy was some kind of religious nut.

With cards, plainer is always better. In fact, avoid cards that have any writing on them at all, unless you decide to have your name, address and phone number printed on them. You can buy unmarked cards at any stationery store. In any case, your thank-you note might read something like this:

Ms. Luscious Jackson
Riot Girl Fashions
2 Thrasher Street
Seattle, WA 00000

Dear Ms. Jackson:

I just wanted to drop you a quick note of thanks for taking the time to meet with me today. I enjoyed our conversation and found it very informative—as a Seattle native, I've keenly followed the music scene there for some time. I think your decision to launch a new clothing line at this time is tremendously exciting. My senior paper on the rise and fall of the grunge look makes me believe that young Americans are hungering for a new direction in fashion. Thanks again for meeting with me. I look forward to hearing from you next week.

Sincerely,

Edward Vedder

You get the picture. Nice, short and to the point. "So few of our young applicants send thank-you letters," says one human resources person, "that those who do really stand out."

That's what you want to do. Yes, there are people out there who could care less about thank-yous. It's just one more piece of paper to toss straight into the bin. But for a minimum of effort, you're not doing yourself any harm by writing one and you may be doing a whole lot of good. One final note—if you are going through a multitiered selection process, be sure to thank everyone who met with you, not just the first or last interviews.

TIP #9:
Everyone Gets Dinged Once in a While

Sometimes, no matter how thoroughly prepared you are, you crash and burn. The interview just doesn't go the way you want it to. Maybe five minutes after sitting down for your interview you get an abrupt "Thank you for your time, Mr. Dud, we'll be in touch." Or even worse, "I really don't think this job would be suitable for you."

Maybe the interviewer is a jerk, or you are just too nervous, or you're having a bad day, or the two of you just don't click.

Don't beat yourself up over a failed interview. Let it go.

It's quite possible that your interviewer didn't think your performance was as awful as you thought it was. You may still have a shot at the job. That's one reason why it's important not to forego the thank-you note or letter. If you flubbed an important question, you might expand on your answer in your note and emphasize strengths you have that may have gotten lost in the shuffle during your interview.

If it turns out that things did indeed go as badly as you feared and you get rejected, don't take it personally. There could be any number of reasons why you didn't get the job. It doesn't necessarily have anything to do with what you said or did—it could be that the son of the company president applied for the same position, or that it was a horse race between you and several very strong candidates. There's simply no point in torturing yourself.

You might want to call the interviewer up and ask why you weren't selected, and if there are things you can do to improve your chances of getting a similar job. Who knows, he may be able to refer you to an internship program or provide you with new leads in your job search. This is an extremely difficult conversation to initiate, especially when you just want to put an unpleasant experience behind you.

"Human beings hate giving bad news," says one personnel director. "That's why it takes some people so long to get back to candidates about jobs. If you didn't get a job, try and find out in a nonthreatening way. Explain you are new at this and want to learn how to improve. It's always good to get feedback."

One last thing—when rejected, be gracious to a fault. Never react in a vindictive manner when you didn't get a job. Don't slam down the phone or write a nasty letter. You will regret it. And if a friend of yours gets a job you hungered for, resist the urge to bludgeon them to death. Keep your bitterness to yourself and congratulate them. You'll only bring yourself grief if you behave badly. Whether you feel things turning

sour in an interview or are totally stunned that you didn't get a job, try to get something positive out of the experience. At least you've learned something for next time—and you may even be able to laugh about it. Remember tip number one. The more you interview, the better you'll get at it. And sooner or later, somebody's bound to show their appreciation with a job offer.

91

WELCOME TO THE JUNGLE: LIFE ON THE JOB

Maybe not today, maybe not tomorrow, but **someday** soon you are going to get a job offer. And believe it or not, it can actually cause you as much stress as looking for a job. Why? Because you'll have to decide whether or not to take the damn thing, and that's not always easy, even if you've been living off gruel and donating your organs for rent money.

Remember, when we talk about "jobs" in this book, we are talking about *career-oriented positions*— not stopgap work you find to keep yourself fed. That kind of employment is easy to say yes to, because you have no expectation of doing it for the rest of your able-bodied days, or even for a considerable portion of them.

> **(You should take a job if you need a job— don't be a snob.)**

Although we hate to fall into the trap of using this language, here goes— we are talking about "real jobs" here, versus "any old job." A real job is anything you want it to be—what matters is that it's important to you. Even what seems to be the most crudball opportunity can turn into something fruitful down the line. What makes it real isn't the money you make, or the clothes you wear, but your level of commitment.

1. NIBBLES AND FEEDING FRENZIES— JOB OFFERS

When you get your first "real" job offer, you should feel terrific. Somebody out there thinks you have what it takes to be an atomic engineer, or a hand model, or a cliff diver. You stud, you. You should feel quite chuffed, but don't let it overwhelm you. Keep these three things in mind.

1. YOU DESERVE IT . . .

Oh, yes you do. You can forget that, especially if you have been looking for a job for a long time. Your natural instinct may be to get down on your knees and lick your future employer's soles in sheer gratitude. ***But remember, you are under no obligation to take a job just because someone was nice enough to offer you one.*** Resist the temptation to leap at a job when someone calls you up and offers it to you on the phone. Even if you have been dying to work for Tammy's Toxic Waste Disposal since you were ten. Even if there seem to be no other opportunities on the horizon.

2. ...SO THINK IT THROUGH

When someone asks you to come to work for them, ask for a little time to think it over. At a bare minimum, you should have at least a day or two to kick things around. Be specific—"I'm thrilled with the offer. Can I take the weekend to consider it and give you a ring Monday morning?"

Most people are completely understanding about this. After all, they have been in your shoes. Once you accept a job offer, you cannot go back to the bargaining table expressing buyer's remorse. ***So think everything through carefully, and raise your concerns before you sign on the dotted line.***

However, you also can't expect eons to pussyfoot around. Employers are under tremendous pressure to fill jobs as quickly as possible. Try not to jerk someone around while you hem and haw. It's extremely inconsiderate, and in the event that you do take a job after several weeks of mulling it over (a miracle if the job's still open and the employer hasn't rescinded the offer), you won't be starting on a good note.

There are some occasions when an employer demands a very quick answer, but never let yourself be pressured into accepting a job on the spot. It's extremely rare for an employer to rescind an offer if you need to sleep on it overnight.

Ask yourself this question for the millionth time—***Is this a company I want to work for?*** Hopefully, after all your research, networking, careful planning and thorough interviewing, you have a good idea. Because nothing, not salary, prestige or what your mother thinks, is more important.

Consider the work environment you are about to enter. Is it the kind of place you'll feel comfortable in? Are the people casual and friendly, or stiff and uptight? Are the higher-ups receptive to ideas from below? What are the opportunities for promotion? Is there a high turnover among entry-level people? Are there a lot of young people at the company? Is there a chance you may be laid off in the not-too-distant future? Can you learn to live with your hours and schedule, or are they going to be impossible for you to cope with?

Think that last question is silly? Ask droves of brilliant young women and men who are annually lured by the big money of jobs on Wall Street and later bail because they can't stand leaving work at 4:00 A.M. and returning at 8:30 the same morning.

Go forward with your eyes open—by now you should know it's not going to be all champagne and pretzel snacks. Work is, after all, just that. No job is all glamour and good times, especially at the rock-bottom rung on the ladder.

Share the good news with any contacts you have made in the industry and ask their advice. You might also want to discuss your options with a trusted instructor or counselor. Feedback is very important, but ultimately you have to trust your gut. If you got a

94

grim feeling about a place from your interview, it may not be the place for you (remember that at least 50 percent of any good interview is checking out the employer). Getting the butterflies is normal — but major queasies are worth a serious examination.

Sometimes, unfortunately, instincts prove to be wrong. You choose to take a position you thought would be perfect for you and it turns out to be hell. Don't worry. You have no pact with Satan committing yourself to a life of serfdom under a miserable boss. As important as the decision to accept a particular job is, it is not irrevocable. In the final analysis, the best way to find out if a job is for you is to actually start clocking in every morning.

3. IT'S OKAY TO SAY NO

If you decide to decline a job for whatever reason, don't feel guilty. You are replaceable. Nobody is going to be up all night weeping because you refused to work for them (unless you have just told your parents you won't be going into the family business). However, it can certainly be frightening to turn down a job when you don't have other firm prospects.

THINK OF IT THIS WAY—IF YOU WERE GOOD ENOUGH TO GARNER ONE OFFER, THERE WILL CERTAINLY BE OTHERS COMING DOWN THE PIKE.

So, when a prospective job doesn't pay you enough to buy toilet paper, or the work environment feels wrong for you, or the possibilities for advancement seem nonexistent, it's okay to politely say thanks, but no thanks, and be on your merry way.

Nobody likes giving bad news. It may seem easier to just blow the person off. **Never do this.** Who did you hate more when you got rejected— the employer who had the decency to call you up and break the bad news, or the jerk who never returned phone calls until you saw the handwriting on the wall? Don't alienate a valuable contact by freezing someone out.

Have the guts to phone someone up, thank them for their kind offer, and tell them politely that you can't take the job. Calling them is absolutely the best way to go. Don't hide behind a letter. If they ask you why you are turning them down, feel free to tell them frankly and courteously what the reason was— even if you are going to work for a competitor.

WEIGHING YOUR OPTIONS

Up until now, you've been told that discussing your salary and benefits is a bad idea. There is a very good reason for this. You would look like a grasping, craven, venal little cuss if you had mentioned these things before someone actually asked you to come and work for them. There's probably nothing that alienates an employer faster. When you are offered a job, your employer will tell you what your salary will be. You should already have a firm idea about this from your research. Your benefits package will most likely come up in the discussion. It's nearly always better to wait for the employer to initiate the conversation about your compensation package.

Believe it or not, money is only a small part of the reason why you should take a job. Think of it as an integral piece of a much larger pie. If

JUST SAY "NO"

your salary seems generous, but you have little else in the way of compensation—that is, if your health insurance, 401(k) investment programs, and other goodies are nonexistent—you had better think twice about this position.

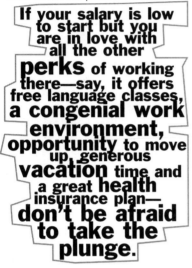

If your salary is low to start but you are in love with all the other perks of working there—say, it offers free language classes, a congenial work environment, opportunity to move up, generous vacation time and a great health insurance plan—don't be afraid to take the plunge.

THINGS TO CONSIDER BESIDES SALARY:

HEALTH INSURANCE

If you have a pulse, you need it. **No excuses.** You are not immortal. If something terrible happens and you must undergo surgery or treatment for an illness, you'll be financially crippled by enormous medical bills. That is, if you can even afford to pay them at all. Having no insurance also means you won't be visiting the doctor regularly, which in turn can mean you may develop a serious illness or may need expensive surgery later on, which leads you straight back to crippling medical bills. Ah, isn't adulthood a bitch?

Health insurance should be part of every benefits package. If it isn't you are going to have to try and find insurance on your own, and the monthly premiums can be more expensive than an uninsured trip to the emergency room—we are talking

hundreds of dollars a month in some cases. Frightening, isn't it? If your employer doesn't offer health insurance, and you still want the job, one thing you can do is check and see if you are eligible for a **group rate** through a professional association, union, guild or fraternal organization. Many associations offer policies for their members at prices that are far less astronomical than individual policies.

Hopefully, you are going to get at least some health-care coverage from a prospective employer. Because they have heaps more money and represent not just one but many individuals, insurers give companies breaks on rates they'd never dream of passing on to you alone. That means when you pay your insurance premiums under a company health plan, your rates are going to be far cheaper, if you pay premiums at all.

Opting for Peace of Mind

An MTV poll underscores how important health insurance is to most of us. Of 800 16- to-29-year-olds questioned, **two out of three** *said they would take a job with benefits and lower pay over a job without benefits and higher pay.* **Seven out of 10 women felt this way.**

In many cases the company picks up all or a significant chunk of your monthly premiums. Health insurance programs vary from company to company—some are quite generous in doling out benefits, others are more stingy. What kinds of treatment are paid for by a medical plan also varies widely. For example, a trip to the emergency room might be paid for entirely by your insurer, while smaller ticket items like having your teeth cleaned or physical exams will require you to pay for a large part (or even all) of the cost of the visit out of your own pocket. Dental care is frequently

"At the first company i worked for, my health insurance was pretty spotty. There was a lot of basic care that just wasn't covered. it was a small organization that simply couldn't afford to offer us much more than a bare-bones policy. My second job has been very different—a regular checkup costs me about five dollars."

—Kiki, 26, marketing assistant

not covered by company plans. Now, generally, large, flush corporations can offer their employees a wide range of health insurance plans to choose from. Many small and nonprofit businesses are going to be far more limited in what they can provide.

You can understand why so many companies today are relying increasingly on freelance and temporary workers. They may pay you fifteen bucks an hour, but they don't have to shell out the really big bucks on the benefits that come with being a permanent employee. A great many companies also do not give new employees access to their benefits package until several months after their hiring. They don't want you to take advantage of their mother lode of goodies until they are certain you aren't going to ditch them immediately.

If employers take benefits that seriously, you should do the same. In many instances you will be given a packet detailing the company package at some point in your interview process. That means you can look it over and answer many of the questions you have about what is or isn't covered by the company health plan before you are even offered a job. These are generally not riveting reads; you may find yourself nodding off as you read about the pros and cons of selecting health-plan B over health-plan D, but it's in your best interest to look over the information *carefully*. If what's on offer seems truly egregious, it might be worth

discussing, but it's almost always ridiculous to try to negotiate for better health benefits. You can't say to an employer, "I can't work for you unless you cover my appointments at the dermatologist." It doesn't work that way. What's available is what's available, not just for you but every employee in the firm. Take it or leave it.

When you accept a job offer at a company that offers more than one set insurance package, you may want to ask fellow employees in your age group what benefits plan they have selected for themselves. There is usually an el-cheapo standard package designed for young, single people with no dependents. If you have specifc questions, you can direct them to a **benefits specialist** in a larger company. They should be able to help you decipher what each plan offers and what the strengths and weaknesses are of each one. Remember, in a big organization your boss may be as overwhelmed by the intricacies of the benefits game as you are, so she may not always be the best person to turn to for advice. Another important kind of insurance you should have is **disability**, which protects you in the event you can't work by paying you your regular wages. (We'll come back to insurance again in the money management chapter.)

PENSION PLANS AND 401(K) PROGRAMS

Okay, you are young and spry, but someday you may be sporting Depends undergarments. **Don't even think about counting on Social Security to see you through your sunset years.** If it's there at all for you to draw on when you hit your late sixties, your monthly check is only going to equal a fraction of what you were making when you were working full time. Because of that, you need to start putting money away, the sooner the better.

When you are offered a new job, you should know what investment and retirement programs are offered by your employer. In the good old days, most big companies offered what are known as **defined benefit plans**, or pensions. Upon your retirement from the glue factory you were rewarded with a check each month for the rest of your life. The amount was decided upon by your length of service with the company, the salary you were making over your last years there, and the age at which you retired. In many ways, it was like corporate Social Security, but with an additional plus. Unlike with Social Security, you don't pay into a defined benefits plan—your employer contributes on your behalf.

Increasingly, employers are backing away from traditional pension plans. Instead, they are asking you to bear more responsibility for your retirement. In a **profit-sharing** arrangement, an employer reinvests a portion of yearly profits in its employees, but you also contribute to the fund. The employer can also suspend payments or cut them in bad years. In **money purchase plans**, the employer contributes a set amount to your account every year regardless of how good or bad business is, and a portion of your earnings goes into the fund as well. Your final benefits are whatever the assets in the account will buy at

retirement. Maybe a house in the Bahamas, maybe a tin cup.

Perhaps the most popular employer-designed investment program is the **401(k) plan**, which, in case you are interested, is named after its section of the tax code. Typically, somewhere between two and ten percent of your **pre-tax salary** is deducted and invested in an account managed by your employer. Under this type of plan, an employer offers several different investment options, and you choose where the money goes.

You pay **no taxes** on your 401(k) money until you withdraw it, ideally at retirement. In some companies, **your investment will be matched dollar for dollar by the employer**. In other cases, the company may contribute 50 cents for every dollar. It's a win/win situation for you—take advantage of it. You save money, and they give you, yes, give you, more money to save with it. Go figure. But go for it.

OTHER BENEFITS

Your new job may come with other scrummy items that sweeten the pot. Maybe there's the opportunity to enter an employee training program that will help you in the long run, maybe your moving expenses will be paid if you are relocating, maybe evening classes at local universities are reimbursed, maybe exceeding a performance quota is met with a bonus. Employees of one media giant in New York City get cut-rate admission at many of the city's museums, movie theaters and cultural events. Quite a few match your gifts to selected charities or your college alumni fund. All of these things can make the difference between feeling like another drone or a valued member of a team.

NEGOTIATING A SALARY

SORRY, BUT **YOU ARE NOT A SUPERMODEL. YOU MUST ROLL OUT OF BED FOR LESS THAN A GAZILLION DOLLARS A DAY.** An applicant for an entry-level job simply doesn't have much room to negotiate a salary. Your starting pay range has pretty much been set in stone, and as someone who is just starting out, you haven't got very much to bargain with.

Sad to say, but young greenhorns are a dime a dozen. Come in making outrageous demands and the only responses you are likely to get are peals of laughter and the door slamming behind you. Once you have been working a while, you can begin to haggle about money.

Entry-level salaries are generally determined by the marketplace. That means they are (big surprise) criminally low. There are a few exceptions, most notably investment banking, where some trainees can make up to $50,000 a year (without MBAs).

Guess what, these jobs aren't exactly easy to get, and are notoriously arduous. "Maybe we make twice as much money as our peers, but we work twice as many hours," says one red-eyed financial analyst. Young people going into business and administrative jobs generally make salaries in the mid-twenties on average, and highly competitive slots in media and the arts are notorious for their crummy money.

Most beginning publishers, journalists, producers and museum curators are lucky to scrape in $20,000 a year. A salary in the teens doesn't go very far in big media towns like Chicago, New York and Los Angeles. Likewise, nonprofit corporations frequently have little money to spare on employees. Frequently, fighting the forces of evil or doing creative work means accepting low wages.

In some cases you may have to get a second job just to keep yourself in peanut butter and jelly sandwiches. You can certainly make it work—just don't be shocked when an exciting opportunity to work at a local dance company means your benefits package is getting to watch performances for free.

"i really don't think it's appropriate to negotiate a salary for your first job. you really don't have that much to bring to the table. As you start getting experience in a particular field, then negotiation becomes important."
—Annie, 25, administrative assistant

"our salaries for entry-level people are pretty much the industry standard. There's not much room for hiking them up. A young graduate should know what their salary range is before they get a job offer. if they don't know, they might ask a career counselor what company x is paying its entry-level people this year."
—Tim, recruiter

Now if you sincerely feel what you are being offered just isn't fair compensation, you can certainly try to ask for more. **FROM YOUR RESEARCH, YOU SHOULD HAVE A SOUND IDEA OF WHAT THE PAY RANGE IS FOR ENTRY-LEVEL PEOPLE IN YOUR FIELD. THAT'S YOUR METER. ASK FOR MORE THAN THE UPPER REACHES OF THAT RANGE AND YOU'LL GET NOWHERE.** The dance company cannot afford to pay you more than $18,000 a year, full stop.

But if they offer you $15,000, you might try a little honesty and say, "Look, I'd really love to come work for you, but quite honestly I'm unsure if I can make it on that salary." If your employer is able to, she'll go back to her superiors and see if she can squeeze a few more bucks out of them. If she can't, well she just can't. There's no harm in asking—if she is really thrilled with you, she's going to try her best to get you on board.

Be very polite in money negotiations. Don't try and play hardball. You haven't got much room to maneuver. You shouldn't even start down this path unless you are truly interested in a position. If you turn somebody down because you can't live with the money, that's one thing. Getting someone to bend over backward for you and then unceremoniously dumping them is quite another. You are going to have one hopping-mad dance company director on your hands. If it happens that after a drawn-out successful negotiation you still can't take a job, apologize profusely and thank the person for their efforts on your behalf.

If you are actually asked about your salary requirements, try and get the employer to name a figure first. You don't want to be pinned down to a set amount right away. For example, ask them what they think would be appropriate; don't blurt out the first number that pops into your head. If you are pressed to give a number, try to give a **salary range**, say between $20,000 and $25,000, if you know from your homework that is standard for the position on offer.

When you are pinned down still further, start on the high side of an appropriate range. If you want $20,000 a year, for example, you might ask for $25,000. If you ask for $20,000 straight off the bat, the employer may counter with $18,000 and you're stuck. By asking for slightly more than you want, you can meet her in the middle—the salary you really are gunning for.

One last word on money negotiations. They are like poker. You can't betray your distaste for a paltry offer or sheer delight at a good offer. Even if you still feel like you're twelve years old inside, don't betray your lack of confidence. You are in the big leagues now.

If you do manage to extract a better deal out of an employer, make a serious effort to **get it in writing**. Not a contract or anything scary like that, simply a letter of agreement stating the new arrangement for your records. Until you have it, or start your first day on the job, you don't have a done deal. So it's in your best interests to have it all ironed out formally in advance.

OTHER JOB OFFERS

What, you have more than one employer biting at your hook? Bonus! That's a terrific feeling, and you should savor it. Sit down and compare your offers. Beyond who's paying what, look at all the various pluses and minuses and decide which employer is better for you.

The Golden Rule of Entry-Level Salaries

If the choice between two jobs comes down to money or experience, take experience every time. Money is nice, but what you gain from your first job in knowledge, contacts and opportunities is far more important in the long run. Pick the place where you'll learn the most and have a chance to take risks. It's better to be a poorly paid low-level peon in that environment than a slightly higher paid one in a rigid bureaucratic organization.

When you get a job offer, it's perfectly kosher to call up other employers you have interviewed with and tell them. In the best-case scenario, you might just start a regular little bidding war. It's also a superb tactic if you haven't yet heard from an employer you **especially want to work for.**

You may be able to force his hand by informing him that you have to give a response to someone else within a few days. If you don't want to work for him, don't lead him on by pretending that you do. You want to make as many allies as you can in a field, even if you don't end up working together immediately.

Trying to start an employer feeding frenzy around you is dicey—especially when there are thousands of eager young people out there willing to take your place. **Don't push it.** You don't hold enough cards at this point in your career. If, after careful consideration, a job doesn't seem right for you, politely decline the offer. **Never, ever, accept two job offers at the same time.** It's bad karma and competely dishonest. Why risk getting burned?

Again, when turning down an offer be as courteous as possible. Phone the person up to give them the bad news yourself. Write a note thanking them again for their interest and consideration. You may need that person's help one day.

SAYING YES

At some point, after weighing all the pros and cons, tossing and turning and thrashing about, you are going to be ready to say yes to a job offer. When the magic moment arrives, handle it the right way. Call up your future boss and tell her you are delighted to accept and can't wait to get started. The two of you will then iron out when your first day of work will be.

Employers usually want you to start yesterday, but if you need a few days of calm before the storm, try and get them. The last thing you want to do is arrive frazzled from an arduous job hunt and interview cycle. On the other hand, don't ask for six weeks to visit the religious shrines of India. Try and be as considerate of your employer's schedule as you can. You surely don't want to piss someone off before you even start working with them by refusing to go along with their start date.

It's good to try and start on a Monday if you can, rather than plopping yourself into the middle of a busy work week. Then again, it can also be good to have your beginning, stressful days be mercifully close to the weekend. In either case, you'll be off and running before you know it.

Again, it's always best to have an official letter from an organization welcoming you to the company and confirming the terms of your employment there. A great many human resources departments send these letters out as a matter of course. You may want to write your own letter to your supervisor, formally accepting the position.

REMEMBER, ONCE YOU'VE SAID YES TO YOUR FUTURE BOSS, BARGAINING TIME IS FINITO, OVER, DEAD, DONE, HISTORY. YOU HAVE STRUCK A DEAL.

If you suddenly realize you are unhappy with your starting salary, for example, you are just going to have to suck it up for a while, or risk appearing indecisive and childish. That's why it pays to weigh your options very seriously before you agree to an employer's conditions.

One last thing. As soon as you accept a job offer, be sure to thank all the contacts who helped you along the way. This is important—you owe them, big time. Maintaining an effective network is tremendously helpful as you build a career. ***Do this every time you change jobs.*** Once you have committed to your first job, you are ready to build a strong foundation.

2. LEARNING THE ROPES IN THE WORKING WORLD

"One of the biggest problems younger people seem to have is that they tend to be very naïve about the business world. They haven't a clue about how organizations work."
—Dena, recruiter

You made it. Jumped through all the hoops. Signed on the dotted line. Bought yourself a good pair of shoes and two ties. Once you get a job, case closed, right? Not exactly. You have entered the commuting, coffee-swilling, antacid-chewing, suit-wearing, clock-punching, migraine-spawning world of work. And the worst part is, you are probably better prepared for a tour of duty on the space shuttle *Columbia*.

Not that it's your fault. For the most part, secondary schools and colleges do a pretty lousy job of getting you prepared for the job market. Other countries are miles (or kilometers, rather) ahead in this department—shoving comprehensive training and apprenticeship programs down the throats of young people before their foreheads blossom with whiteheads. In fact, a national commission declared America at the musty rock bottom of the heap in comparison to countries such as Germany and Japan when it comes to preparing students for work.

Alas, that frequently means your first job is akin to parachuting into the jungles of New Guinea without a compass, machete, map or bug repellent. All by your lonesome, you have to find your way through the bush and understand a totally new culture without being devoured by crocodiles, stung to death by fire ants or having your head severed, shrunk and thunked on a pole. Your goal? A successful and rewarding career. Quite a daunting prospect, pilgrim.

Nobody has to tell you that school and work are different worlds, but the ways in which they are different can be hard to detect, especially if your exposure to working life has been minimal before graduation.

You will eventually master your new environment, by stumbling down blind alleyways and smashing your head against the odd concrete wall. No matter how rocky your first days and weeks are, you'll get the hang of it. But go in **prepared**, because there are some miscalculations that can cost you, big time.

Everything you projected before you got the job—competence, professionalism, clean teeth—has to remain in place, of course. In addition, you have to figure out how your particular organization works, how to advance your career, build strong relationships, get the actual job done and still be the all-around chip off the old block that we know you are. Think back to the New Guinea analogy. You are off on a grand Indiana Jones–like adventure. Now, let's make sure to get through it in one piece.

GO IN WITH REALISTIC EXPECTATIONS— EVERYBODY PAYS DUES

Starting your first week of work and no keys to the executive suite yet? No reason to pound this point into rubble, but **everybody pays their dues**. As the new person you can't expect to be given huge responsibilities or the most difficult projects right away.

"one of the most irritating duties i had when i started my first job was taking the postage meter to the post office to get it refilled. it was heavy, and the post office was blocks away, and i had to wait in a long line there with this thing, and haul it all the way back. i also was always called upon to try and fix it when it was jammed, which was all the time. God, i hated that thing!"
—Holly, publicist

103

"photocopying huge manuscripts is the most odious task i have. odious! Evil! i was at the copier the other day and smelled something burning. i couldn't tell if it was the machine or my soul rotting!"
—Leah, editorial assistant

Quite frequently you'll be given scut work—the cruddy stuff nobody else wants to do. Naturally you should execute these tasks cheerfully and without complaint. That's easy at first. But then weeks drag by, and you may begin to chafe at some of your more menial tasks.

It sucks answering other people's phones, or spending months filing, or scraping the gum off your supervisor's Joan and David pumps. Here you are, this bright, well-educated, beautiful ball of energy, and you are being treated like Cinderella, pre–fairy godmother. You'll hear a little voice in your head that says **"But I wasn't hired to do this"** every time you are asked to run out and buy lunch, or extract jammed paper from the photocopier.

If you like, complain to your mother, or friends, or to your analyst. But avoid getting all sullen and whiny at work when you are asked to change the light bulbs. Recognize that your more boring and tedious duties are going to be with you a while. The trick is to do them quickly and efficiently, and take on new and more important responsibilities whenever you can.

Everyone has aspects of their jobs they loathe. There may be some point down the road where you feel you are only given the dumb jobs, and denied chances to prove yourself.

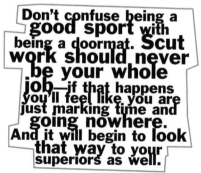

Don't confuse being a good sport with being a doormat. Scut work should never be your whole job—if that happens you'll feel like you are just marking time and **going nowhere.** And it will begin to look that way to your superiors as well.

At some point, you may want to talk to your supervisor and ask for more responsibility. But you can't have that

discussion early on in your new job. For now you have to do some grunt work, and act like you like it.

This will pop up again and again— no matter how smashing your qualifications. **You must earn the confidence of the people you work with.** When you gain the reputation as a diligent member of the proletariat, more opportunities will follow.

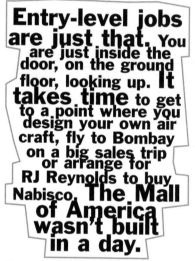

Entry-level jobs are just that. You are just inside the door, on the ground floor, looking up. **It takes time** to get to a point where you design your own aircraft, fly to Bombay on a big sales trip or arrange for RJ Reynolds to buy Nabisco. **The Mall of America wasn't built in a day.**

No matter how mundane a task it may seem, if it's important to your boss, it's important for you to do it quickly and well. Say yes to whatever humble chore she asks you to complete. And yes, **that means you get coffee.**

HAZING

Just because you do scut work doesn't give everyone license to dump on you. "If you feel people are throwing *all* their garbage work on you," says one human resources officer, "pleasantly tell them you'd really like to help them out, but you can't right now—give them a specific time frame when you can. You might say, 'I'm very busy now, but I'll be able to help you with that in three days,' for example."

Go to your boss and ask her if you are meeting her expectations. Is the junk work getting in the way of your real job? If your supervisor says that all the busy work is part and parcel of what you were hired to do, don't argue with her.

However, like the army, or fraternities and sororities, some organizations haze their new recruits. Let's define hazing as something above and beyond paying your dues by doing scut work, though many people at these companies wouldn't necessarily make such a distinction.

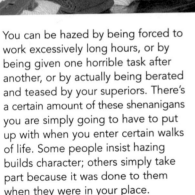

You can be hazed by being forced to work excessively long hours, or by being given one horrible task after another, or by actually being berated and teased by your superiors. There's a certain amount of these shenanigans you are simply going to have to put up with when you enter certain walks of life. Some people insist hazing builds character; others simply take part because it was done to them when they were in your place.

You are a grown-up, not a pledge. Stand up for yourself. If you feel harassed, bullied or someone's behavior has become entirely inappropriate, you have every right to call them on it. If it becomes truly serious, you should make a complaint to your supervisor or the human resources department. You don't have to put up with any kind of sexual harassment or slurs. (More on that later.) In any case, don't let the

bastards get you down, or curl up and die. These responses will surely make things worse before they get better.

REPORTING FOR DUTY

Your first day of anything, from nursery school to your first job, is often a bewildering and more than slightly sick-making experience. There's so much to process—a blur of people introducing themselves, copious forms to fill out and detailed instructions to follow—that you wish you were back home under the comforter.

ASK
QUESTIONS

You are going to feel like a big goober for a bit. It's an awkward situation, for both you and your new boss. You don't know where the bathroom is, or have anybody to take lunch with, or know how to get messages from your voice mail. Throwing yourself out the window is an option, but it's far less messy to simply swallow your fear and start **asking questions**.

In every workplace there is *at least* one haggard veteran who can tell you what to do if the fax breaks down, how to fill out your time card and where to request a stapler for your desk. Nobody is going to think you are stupid for admitting you don't know how to work the copier, or for not knowing where the stationery is kept. You are a rookie—asking for help when you are at a loss is in no way a sign of weakness or incompetence. Remember, every organization has its own peculiar culture. Your first days are going to be consumed with trying to decipher it. Smile, be polite and muddle your way through. Don't beat yourself up every time you make a mistake. Start paying keen attention to how things run. Being an astute observer of what goes on around you is often the best way to learn. The more days that pass, the less of an outsider you are likely to feel.

to work in a decaying halter top. But appearance carries over into other realms besides dress and hygiene. When you sit at a desk, try and keep it from looking like a bombed-out section of Sarajevo. If your papers look well ordered, you'll look efficient.

FIRST DAY
FIRST IMPRESSIONS

On your first day of work, dress as professionally as you did in your interview. You are meeting loads of new people, and you want them to believe that you are not a serial killer, heroin addict or moonlighting lap dancer. Again, first impressions are important—get started on the right foot.

You may not have to wear a tie or skirt every day at your new job, but on your first day come dressed a little more conservatively than you might in the weeks to come. Everybody is naturally going to be checking out the fresh meat, and it's preferable not to be remembered for weeks and months afterward as the moron who showed up for his first day in the white leisure suit.

If you are still confused about what the dress code is, ask your supervisor or one of your new colleagues. Follow their lead in the weeks to come, and you'll be okay. Some career experts often advise people to copy the wardrobes of those in senior positions you'd like to hold one day.

Even in very casual work environments, looks count. Of course you can't come

You will also *feel* less frazzled because you will hopefully know what piles you neatly stacked things into.·

Here's another appearance matter you should be highly aware of—punctuality and how much time you give to your work.

Pull the oldest trick in the book—get in the habit of coming to work before your boss does and leaving after she's out of the building. Even if it's only a matter of minutes.

Eeew, only a complete brownnose would do that, right? Wrong. Unfortunately, we live in a country that places inordinate value on **time**. It's highly important to continually demonstrate what an asset you are as an employee, and one way to do that is to work a little more than your assigned hours. At school you could simply show up and do good work and be recognized as a stand-up cat. In a work environment you have to be more assertive, and **show** your dedication to employers. We are talking about visible evidence of how reliable and hardworking you are. Rolling in late is not going to do it.

DAMN GLAD TO MEET YA

Introductions can feel like running a gauntlet over your first days on the job. It's hard to remember who everybody is, and you may spend days poring over your phone list trying to match names and faces. Take the initiative to introduce yourself to people—don't passively wait for your boss to do it for you. When you run into someone you haven't met, do your father proud. That means the hand goes out for a firm shake, you lock eyes with theirs, and something like this comes out of your mouth: "Hello, I'm Sidney Vicious. I've just started working with Nancy Spungen in purchasing. I don't think we've met. . . ." Lame? Guess what, that's what civilized people do.

If a really big wheel rolls in your direction, says a Ms. Chairman of the Board or a Mr. Vice President in Charge of Terrifying Underlings, don't hesitate to introduce yourself. Oh sure, it's easier to burrow into the nearest supply cabinet until they have made their rounds, but they will undoubtedly be impressed with you if you come straight up and say hello. You are working together now.

Still, it's rather uncomfortable, especially when the person is a big shot. Use your bean and ask someone else what that person's name is when you see them barreling down the corridor.

Sometimes you get trapped. Well, don't dig your hole any deeper. Just fess up. "I'm terribly sorry, but I seem to have forgotten your name" works fine. Only a royal putz would hold that against you, especially when you have just started a new job.

By the same token, expect that people may sometimes forget your name. Be as gentle with them as you would want them to be with you. Politely reintroduce yourself, or correct their mispronunciation—*subtly* remind them your name isn't Laura, it's Lara. Stifle your urge to jump all over somebody because they have a hard time with your moniker. Even if you have hated being called Laura since childhood, or your blood boils when somebody calls you Bob and not Robert, keep your shorts on and cut people some slack. It happens.

Sometimes it's better just to let it go and hope the person will stop calling you Kristen instead of Kirsten by hearing you and others say your name correctly. We've all known someone who gets hopping mad every time a stranger fudges their name. As sympathetic as we may be to their plight, a little warning bell goes off in our heads that says, "Uh-oh, way too anal." In all areas of human endeavor, resist the compulsion to correct people over and over again.

Many of your new colleagues are going to welcome you warmly to the fold. But others are going to be too busy that day to have time for pleasantries, or are just not socially adept. Your first few days can be a lonely time. Try not to judge people too quickly when you meet them. After all, they have work to do.

DOING THE PAPERWORK

In many large companies your orientation to work may include a formal program planned by the company. Along with other new hires, you could be asked to file down to the human resources department to watch a corny video about how great it is to work for Swedish Undergarments International. The benefits plan and personnel policies will be explained to you, and you'll be issued a company handbook or information packet. Even if you have heard all the information three times before, don't skip your orientation. They are often mandatory, and you are going to be needled to go until you go through it. Sometimes you won't be getting a paycheck if you don't participate. And besides, being labeled as "difficult" is not a great way to start out at a new company.

Orientations can be a nice structured respite from all the craziness of your first days on the job. At least you don't have to figure out what to do with yourself. You'll get the rundown on what the company's antidiscrimination and harassment policies are. And it's also a good time to ask any outstanding questions about how the payroll system works, what the policy is about sick or vacation days, and what health plan you should sign up for. The event's been set up to address those issues.

In some cases companies require new recruits to go through specialized **training programs** from a few hours long to several weeks in duration. Each organization's training program is unique, but many use a standard classroom and lecture format, just like back in school. On-the-job training might require you to work in a different division of the company, far from where you will actually be working, with your hotel bill footed by the company. Sometimes your training classes will coincide with actually working at your new job. Whatever form your training takes, try and get something out of it. There will undoubtedly be loads of hoo-ha that will turn out to be utterly useless. But some things you learn will help you get up to speed faster.

Whether or not you not have to attend a formal orientation or training, you will be asked to fill out payroll, health and tax forms sometime over your first few days. Since we have filled out forms before, this needs little explanation. You may be given the option of having your paycheck deposited directly into your bank account or with your **company credit union**, which generally provides the same services as a bank or savings & loan at lower cost. (More on this later.)

For health forms, remember to bring the names and addresses of people to contact in case of an emergency. In addition, your employer just might pay for you to have a physical exam, which is a great little windfall, or order you to take a urine test, which is most definitely not.

Drug testing is serious business.

Generally speaking, companies have a legal right to find out if you are free of illegal drugs as an employment requirement. If you are required to take a drug test and the results show that you have been indulging in *the herb* or other contraband substances, you are toast. Courts have largely been sympathetic to employers on the issue. You probably don't want to be the next test case.

Most employers still don't do drug tests, but if you have any suspicion that yours does, abstain or you're going to be one out-of-work stoner. *One possible exception might be if you have a drug habit and are in a legitimate program designed to get you clean.* Drug addiction is covered under the *Americans with*

Disabilities Act; that means your employer cannot summarily dismiss you because you are trying to **rid** yourself of your dependency any more than he can sack you for being deaf. If you are on any prescription medication, be sure to inform your employer before you take the test.

Federal law requires employers to show that their employees are citizens or legal residents of the United States, so you will be asked to provide the necessary documentation to complete a federal I-9 form verifying your immigration status. A passport, green card or birth certificate is usually considered ample evidence. Remember to bring this stuff in, or you may have to wait on your first paycheck.

If you are not eligible to work in the United States, you are going to have to convince your employer to fill out the necessary forms on your behalf. Canadians are not exempt from these requirements. This is a big risk, but it's better to come clean than misrepresent your status—your employer can be severely penalized for employing undocumented workers. You'd be surprised how many people are willing to wade through heaps of intimidating bureaucratic mumbo jumbo for a good employee.

Then there will be those handy-dandy federal, Social Security, state and sometimes local tax forms to fill out. Just in case you've **never** been paid over-the-counter in your life, you fill out these forms so that your employer will know how much money to deduct from your paycheck, based on the number of personal allowances you claim. An allowance reduces the money you pay in taxes. If you have no dependents, you can put zero in the little box. Unless you are making heaps of money on a trust fund or your investment portfolio, most likely you can be on your merry way until refund time, when the government throws all the money it owes you back at you. The great thing is, you

never even really knew you had it. It's like a present. Think of it as Christmas in springtime. Of course, you don't get any interest on the money the government has been holding, so if you have a reason to claim more exemptions, you might want to.

Read the paperwork through carefully and tick the appropriate boxes. It's not difficult, but the forms seem specially designed to make your eyes glaze over. Don't be afraid to ask a personnel or human resources person for help. (More about taxes in a bit.)

WALKING A FINE LINE

You have to be cautious during your first weeks on a new job. You don't know how the system works yet, how decisions get made, where all the fault lines are. A natural instinct might be to keep a low profile and get acclimated to your new surroundings before you get your feet wet. Here's the problem—you don't want to appear too timid or withdrawn. Then again, plunging in without knowing what you are getting into can be even worse. Some people find nothing more insufferable than an impertinent underling. You can hear all of your co-workers now, whispering by the water cooler about that wretched know-it-all kid.

You need to find a balance between shrinking violet and gung-ho jerk.

Don't ride into town like Clint Eastwood, blowing away every *bandito* in sight. If you bite off more than you can chew, you risk floundering and stepping on people's toes. Here's yet another wrinkle, though. No matter what they tell you, employers **do** expect you to be productive straight off the bat. You can't twiddle your thumbs all day, looking idle and waiting for the phone to ring.

Chances are you wouldn't want to either; it gets old awfully fast. The answer? Complete all those dues doing assignments in a crackerjack way and take on bigger projects when you have truly gotten your bearings. If you find it takes you five shakes of a lamb's tail to get those chores done, ask your boss for more. If she hasn't got anything, start anticipating what she'll need to get done. Find ways to make yourself useful.

Make yourself a standout in tiny visible ways. Here's an example. Shelly started a new job as an administrative assistant at an advertising company. It was a laid-back and convivial atmosphere, and she wanted to show her colleagues that she could do more than answer their telephones. One of her more mundane tasks was to keep the minutes for weekly department meetings. What a drag. She could have done the bare minimum, cranking out notes for her colleagues that might as well have been titled *Please Throw Me Away*. Instead, she pulled out all the stops. She wrote lively, thorough and sometimes even funny accounts of what went on in the meetings.

People adored her minutes. Executives in far-flung parts of the company would call her up just to compliment her. Suddenly they were required reading. Everybody knew who Shelly, a lowly assistant, was. In a creative field like advertising, she demonstrated she was a sharp person who had a way with words. By taking

a seemingly insignificant task, and by doing it well, she proved her mettle to an entire organization. Suddenly she was perceived as a valuable member of the team. Bigger responsibilities, promotions, bonuses, beach houses, silver sport cars and fabulous Hollywood parties followed.

Had Shelly come in and tried to **run** her first department meeting, her colleagues wouldn't have been nearly so receptive. She would've looked like an upstart who didn't know her place. Completely inexperienced and with no allies in her organization, her credibility would have been shot immediately. Instead she got a sense of her work environment, saw what would fly and what wouldn't and picked a small, nonthreatening way to prove herself.

Big surprise here—a **huge** portion of becoming **successful** in your new job is learning to **work well with others.**

When you are the new gal in town, you haven't got much of a sense of how people complete tasks, whose opinions matter and where the bucks stops. It can take you months to sort all that out.

Remember New Guinea? You have just happened on a previously undiscovered tribe. They may settle conflicts in a unique way, revere some individuals in the clan and have no respect for others, expect new members to show profound respect for the hierarchy and insist on convoluted methods to complete relatively minor chores. They may even communicate differently. Your natural instinct may be to shake things up and say, "Hey, you people are utterly stupid. Why don't you just do it my way? It's much easier." Do that and they will eat you for supper with fava beans and a nice Chianti.

Your colleagues **like** the way they do things. Or at least they are comfortable with their tried-and-true methods. Don't piss them off right away by trying to turn their world upside down. Show respect for the old order and understanding for the way things work, and you will win their admiration and acceptance. As you gain both your footing and their trust, you will be able to take bigger risks and be more of an innovator. This isn't simply about toeing the line. You need to educate yourself about your workplace and know it like Beverly Hills' zip code before you can truly diagnose what its big needs or problems are.

3. THE SCHMOOZE FACTOR— GETTING ALONG AND GETTING AHEAD

Have you ever heard someone say, "My work isn't my life. I just put in my time and look forward to the weekend"? They are only partly right. Your work should never be your *whole* life—what an empty existence that would be. There's far too much to enjoy in the world to simply meld with the papers on your desk and never come up for air. But it's equally foolish not to admit that *work is a hugely significant part of your mortal existence.* You probably spend at least 40 hours of your week working. That leaves two piddling days a week for your "life." Talk about depressing.

You certainly don't have to enjoy your job every second of the day. Who does? But hopefully you've chosen a field that excites you and are at least trying to find out if you could turn your boring entry-level job into the beginnings of a rewarding career.

Successful people manage to fully integrate work into the rest of their lives. When they are at work they are truly **there**, not staring off into space waiting for the bell to ring. Of course everybody feels that way sometimes, and you needn't spend every waking hour plotting your path to the top, sacrificing contact with family and friends. But you have to do more than just what's written on your job description.

That doesn't just mean dotting every "I" and crossing every "T." The people you work with are critical to your success. Alienate them and you will surely fail. Good work relationships are extremely important. After all, you spend all week with these people. Count up the hours and you'll find they usually bask in your aura longer than anybody else you know, including the person you sleep with. If you hate them all, or they all hate you, you have a serious problem.

Being good at your job isn't all about being **Mr. Popularity**. You still have to be able to deliver the goods. But sacrifice good relationships with your colleagues and everything gets harder. You are a part of something larger than yourself—going it alone isn't an option.

Don't sell out, or smother your unique and wonderful personality in the name of filthy lucre. Just don't underestimate the human factor.

"A lot of work is really about—i don't want to say brownnosing—but working the right people. it's definitely who you know. in the company i used to work for, everybody wanted these big assignments that included travel all over Europe. i found a mentor who was able to give me those opportunities. you have to schmooze and play the political game in order to get noticed."
—Chaton, 25, screenwriter

113

Politics is a pretty filthy word these days, and it's usually considered doubly heinous when smooshed right behind *office*. It conjures up images of some unfortunate resident of *Melrose Place* getting a pair of scissors plunged in her back over at D&D Advertising. In fact, a lot of career books are filled with advice that could have been culled from a showdown scene between that vixen Amanda Woodward and whiny Allison Parker. It's all "watch your back," "learn how to play the game," "don't get screwed," "cover your ass" and "know who your enemies are." **Blah, blah, blah.** If only people were that inventive and sinister.

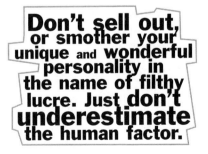

Here's the deal. Whenever human beings get together, politics spawns like a fungus. We are not talking about storming abortion clinics, pork barrel projects in Arkansas, or smoke-filled rooms on Capitol Hill. The politics of our everyday lives is far more subtle. It consists of jockeying for position, pleasing others and smoothing down ruffled feathers. Whether you like it or not, you play politics—at home, at school and at work. From the time you're born, you are a political animal.

No organization is free of unwritten rules, intrigues, gossip, bickering and cliques. **None**—no matter how cravenly capitalist or saintly and altruistic. *Being aware of the particular politics of your work environment is part of doing a good job.* You are not being slimy, you are being sensible.

Let's say, you lucky thing, you, a job comes your way as a copywriter at D&D. You know that Amanda is the Queen Bee, cross her and you and your Mandee wardrobe go limping straight back to whatever tanning salon you crawled out of. Allison goes out of her way to be nice to you. Soon she's gossiping about the fact that Amanda frosts her hair, that her skirts are too short for work, what an utterly horrible person she is and how much she hates her. Here she is, being so nice to you, you find yourself joining in. Yeah, that Amanda is such a tart, isn't she?

Mistake. Warning. Stop. Desist. You have just gotten mired in the thick of a very nasty conflict between two senior people. Even worse, when it hits the fan, you are going to be on the losing side. If you had been more clued into the culture of your new job, you would have known that Amanda holds all the cards in her complex relationship with Allison. She can unceremoniously sack her (and you) in a heartbeat.

You don't want any part of this mess. You want to do your job, maybe talk sports with Billy at the water cooler, and be appreciated all around. Mediating catfights is not what you collect a paycheck for. Life is already too complicated.

The solution to the problem is not to go butter up Amanda and dish on Allison. The solution is to be polite, neutral and pleasant. Think of yourself as Switzerland. Avoid the impression that you are one "side" or another. Never gossip, meddle or suit up for battle, especially when you are the new blood.

Understand Amanda is the big boss. Recognize and respect her authority. She's also a rising star in the company. You want to get to know her and win her respect. Maybe one day she can help you along. But respect Allison, too. You want no enemies, only allies. It's easy to be drawn into larger conflicts we have absolutely no understanding of. And it can be deadly.

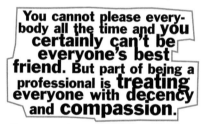

You cannot please everybody all the time and you certainly can't be everyone's best friend. But part of being a professional is treating everyone with decency and compassion.

Some people are far easier to like than others. There will be some individuals, in every workplace, that frustrate or annoy you. *Save your bitching about them for after hours.*

There are people out there who are convinced that you need to grab every potential rival by the nuts in order to claw your way to the top. That seems a rather grim, brutal and nasty way to live life. It may work on *One Life to Live*, but it almost never works in real life, especially when you are the rookie. If you come on like a shark, people will avoid swimming with you, and you can't afford to be a pariah.

When you simply take a few minutes to be friendly, you find that most people have redeeming qualities and respond when you show a genuine interest in their lives. It can be as simple as asking someone how their evening was, or bringing in a big box of donuts. And it makes work a hell of a lot more fun, too.

Do not, however, become a big bubbling vat of sickly sweet phoniness. You remember that one cheerleader in high school—let's call her Bambi—who always ambushed you in the hall, gushed about how cute you looked (even when you looked like a lump of tapioca pudding that had been left in the blazing sun for three days) to your face, then talked trash about you the minute your back was turned? **Everyone knows a Bambi.**

Become Bambi and people will spot the routine a mile away. By all means be genial and compliment people. Falling over yourself to get "face time" with higher-ups, and being a general ass-kisser and sycophant, however, is a great big minus. Your peers won't trust you and your superiors won't respect you. Don't be afraid to have an opinion, and stick to it. If you suggest an idea that gets shot down in a meeting, congratulate yourself for having had the guts to bring it up. Don't be a weather vane and blow whichever way you feel a powerful person wants you to. Toadies are always despised, even by the people they serve.

In work, as in all aspects of your life, you will run into scumbags who seem to be pure evil and succeeding because of it. Ignore them. If someone appears to be lying, cheating and sleeping their way to the top, don't

 compromise yourself by sinking to their level. That is truly selling out. It does seem sometimes that **Evil Wins**. But in the

end, those who connive their way to the top will get what they so richly deserve. Look, there is no empirical evidence to prove this; you just have to believe it's so.

If you can get there by playing by the rules and being true to yourself, the rewards will be ever so much richer.

What is absolutely true is that if you step on people in your mad dash for the brass ring, they will never forget it. If you need their help, or if your fortunes take a turn for the worse, they are going to be gathering kindling together for your inevitable roasting at the stake. Be smart and realize that some unscrupulous people resort to gamesmanship and treachery. Don't give in to it. At the end of the day, all the material success in the world means nothing without a sense of honor.

GOSSIP

If you never gossip, you don't have to read this.

Hey, wait a minute— get back here!

Everybody gossips. Don't get all high and mighty. Come clean. How can

anybody *not* gossip? Gossiping is one of life's great pleasures. It's fun, it's free, and you can do it practically anywhere. A workplace without a lush and fruity grapevine is not inhabited by humanoids.

It's next to impossible *not* to gossip at work. You can start out determined not to, but sooner or later you are probably going to wallow in this guilty pleasure. We could be sanctimonious and tell you that engaging in gossip is completely unprofessional (which it is) and morally wrong. But that would be pointless. And heck, sometimes gossip makes work quite entertaining.

So let's assume that, despite the fact that you know **you should never contribute to the rumor mill**, one day you are going to go to lunch with a friend and bond over the fact that your boss is wearing a horrifying tie, or that Sadie in special orders has the most grinding nasal voice you've ever heard, or that Chip, the mail boy, is having a torrid affair with a top-level executive.

Gossip is a wicked good time, but it's dangerous. If you give into it, be very careful. Never huddle in corners and corridors to whisper and cackle. Not only will people become more guarded around you (even if they aren't the people you are talking about), but it looks terribly childish and unbusinesslike. Have you ever been caught talking about someone?

There's nothing worse than having your boss show up behind you at the water cooler while you are describing the disgusting way he picks food out of his teeth. Take your juicy tidbits outside, and away from potential scenes.

It's deadly to become known far and wide as the office gossip. That's certainly not a person you'd trust with confidential material or a difficult project. When a supervisor or customer shares top-secret information with you, keep your big floppy lips zippered. You may get a sudden rush from leaking the information, but you could wind up collecting unemployment for the pleasure. Be honorable and discreet.

Some gossip is harmless, and some is actually quite useful. It's good to have an ear tuned to the business grapevine. You'll know when a big shake-up is happening at the top levels of your corporation, or when a new manager is being hired or promoted. All that can help your own career. "You should have an ear on this kind of grapevine," says one careers expert. "But never pass on the information or contribute to the rumor mill until the facts are confirmed. Then you are relaying information, not gossip." Never take grapevine rumors for fact until you are certain they are true.

That said, some gossip is absolutely poisonous. Never spread vicious rumors about a co-worker's personal life. If it gets back to them and they trace it to you—ouch. This may seem like the most delicious gossip of all, but it leaves a terrible taste in your mouth. The great thing about gossip is the thrill of revealing a secret, not hurting someone.

A related point—if you **do** surrender to your baser instincts and gossip about someone, know when to stop. *If you find yourself spending a whole lunch hour tearing someone apart, it's more than time to quit.* There may be one woman in the office you absolutely cannot stand. Neither can your friend. At first you resist the temptation to dish about her, but finally the dam bursts. Soon you are noticing every little thing she does and storing it up for a bitch session. The more you talk about her, the more she annoys you. You and your friend tell each other that you really have to stop, but then she'll go and do something else you simply have to comment on. Pretty soon you find that whenever you are in this woman's company you reflexively snort or roll your eyes. You can't help snickering with your friend dangerously soon after she leaves a room. You both try and reassure each other there's **no way** she could overhear you or know what's going on.

Chances are, she does, you louse. You may think she's dumb as a post, but people are all built with extrasensitive antennae that are specially designed to detect when others are having a laugh at their expense. Pretty soon it'll be open warfare. And one thing is certain—if she can make your life one-tenth as miserable as you've made hers, she certainly will. You may never, ever, like this woman, but you have done yourself no favors by working overtime to turn her into an enemy. You can make your own life hell by turning work into a seventh-grade classroom.

KEEPING SECRETS

Here's the 411 on human beings. They are lousy at keeping secrets. Remember that every day of your working life. Sordid details about your personal life—*like who you are dancing the naked mambo with*—should never be discussed at work. Not only is it completely inappropriate, but your information will get spread faster than a rabid flesh-eating virus. Nice people, decent people, people who earnestly mean it when they swear on their mother's health that *they'll never tell anyone* your secret passion for whips and chains, are going to spill the beans.

Ascribe to the peas-up-your-nose theory. You are seven years old. Your mother is forced to leave you alone in the house. She tells you to stay out of trouble while she's gone—and to please, please, not stick peas up your nose. She's off to the supermarket in the station wagon, and there you are, with an evil seed planted in your brain. Why not put peas in your nose? It soon becomes an irresistible tractor beam of temptation—you are shoving the little green suckers up your sniffer like there's no tomorrow.

It would never even occur to you to do this if your mother hadn't specifically told you not to. Don't tempt a person to put peas up his nose by serving up a bucket of spicy dirt about yourself. You may as well take out a full-page ad in the newspaper. "If you want information to spread," says one human resources officer, "tell someone it's a secret. If you want to keep it secret, don't tell."

Never expose yourself to the rumor mill. If you blab about your pierced nipples, it will get out. If you get sloshed at the Christmas party and make out with your boss, it will get out. If you flirt shamelessly with everything in trousers, or drool over anything in a skirt, it will get around.

117

Try not to give people an opportunity to make professional judgments based on the sordid details of your private life.

whine, whine, whine

Like gossip, another enjoyable way to pass the day is complaining. Here's another bit of useless advice—**never complain about your job.** **Yeah, right. And stop breathing that oxygen crap, while you're at it.** Complaining is innate and something some people have refined into a high art form. Cut out complaining and gossip and we would be a nation of mutes. Nevertheless, there is a time and a place for complaining. Most of the time, work is the worst possible venue.

Jack was a nice guy who worked for a market research firm. He had some wonderful qualities, and he put in long hours making sure his work was well done. But Jack couldn't help himself. Engaged in any conversation for more than two minutes and he would begin harping about how put-upon he was, how nobody ever appreciated what he did for the company, how his back hurt all the time, how his dog had a malingering tumor and how he couldn't get dates.

Sometimes he'd even stun his listeners by saying something like "Well, it's no wonder my life turned out this way—I mean, I'm so pathetic."

People began to avoid Jack, and when projects came up that he would have been perfect for, he was passed over. Nobody thought he could handle them, because his life was such a mess. The truth was, Jack's life was just fine. He just got into the nasty habit of harping on and on about every little thing that didn't go perfectly for him. Not only did people read that as unwillingness to do work, others saw it as proof that he had absolutely no self-confidence. Soon he had nothing to do all day, which made him complain even more.

When people began to develop elaborate methods of bypassing his cubicle on their way to the bathroom, Jack sought them out. He'd linger at someone's office door, waiting for his moment to launch into a long-winded account of how his computer ate all of his most important files or how yet another woman stood him up. Finally one of his cornered victims beat him to death with a hole puncher in order to save herself the agony of having to endure yet another story about how Jack's parents never remembered his birthday. No one from the office attended the funeral.

Don't get dubbed *"The Complainer."* It's extremely difficult to shake this mark of shame. If every word that comes out of your mouth is part of a never-ending saga of misery and woe, you are going to be treated like the pox. If you have a professional beef, find an appropriate party to air your complaint to and try to have it redressed. When things don't go your way, accept it. Don't hang around the water cooler whining to everyone you can ambush.

Likewise, your co-workers will be utterly (and justifiably) mortified by convoluted forays into your wretched childhood or unhappy love life. **This material should never be the stuff of office banter.** Save the game of true confessions for your close friends.

Moderate any instinct you may have to cut yourself down. Self-deprecation is a bad habit many of us pick up in high school. We say "I'm so stupid" or "I'll never be any good," and pretty soon we start to believe it. Even if we don't believe it, and are simply fishing for compliments—"Oh Jane, you *are* beautiful, you *know* you are"—continually making these kinds of comments all the time in the workplace is as wrongheaded as bragging about how stupendous you are. News flash—this is not *Ricki Lake*. Don't ask your boss or colleagues to patch together the fragments of your shredded psyche.

"Relationships are going to happen at work," says one human resources director. "The key is to be practical." When they do, remember these ground rules:

NEVER DATE YOUR SUPERIORS . . .

Your boss, your boss's boss, the chairman of the board and any other more senior person in an organization are most definitely **not** who you want to end up smooching. You are violating so many taboos here it's ridiculous. If people find out you're sleeping with the boss, you have reduced your credibility to zero. If the boss and you have a messy breakup, you could be out on your ear. We could give you one horrifying scenario after another—but you get the picture. Don't go there.

Work and *Sex*

Hook up with people you work with, and life can get **very** complicated. If you are looking for love, buy someone a fruity drink at *Get Lucky's Bar and Meat Market* or take out a personal ad. No matter how gorgeous a colleague may be, attempt to gird those loins. A casual fling never ends up being casual at work. You can rest assured that people will find out about it—and *quick*. Then there's the fact that working with a spurned lover is about as pleasant as having a boil lanced.

However, the fact is that our hormones often lead us where common sense has told us not to tread.

. . . OR PEOPLE YOU SUPERVISE

This may even be *more* important than the first point. You have power over people who work under you. If you pursue such a person romantically, you may be crossing the line into that very nasty stretch of the woods called **sexual harassment**.

"Sexual harassment is about power," says one human resources officer. "Even if it seems your affair with your assistant was consensual, after you break things off things can change. She may claim that she felt she had no choice but to enter into the affair because you had power over her. She may claim that after you dumped her you hurt her career opportunities. This kind of relationship is a huge no-no." Okay, most of us starting out don't have people working under us. But it's important to be aware of this from the outset.

Who does that leave? One less hazardous source of dates are clients or freelance people whom you meet and work with for only a short period. **The least risky office romance is going to be with a peer**, hopefully in another department. If you fall for Gino, the sexy guy in hair transplants, and you work in liposuction, there's no real conflict of interest. But when you and Gino work side by side every day, you may have a harder time of it, especially if things don't work out.

If you enter into a serious relationship at work, you may want to tell your boss. Give your supervisor an opportunity to advise you. She may recommend you break off the relationship, or be able to help transfer you or the other person out of the department, or give you her blessing and tell you to be careful. What you don't want is to surprise her with the messy after-effects of your breakup a year later.

Making your boss aware of the situation doesn't mean giving her the steamy lowdown on your affair, obviously. You are just letting her know about a situation that may change group dynamics in the workplace. A good manager appreciates the information.

Whether you choose to tell your boss or not, **be very discreet**. If you are in an office relationship, keep it out of the office. In other words, when you are at work, you are colleagues, not lovers. You should appear to be no more than friendly co-workers to your associates. No kissing, petting, hand holding or goo-goo baby talk.

Try not to go too public with the relationship until one of you moves out of the department or organization. Even if word gets out, don't come skipping to work holding hands. Keep your daily interaction all business.

DISCRIMINATION AND HARASSMENT

These words get bandied about an awful lot. They are grave terms, and they can wreck careers. Accuse a person of discrimination and there is no going back—it will be next to impossible to salvage the relationship. So know what these words mean and employ them only when you absolutely have to.

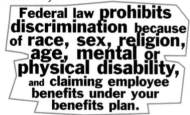

Federal law **prohibits discrimination** because of race, sex, religion, age, mental or physical disability, and claiming employee benefits under your benefits plan.

If you blow the whistle on illegal practices in your organization, you may also be protected from retaliation by your employer. The state and city you work in may also have antidiscrimination laws that prevent you from being discriminated against on the basis of sexual orientation, marital status and filing a worker's compensation claim, among other things. Know the law in your area.

Beyond that, nearly every organization of any size has its own antidiscrimination policies. You are surely familiar with the phrase *"**Company X** is an Equal Opportunity Employer."* You should have a copy of the company policy somewhere in the reams of material given to you when you started the job. **Read it.** If someone refuses to promote you because you are Korean, fires you because you are gay or denies you a salary increase because you are pregnant, your organization may have elaborate mechanisms to deal with the problem. However, if you are in a small business or startup organization, there may be no such fleshed-out policy.

In either case, if you feel you are a victim of discrimination of any kind at work, you must go to your supervisor and **tell him about it.** Some companies have specifically designated employees to hear all grievance claims. Check to see if your employer has a grievance policy you should follow. Your human resources department can provide you with this information. If your company does not have a human resources department, and it's your supervisor who is the source of the problem, go to his boss. It's smart to keep a record of every conversation and correspondence you have about your problem. In the best-case scenario, the company will act quickly to resolve the situation. If for some reason they aren't, you have established that you were serious from the outset about ending the discrimination should you, as a very last resort, have to take them to court.

Harassment is a *form* of discrimination. As high as its profile has been in the media lately, people still get very confused when the issue is discussed. The simplest way to understand harassment is to split it into two types: let's call one *direct harassment* (lawyers call this **quid pro quo harassment**):

the other is commonly referred to as **hostile environment harassment**. The first type of harassment is easier to grasp. A woman is told by her supervisor she won't get promoted unless she rolls in the hay with him. That's a clear case of **sexual harassment**.

If her supervisor made lewd remarks about women in general, pinned up cheesecake pictures on the office wall or continually called her a dumb broad, she can also claim she was sexually harassed. This is hostile environment harassment—her boss's actions created an atmosphere that could easily be perceived as antagonistic to women. Whatever your gender, this is one more reason to leave lurid stories about your kinky sexcapades in the locker room.

If you **willingly** enter into an affair with your boss, you are going to have a devil of a time proving sexual harassment. However, if, for example, you break things off and she begins to threaten you or continues to pursue it, you can make a good case for it.

Likewise, if you are black, and you are in a workplace where "nigger" is used frequently by fellow employees, you could make a compelling harassment claim, even if it is not aimed at you and **even if the employees using that word are black**. That language doesn't belong in the workplace, full stop. A nasty caricature of the Pope that a Catholic could find offensive could also be construed as religious harassment. A person doesn't have to come out and say "I hate you because you are Catholic and I will never allow you to advance here because of it" in order to be guilty of harassment.

121

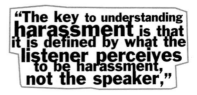
"The key to understanding harassment is that it is defined by what the listener perceives to be harassment, not the speaker,"

says a human resources officer. At work, stay a mile clear of racy conversations, lewd jokes, ethnic humor—in short anything that might be taken the wrong way by another individual. If, for some reason, you blunder into a statement that might possibly be construed as harassment, do what any well-mannered person does when they are unwittingly rude. **Apologize immediately.**

Uh-oh, we hear it now. People accusing us of being Big Brother's P.C. Thought Police. Look, this has nothing to do with being politically correct, and everything to do with decent manners, accepted standards of ethical behavior, professional conduct and **the law**. Civilized people don't talk this kind of trash, whatever their politics.

And again, before you ever lodge a complaint against someone, it may make sense to attempt to work the problem out.

BULLIES . . .

Like schoolyards, some workplaces come complete with bullies. Office bullies throw their weight around—no matter how insignificant their authority. They are territorial—if they perceive that you are poaching even the tiniest responsibility from them, you are going to get it with both barrels. Bullies humiliate you in meetings with condescending comments or in out-and-out tirades. They take credit for your work, while cutting you down. They complain about you to higher-ups.

Some people bully you because they are just horrible, others because they are threatened by you. They may think you are after their job, for example. Most of them are easily cowed. Don't stand for any monkey business. You didn't take a job to get screamed at all day or to be treated like a moron. You'd be surprised how contrite many bullies become when they realize you won't be pushed around.

Don't cower in the bathroom crying because the office dragon lady lit into you. Never lose your temper in front of a bully, or break down. Stay calm, and don't engage in an extended argument or shouting match. "I'm willing to discuss this rationally, but I won't stand here and be harangued," might be the ticket if you are feeling especially ballsy. Or you might try and defuse the situation with something like "Are you having a bad day?" If that pisses the person off further, walk away until things cool down. "Always try and resolve the misunderstanding with the person," says one human resources officer. "Try and talk it out. Most people don't mean to be nasty. Really."

If you have a serious problem with a person that seems to defy resolution, go to your boss and tell her about it. The worst possible bully to encounter is one that is your boss, especially your first boss. Don't slink around muttering about how horrible she is to you—confront her and ask if there is some aspect of your work that needs improving. You and your boss need to have open lines of communication. If after an exhaustive attempt, the two of you can't work it out, it may be time to talk to her boss or to human resources. And if things are simply unbearable, it may be time to start thinking about moving on.

Sometimes people lose their tempers at work. Don't take it personally. Conflicts flare up and quickly die down. When you spend time with people every single day, things can get a little hairy at times. Your boss may be going over a complex set of instructions with you the day before a big meeting, and you can't manage to get your head around them. He sighs in exasperation or snaps at you. He's not a bully or a monster, he's just tired and grouchy.

If you feel yourself getting sharp with people, catch yourself. Apologize. Explain that you were testy earlier because your car broke down on the way to work, or whatever. If someone seems annoyed with you, throw out an apology for any misunderstanding you may have unwittingly caused, and ask if you upset them. Apologies are wonderful. Don't be a child about them—even if you feel you were 100 percent in the right, opening a conversation with an apology signals your willingness to work things out and get the problem behind you. Take the initiative, and be the first to say you are sorry.

Talking things out is not a second chance to win your argument. If you come back to someone, accusing them of all kinds of horrible wrong-doings, you are going to get their back up and fast. You may never see eye-to-eye with someone, but you can work together. Don't get personal—avoid putting them on the spot and blaming them for what went wrong. Keep the focus of the discussion on the project you are working on together, and how you both might best complete it.

Never stew over a misunderstanding. Think of all that bad karma flying around. You've got better things to do, and you will feel absolutely lousy. People who scream and yell their way through the work day are mercifully few. Most of us hate conflict far too much. But if you encounter a bully, don't become their doormat. They are behaving inappropriately, not you.

. . . AND BUREAUCRATS

Bureaucrats are a whole different jar of salsa. They cling to forms and procedures, are highly protective of their turf and zealous about doing things according to the book. Most bureaucrats are not bullies. They simply need to be reassured that they are important, and that their contribution won't be minimized by hotshots and cowboys.

Here's a textbook bureaucratic encounter. You send a package to the mail room and it gets sent back with an angry note attached because you stapled the package shut, instead of sealing it with tape, per regulation 456G. Milliseconds later, Mail Room Bureaucrat is on the horn to yell at you for this seemingly minute infraction.

This is ridiculous and anal, so your first instinct when he calls may be to snort in derision. Don't do it. The one thing bureaucrats *hate*, more than anything, is to be belittled. Your pack-ages will mysteriously stop getting where they need to go. You'll end up spending hours screaming on the phone, start losing your hair in clumps and getting stressed out over the most insignificant aspects of your job. The bureaucrat has been around a long time. He knows how to make your life a living hell, simply by slowing things down or harping over regulations.

Here 's a better response: "I'm so glad you called, Mail Room Bureaucrat, because I was just about to call you. I'm really sorry I didn't seal the envelope correctly. You see I'm new here, and I'm just figuring things out. Thanks for pointing it out to me. It won't happen again." Mail Room Bureaucrat feels great. He isn't someone you can just kick around. Presto-change-o, you've got a friend.

If a bureaucrat gives you a hard time no matter how nice you are, write

them off as a grouch. If you are getting nowhere, your critical packages are piling up and you are about to have a nervous breakdown over the whole thing, go to your boss and let her breathe a little fire on him.

Some bureaucrats are paranoid—they see conspiracies to undermine their authority at every turn. Or they simply feel they get no respect. Send a little flattery their way, and you are usually in business.

MAKE FRIENDS

You want to build friendships at work, and lots of them. Forget politics for a nanosecond. If you don't enjoy at least some of the people you work with, you are going to hate your job. There's no denying it. One of the best aspects of any entry-level job is hanging out with other young people like yourself. You go out together for beers on Friday, or long after you've moved on you gather together to laugh about an old supervisor's tantrums. These people are a huge part of what makes life worth living. Without them, success is pretty empty.

Even in the most competitive workplace, make friends with your peers. Don't lord your accomplishments over them or ignore them in order to spend your time courting the top brass. You will be forever remembered as *"The Climber."*

IT MAY BE FRUSTRATING TO YOU, BUT A PARADOX OF WORKING LIFE IS THAT WHILE AMBITION IS HIGHLY VALUED, BEING PERCEIVED AS OVERLY AMBITIOUS IS ALIENATING. BRAGGARTS AND USERS BE WARNED.

Alix was a bright young thing out to make her mark on the fashion world. She lucked out by getting a trainee buyer position at a prestigious department store. Her eyes set firmly on the prize of trips to New York, Paris and Milan, she came on like an armored personnel carrier. She felt if she behaved like an executive, she would get noticed. Alix also thought that if she was seen socializing with other trainee buyers, she would be perceived as an underling, so she made no effort to bond with her peers.

Alix **did** get noticed by the top brass. She was unafraid to make demands of her superiors and they usually acceded to them. If she needed a day off, she got it. If she wanted a raise, she got it. If she asked for a responsibility unheard of for someone in her position, she got it. People were often too stunned to say no to her. Many of the store executives were impressed—they saw Alix's enormous drive as an asset to the store.

But the other trainee buyers hated her guts. Her brazen behavior became the stuff of legend among her colleagues. **She may have called bigwigs by their first names, but no one her age would have lifted a finger to bail her out of a jam. They resented her achievements, talked about her behind her back and fantasized about her eventual comeuppance. Middle-level managers also began to distrust her.** They felt she would drive a stake through her grandmother's heart in order to get to Paris.

You can see where this is going. Alix quickly became the most unpopular person in a once-pleasant workplace. She saw people's frosty behavior as merely a manifestation of jealousy and chose to disregard it. She did move slowly up the ladder, but her Concorde to the Fall Collections never arrived. A few years later, she found out that an old colleague was in a high-level job at a competing store. She called her to touch base and discuss possible job opportunities there. The woman flatly refused to help her. After all, she hated Alix's guts.

You cannot ignore someone because you think they are unimportant and rediscover them when they make it big. People really hate that and will pay you back for your lousy behavior. There is nothing wrong with striving for what you want. But never forget your peers are instrumental in helping you get it. They may be in positions of power one day. It's also no fun to have nobody to grab a bite to eat with. When you are around your peers, don't go on ad infinitum about your career ambitions. We are only human, after all. You may inspire resentment and fear.

HAVE A LIFE

No matter how close you and your co-workers become, don't neglect your social life outside of work. You'll go crazy otherwise. You need to be able to escape the same faces every day and talk about things other than your job. Have you ever met someone who is unable to talk about anything but fiber optics, or tires, or nylon stockings or Mortal Kombat? You find yourself nodding off as this person talks, and praying that God will send down a thunderbolt to incinerate them.

Sacrifice everything for work and you will inevitably become Johnny One Note. When you are in school it's easy to have friends with a diverse array of interests and goals. When you are locked into an industry with people on the same track as yourself, you need to go out of your way to maintain contact with the outside world. How boring to hang out only with lawyers or bankers, filmmakers or shoe salesmen.

Just because you work behind a desk or punch a clock doesn't mean you cease to be an interesting, involved and dynamic person. Push yourself to get out of the house after work to volunteer, go to bookstores, hang out with the old crowd, see a movie or catch a ball game. At work and away from it, the most interesting people are always the ones with diverse interests and experiences.

4. YOUR BOSS

The most important relationship you have on any new job is the one you have with your boss. Now, some of us have been blessed with real mensches as supervisors, and some of us haven't been so lucky. Like any close relationship, chemistry is part of the mix. But even if you and your boss have absolutely nothing in common, you can forge a strong and productive alliance.

KNOW YOUR BOSS'S JOB AS WELL AS YOUR OWN

Your boss told you generally what your duties would be when you were hired, but she may not have gone into great detail about her own job. You need to understand your boss's responsibilities just as well as your own. She's got a boss, too. She's under pressure and has a huge list of priorities to muddle through. She's pressed for time. If you know her schedule and all that she has on her plate, you can better anticipate her needs and fill them. She'll love you for it.

Only by working together will you get a true sense of who your boss is and what she likes. She may be the type who likes to work long hours or someone who rolls out of the plant on Friday at noon. She may be all business or walk around the office barefoot. A large part of your job is adjusting to her particular rhythm.

Get to work before her, leave after she does and go with her flow all day long. You needn't turn yourself into a junior version of your supervisor, but dancing well together is easier when you aren't stepping all over your partner's toes.

UNDERSTAND YOUR BOSS'S EXPECTATIONS

"My first boss never sat me down and went over my responsibilities with me. She was a very nice person, just not good at giving orders. I had no idea what i was doing for the longest time."
—Cheryl, 22, receptionist

"you have to have open lines of communication with your supervisor. if you don't have that, unexpected things can happen, and you never want to surprise your boss."
—Marie, human resources director

If for some reason your boss has not sat you down and gone over exactly what he expects of you on the first day, you need to go to him and hash things out. Good communication is essential if you are going to have a pleasant and productive relationship. This sounds easy, but it can be a real bitch. Many supervisors are very explicit about what they want, others expect you to pick things up through telepathy.

You may work for a shy, sweet fellow who just can't bring himself to ask you to do things. Resist the perfectly human temptation to jump up and down with joy over what a sucker he is. Chances are he still expects you to be producing even though he doesn't give you directives. Which means while you are kicking back doing nothing, he's sitting at his desk stewing over what a lousy worker he's hired. He may be too shy to confront you, but he's probably not clueless.

Never let this situation develop. In the first place, you should be *pro-active* in all of your business relationships—that is, you should take initiative and not passively wait for orders. If you find that despite all of your efforts to drum up work, you still have plenty of time to take naps, gossip on the phone and sneak out for three-hour lunches, go to your boss and ask him if there is more you ought to be doing.

Pin him down to specific tasks—too many of us walk out of a supervisor's office feeling more confused about our performance than when we entered. Don't be afraid to ask a supervisor to evaluate your work— you can take it. If there is something in particular that you are having problems with, tell him. If you feel you need more direction than you are getting, diplomatically let him know. Bosses are just people who got their first jobs a few years before you did. Help 'em out. They'll more than appreciate you for it.

ASK FOR FEEDBACK

Many people dread these kinds of discussions, including bosses. Believe it or not, some folks shrink from giving people more things to do. It makes them feel, well, mean. And they dread delivering bad news— maybe they hate the way you photocopy, clean cars or wait tables— but are afraid to say so. Or you may have a grumpy curmudgeon who never talks to you except to bark a few vague orders. Meek bosses and poor communicators need you to make the extra effort and take the first step. Find a convenient time to sit down and go over your responsibilities, even if that time is after work hours or at lunch. Offer to take on more, and **ask for feedback**.

Depending on your personality, this may come naturally to you. Or it may make you feel all oogie. You may be nervous asking for criticism—after all, nobody likes to hear negative comments about their performance— but you have to swallow your fear and ask for it anyway. You must be assertive at work. If you are doing a lousy job, find out *now*. Not when your performance is up for formal review (more on this later), and not when your frustrated boss has no other choice but to call you in and give you a warning.

BE RECEPTIVE TO CRITICISM

Never get testy when your boss criticizes your work. Your boss is not your mother. She is a manager. If she thinks you need to improve in an area, listen carefully to her advice and **follow** it. Don't pout, bristle or start a debate. Ask her for specific tips on what you should do to improve, or ask how she would handle a particularly difficult situation.

Again, nobody likes to be criticized. You may feel an urge to leap across the desk and punch her in the chops while your boss is droning on about what a mediocre filer you are. Betray an ounce of your hostility and you have slid down yet one more notch. Once you were merely *"lousy filer."* Now you are *"lousy filer"* **and** *"responds poorly to criticism."* Think of those descriptions as entries in your performance review.

In case you have missed it so far, you can't walk in the door of any corporation these days without drowning in trite slogans about TEAMWORK. It may sound hackneyed, but organizations take a person's ability to be a "team player" very seriously. Avoid getting labeled as difficult—or worse, someone too intimidating or scary to ever criticize.

HONESTY, STILL SUCH A LONELY WORD

Yes, we've resorted to paraphrasing Billy Joel. Honesty is especially important in your relationship with your supervisor. Always be upfront with your manager. If you get in over your head, see yourself about to take the company into bankruptcy, or have just erased her very important voice mail, tell the truth. Don't start lying.

LOOK, LYING IS EASY, AND FRANKLY, SOMETIMES IT IS BETTER TO TELL YOUR BOSS YOU HAD CAR TROUBLE THAN THAT YOU WERE PUKING YOUR GUTS OUT AFTER A NIGHT SWILLING SCOTCH AND TABLE-DANCING TO ABBA SONGS AT SOME ROADSIDE FLESHPOT. BUT WHEN IT COMES TO YOUR PERFORMANCE, DON'T PASS THE BUCK OR MAKE EXCUSES. IF YOU BUNGLED SOMETHING, BE UPFRONT ABOUT IT.

Don't shift the blame to some other poor sucker or launch into a long-winded rationalization. Most likely, your boss will know exactly what you are doing—and that looks very bad indeed. When something goes wrong, it's like we are eight years old all over again, denying that we spilled the milk, wet our pants or crammed a toy army man down our kid sister's throat even when it's perfectly obvious that we did. Unfortunately, most people in the working world react in the same kindergarten fashion when something goes haywire. Stop making excuses and come clean. You'll feel better about it.

YOU AND YOUR BOSS ARE PARTNERS

Pancho and Cisco, Batman and Robin, the Green Hornet and Kato, Siskel and Ebert. Think of yourself as the junior partner in your relationship with your boss. Your object, as one personnel specialist puts it, "is to always make your supervisor look good." Never forget who you work for—your primary loyalty is always, always to your boss.

If the project you put together for her to present at an annual sales meeting is falling apart, let her know in advance, defuse any new bombs that might blow up in her face. If you have just learned critical information that will drastically alter the outcome of that sales meeting, get it to her faster than a speeding Camaro. Be ready to stand in for your boss when she needs you to. When you know her projects as well as your own, you are in business.

Keep in mind that while you work in tandem, your boss has career goals of his own. Most of the time they coincide with yours, but sometimes they don't. Remember, a successful partnership is not entirely based on what you want or can get out of the relationship. Nor is it about sacrificing your ambitions for someone else's success.

On the other hand, if you ever saw the movie *All About Eve*, you remember what a nightmare wench Eve Harrington was. That hussy began as the protégé of a famous actress, then started pilfering everything her mentor owned that wasn't bolted down.

A barracuda is a lonely fish, and a baby barracuda is going to get gobbled.
Never try to steal your boss's thunder, badmouth her, humiliate her, undermine her authority or gun for her job. It's totally despicable and, outside the realm of daytime drama, an entirely self-destructive course of action.

Suck-ups are not the same as loyal sidekicks. A suck-up says only what she thinks her boss wants to hear, then abandons him when she feels he's lost power or influence. A suck-up has the ethics of a Norway Rat. When your boss solicits your opinion, don't parrot his ideas— be honest and helpful. This is

still a democracy—dissent is okay. But should your boss disregard your advice, support him. He needs you backing him up in meetings with other colleagues and clients—if you have found a hole in one of his ideas, wait until you have a moment alone together to point it out.

DON'T HOVER

We have stressed having a hands-on relationship with your boss. But don't stalk the poor fellow. Keep out of your supervisor's face. That's not being helpful, it's annoying. Always *ask* for a convenient time to sit and talk if you need to go over something in detail. Never go barging into someone's office and start blabbing away. Even in casual settings, respect your boss's limited time and personal space.

Choose your moments carefully. You should be able to tell when your boss is stressed out, or know what time of the week always gets chaotic for him. Having your superior's ear is useless if he's not in a receptive mood. When you do talk, be direct and to the point.

Spare him long-winded accounts all decked out with *ums, ahs, likes* and *you knows*. If you tend to get nervous around your boss, think through what you are going to say before you go speak with him.

OF MENTORS AND MUSSOLINIS

If bosses were lined up in a showroom, like so many spanking-new cars, the model you'd want to go for would be the **Mentor**. The ideal boss shows you the ropes, wishes you well when you move on, frequently helps you to move into a better position, writes you glowing recommendations and throughout your career serves as an inexhaustible font of wisdom. That sounds like a tall order, but there are hordes of potential mentors out there. Always be on the lookout for them.

Some bosses are naturally nurturing types. But most mentor relationships are usually developed over time, not after your initial interview. How do you transform a boss into a mentor? The best answer to that is to simply work hard and use your fabulous personality to charm the socks off someone.

If you deliver the goods, your boss is going to respect you. If you truly bond with your supervisor, even better. But having a lot in common with your boss is not a prerequisite. You could be from Mars—be pleasant, conscientious and dedicated, and any good manager is going to love you. Most supervisors of entry-level people do not expect them to be glued to their current jobs for all eternity. A good supervisor certainly doesn't.

A good boss wants to see you do well and move up the ladder. It's good for them in the long run—the better you do, the better they look. And it's frankly nice to see a protégé go on to greater glory. Tell your boss what your career goals are. Don't lie and pretend that you want to be working under them until the end of time—they wouldn't buy that, anyway. If you have an *especially* close relationship with your boss, you may want to go to her when you are considering moving on and ask for their help and counsel. They'll appreciate the notice and may be of invaluable aid. Sure, they'll be sad to see you go. But nine and a half times out of ten, they'll give you their blessing.

Besides your immediate boss, any senior person you click with is a potential mentor. Your boss should

never be your sole ally in an organization. Think about the executive you talk baseball with in the elevator every morning, the head of another department you speak with on the phone every day who covets your vintage Dexy's Midnight Runners album, the human resources executive who helped you get the job. They are all potential mentors.

Cultivate these relationships—you can grow good mentors like geraniums. This, of course, leads us back to the phoney-baloney issue.

MENTOR RELATIONSHIPS ARE BASED ON RESPECT, AND EVEN MORE IMPORTANTLY, AFFECTION. YOUR MENTOR HELPS YOU BECAUSE SHE LIKES YOU, NOT BECAUSE YOU KISS HER BUTT.

Mentors are central to your ever-expanding network of contacts. Many people still call their first boss and ask for advice many years into their careers. That person gave them their start and helped them along the road. Long after their professional relationship officially ended, they are still maintaining an enduring, productive friendship.

The real lemon in the supervisor showroom is the Mussolini-type boss. This person has all the finesse of Saddam Hussein when it comes to management style. No matter how hard you work, Mussolini will not be satisfied. You can take her kid to see Joey Lawrence in concert seven times in a row, pick her Saab up from the garage, cater her chi-chi dinner parties and she's still not happy. You spend all night working on something, and she takes all the credit. Mussolini bosses are bullies—they may flatter you from time to time, but you always wind up feeling used and abused.

You can try to flatter this sort of person, let them think they are brilliant even if you are doing 99 percent of the work, and hope you will be rewarded. But don't be surprised if you are not. That's another reason to spread yourself around and develop other relationships in an organization. The hardest part about getting a supervisor from hell like this right off the bat is that you are inexperienced. You may blame yourself for having a psycho boss, work frantically to earn his respect and grow even more miserable when you fail. There are loopy people in the world, and you may very well end up working for one.

Luckily, most supervisors are not irrational or evil. Again, tempers flare occasionally for any number of reasons—try not to take the odd tantrum personally. A little spat does not mean your boss hates you or wants to fire you. If you feel you aren't getting what you want out of your relationship, set up a time to talk about it. As with any other problem at work, try and solve the problem *mano a mano*, and if that doesn't work, find someone who can help you solve it—either a more senior person or a human resources officer. Don't sit on your anger or resort to sabotage in order to get revenge. If you are in a small operation, and there is literally no one to turn to but an abusive boss, you may want to start looking elsewhere. You never have to become a wage slave in order to make a living.

Beyond these two generalized types of boss there are a myriad of others— as many as there are individual quirks. There are grandmotherly bosses, stuffed-shirt bosses, manipulative bosses, geek bosses, dead-head bosses, control-freak bosses, ditzy bosses, invisible bosses and absent-minded-professor bosses, just to name a few. With time and observation, you'll be able to do a very thorough armchair analysis of your boss's various personality flaws.

Now, you can either use that knowledge as fodder for gripe sessions or as a tool to help you better understand your supervisor and serve her better. You'll definitely do the former—attempt to do the latter as well and you'll have a more productive relationship and further your own ambitions.

REMEMBER YOUR BOSS'S BIRTHDAY

Hopefully you realize by this point that your boss is not a robot, specially designed and built by your employer to come and harass you all day. As you work together, you will begin to learn more and more details about his life. Show a polite interest in your boss's family and extracurricular activities. Some people decorate their offices with model sailboats and photos of their children, get phone calls from their husbands all day long and invite you to family barbecues. Others are much more hands-off. Never pry into your boss's private affairs, but a holiday card or an inquiry after a sick child is usually greatly appreciated.

Remember your boss at holidays and on their birthday. You don't have to be lavish. Just a card, some flowers, or a good book is more than fine. In some offices, assistants are expected to plan little parties for their supervisors on their birthdays (and vice versa). If your boss is pregnant, or having marital troubles, you will be among the first to know. Don't gossip. Be kind, and go out of your way to help them through a difficult period. That might mean picking kids up from school or taking over key responsibilities for a time.

Your boss, by virtue of seniority, can inflict her personal life on you in ways that would be totally unacceptable if turned the other way round. You may even become an unofficial member of her family. As the two of you work together, you will learn more and more about each other's lives outside work. And you'll become closer because of it. Keep your distance from your supervisor's family politics, feuds and sex life, though. That material brings new meaning to the phrase "taking your work home with you" and is absolutely no fun at all.

BE CORDIAL, BUT DON'T GET MESSY

As close as you and your boss become, remember to keep the mix from getting messy. Blending business with pleasure is fine, but no matter what the festive occasion, never get drunk in front of your boss. Even if your boss is getting plastered. Strike that. *Especially if your boss is getting plastered.*

Mind all the other taboos we've already discussed—sex talk, intimate problems and other sensitive areas of your life are best left outside of work. Never relax so much around your boss that off-color jokes come tumbling out of your mouth. A good-ol'-boy boss may well expect you to swap lurid jokes with him. In most cases you should smile politely at his gags and keep your trap shut. Just in case you missed it, sleeping with your boss is a bona fide awful idea.

You and your boss may become very good pals. But even if you hang out together outside work, never forget who has the power in your professional relationship. That means you can never treat your boss like any other buddy. No matter how cool he is, he is still your boss. Don't give him material after hours that you wouldn't want any other colleague at work to know.

KEEP YOUR BOSS IN THE LOOP

On the other hand, if you and your boss never seem to have contact with each other, do your best to keep her posted about your activities. It's easy to go your separate ways and let communication between you suffer. Touch base often, especially when your boss supervises other people and deals with you infrequently. Not only will this contact prevent unpleasant surprises down the road, but the more she knows about your accomplishments, the better your chances for advancement.

You might only have a few minutes together in the morning, but give your boss a quick rundown on where you stand on certain projects. Don't give a busy manager the opportunity to forget about you. Again, save the involved discussions for a time when you can sit down together and chat.

GO FOR EXTRA CREDIT

By this point you should have this lesson ingrained in every fiber of your being. YOU CANNOT SIMPLY COMPLETE YOUR ASSIGNED TASKS AND EXPECT TO BE REWARDED. EXTRA CREDIT IS IMPORTANT, AND NOT OPTIONAL, WITH BOSSES. Volunteer to take on more responsibilities. If your boss is running late for an important meeting but has to make reservations for a business lunch first, tell her you'll do it. You know the drill here. Become indispensable.

Subtly toot your own horn every once in a while. *Show* your boss how much you have accomplished—don't expect her to be Sherlock Holmes and figure it all out. If your boss is regularly kept abreast of your progress, she has more chances to make positive note of your various achievements. She'll also see how dedicated and enthusiastic you are. Share the glow with people who helped you complete difficult tasks, of course, and don't become an arrogant blowhard. But if you don't take credit for some marvelous achievement, nobody is going to give you a bonus prize for modesty.

5. ODDS AND ENDS OF OFFICE ETIQUETTE

Eating and working at the same time—surely a diabolical torture designed by Torquemada. If you are in a job that requires you to regularly wine-and-dine customers, you have a whole new world of manners to master before you ever bite into your first tofu supreme with a client. But even if you only go out to lunch with your boss every great once in a while, or your sole business function is the annual holiday party, keep the following rules in mind.

STAY AWAY FROM FIRE WATER

Americans are a bizarre and puritanical people, and unfortunately we are getting worse in both departments. Around the time that we were shipping automobiles with tail fins around the world, no red-blooded businessman would have turned down a chance at a two-hour lunch crammed with great stuff like nicotine, bloody red meat, and a veritable Niagara of martinis. Unfortunately, these guys are now about as common as mastodons.

If your boss takes you out to lunch on your first day of work, don't order a vodka tonic or a pint of strong mead. It's just not a smart move. Obviously, drinking etiquette varies from business to business and from region to region. Generally speaking there is more lunchtime drinking in East Coast cities than on the West Coast, for example. No matter where you work, play it safe and abstain.

Even at the company party where everyone else is drinking, moderate your intake. You shouldn't get drunk, even if you can hold your liquor, you don't want to look like a drunk. Order more than two or three drinks, and some stick-in-the-mud types may think you have a serious problem, silly as it sounds.

NO SMOKING

Smoking is now basically tied with heroin addiction in the great list of unattractive personal habits.

It's virtually impossible to smoke at work nowadays—you are usually forced to go stand outside the building you work in to have an illicit puff, like some pathetic junkie. Walk through any business district in the land and you'll see these sad people standing outside in blizzards and heat waves, stamping out cigarette after cigarette on the sidewalk.

This is not meant to be yet another starchy lecture on the evils of smoking. Everyone is rightly sick of those. Indulge the demon god tobacco all you want on your own time. Just remember that many people find smoking offensive and distracting. Be cautious and always assume that smoking is not acceptable in your working life.

Even if you love cigarettes more than life itself, try not to smoke at work. Wait until your commute, or at least until your lunch hour, to light up. Smoking rules and mores vary from workplace to workplace, but try to never join the sad ranks of sidewalk puffers. The street is not your ashtray. Littering your nasty butts all over the pavement should be a capital offense. Stamp out the finished cigarette and place it in the garbage.

If you're hooked, you're caught between a rock and a hard place. You can't smoke at your desk. Even if it's officially allowed, the stale odor will hang around your work station like a toxic cloud. Although it's tacky and lowbrow to smoke on street corners, if you must, at least don't camp out right in front of the building where you work.

> Any habit that forces you to leave the building every hour or so is a black mark against you—so indulging it at the main entrance MAY BE HAZARDOUS TO MORE THAN YOUR HEALTH.

Many managers view habitual smoking as a weakness and a drain on productivity. Smokers should also be zealous about avoiding smelling like an ashtray. Make sure that your breath and clothing don't reek of your habit.

Business dinners and lunches are not the best venues for puffing, either.

You never know who you might offend. Insisting on smoking, or sitting in a smoking section, makes you look selfish and addicted. Make *sure* you know if a client smokes or not before you make a dinner or lunch reservation.

Now, if your boss or client lights up in front of you, don't get your undies in a bundle, or start hacking and gagging. It is as rude as blowing smoke in someone's face. If you are truly sensitive or allergic to smoke, delicately tell the person so, and be *very* nice about it.

Thoughtful managers who smoke are sensitive about indulging their habit in the company of people who do not. They usually ask permission. You are well within your rights to politely let them know you don't like to work in a cloud of noxious, smelly smoke if it bothers you. But never lecture. No matter how vile you find smoking, haranguing someone is just not on. To put it bluntly, you'll look like a militant tightass.

ORDER SAFE FOOD

No matter what kind of business lunch or dinner you attend, from the most casual lunch with your boss to the most formal evening affair, be careful about the food you order. You don't eat a Sloppy Joe when you are trying to sell someone advertising, for example. Food that's likely to make a big mess when you eat it, or that reeks of strong seasoning, is just one big nightmare.

Think about how mortifying it would be to have barbecue sauce all over your face when you are talking to some bigwig. Or to have chunks of your lunch caught in your teeth when you speak. Or to inflict onion breath on everyone at your table. Eating is always secondary at these affairs. No matter how hungry you are, save your big pig-out for later.

WHEN YOUR BOSS TAKES YOU OUT

Your boss may buy you lunch to welcome you to the company, to reward you or to give you a send-off when you leave. She might also take you to lunch to go over your performance or to give you bad news. You truly have to have your head in the sand to not know why someone is buying you a meal. Attempt to figure out the reason in advance—you don't want to be caught off guard.

If your boss asks you to pick the restaurant, use your head. Pick some place nicer than a fast-food joint, but not the most expensive place in town. If your boss hates sushi, don't pick a Japanese restaurant. Wherever you go, bring your best manners with you. Don't start eating until your boss does, and don't pick the most expensive item on the menu.

Almost always, your boss is taking you out on the company—you needn't worry about paying. But you should offer to pay just the same. Only a dolt takes you up on the offer. Offering to pay when someone treats you to a meal is a hallmark of American manners. Go through this silly pantomime, or risk being viewed as inconsiderate.

WHEN YOU TAKE SOMEONE OUT

In many professions, you will be expected to court clients with dinner or lunch. Obviously you are expected to pay, and not to take the person for take-out. Always pick a restaurant where you can make reservations, and if the purpose of the meal is to work out a business deal, pick a venue that will be conducive to conducting business. If you know the restaurant, pick a table that will be suitably quiet, or ask the maître d' to set one aside for you.

It is critical that you find out in advance what the client likes and dislikes in food. You could be saving yourself loads of embarrassment. Here's an example. A young professor was asked to entertain a visiting academic from Malaysia. Instead of taking the man out, he decided to have him and his wife come over for an authentic American meal. The professor prepared a delicious Virginia ham using his great aunt's recipe. Just perfect, right?

Unfortunately, the poor guy failed to realize that most Malays are Muslims, and their religion forbids them to eat pork. His guests politely declined the ham, and all he could do was order a pizza at the last minute and apologize profusely. Doing a little groundwork in advance can save you—and your guests—considerable discomfort.

The customer is your guest, and you should treat him to your best manners. He orders first, and he eats first. Never tell a client he cannot have something on the menu. He can go right ahead and pick the most expensive item— don't you dare say a word about it. When the check comes, lunge for it. Okay, that's an overstatement—politely signal the waiter to bring you the bill. Don't make a big fuss over adding up the bill or calculating the tip. Even if the bill was a doozie, don't break out into a sweat or get hysterical. Calmly pay the tab as if it were nothing special.

A polite guest is going to go through that pantomime we just mentioned above and offer to pay. **No matter how hard he insists, you pay the bill.** If you give in and say, "Okay, let's split it," you have committed a mega faux pas. Clients expect you to pick up the tab. Remember to save your receipt for your expense report or income tax (you can write off the evening's entertainment as a business expense).

Keeping in Touch

Welcome to the telecommunications revolution. There is now nowhere you can hide. These handy-dandy tools keep you in touch with your colleagues and can be life savers. But, use them wisely.

E-MAIL

Having e-mail at work can make your job much easier. You can communicate with people all over the company in an instant and send documents across the world. You can also gossip. Don't take risks on your e-mail. Catty comments can end up in the wrong hands with a slip of your finger. And in some companies, your e-mail may even be monitored. Print out all your important e-mails and keep them on file.

BEEPERS

Are annoying. They don't say doctor anymore; they say "drug dealer." Still, they can be useful. If you use a beeper, make sure you have one that has a silent vibrating alarm as well as a sound alarm. That way you can turn the sound off at work and in meetings.

PROPER ATTIRE

For most business engagements outside the office, you must still wear business attire. That should be clear. Office parties are a whole new tub of muck. If they are straight after work, come as you are. If it's later in the evening or on a weekend, find out what dress is appropriate. Remember who your audience is—these people are going to take note of skimpy outfits or blue tuxedos. You still have to face them on Monday morning.

CELLULAR PHONES

Worse than beepers. If by some misfortune you are given a cellular phone to use for work, don't flip it out on the sidewalk or at lunch to impress people. We are not impressed. Use it when you need to, and be discreet about it. Don't wield it like a phallic symbol.

VOICE MAIL

Voice mail is a good thing. Really it is. You may have to spend three weeks learning how to use yours, but once you've mastered it, you are set. Of course you can't leave some cutesy-pie puke-ball message on your voice mail—this is work. Give your full name, speak clearly and don't feel silly about recording it a million times until it's just the way you like it. It's your greeting, right?

Admittedly, some people get a little crazy about their recorded voices—they dread hearing them so much they use the preprogrammed greeting that comes with the voice mail program. Just make sure it's clear that a person is calling *your* phone number.

Voice mail is not an excuse to ignore people's telephone calls. Always try to return calls immediately. It's annoying to play phone tag, and think of how frustrating it is when you continually hit someone else's voice mail when you really need to speak with them. Be considerate.

One other thing. Always identify yourself when you pick up your work phone. Give the caller your first and last name as a greeting. Don't simply say "hello" or grunt. It's confusing and rude.

Flashy clothes can be alienating to people—you want to look nice, but *too* nice can also be a problem. Dress as nicely as your boss does, but don't try to outdo your superiors with your Donna Karan suits or Hermès ties. People might start to wonder if they are paying you too much money.

CASUAL FRIDAY

Conformity has its good side. After all, you don't have to worry as much about what you are going to wear. There's something ever so comforting about gray flannel. Unfortunately, some sick mind dreamed up Casual Friday.

IN RECENT YEARS, MANY LARGE, BUTTONED-DOWN AND VERY UPTIGHT COMPANIES HAVE RELAXED THEIR DRESS CODES ON THE LAST DAY OF THE WORK WEEK. APPARENTLY, IT'S SUPPOSED TO BOOST MORALE. NOW INSTEAD OF WEARING YOUR BORING OLD SUIT TO WORK, YOU HAVE TO SCRAMBLE TO PIECE TOGETHER A BORING OLD CASUAL ENSEMBLE ONCE A WEEK.

Actually, there's very little that's casual about Casual Friday. You usually can't come to work in your cutoffs or a torn Stone Temple Pilots T-shirt. You have to wear "dressy casual" clothes. You know, khaki trousers, cute little flowered dresses, maybe even Doc Martens or penny loafers without socks. Whoo-wee, what a party. There's nothing better than coming to work in your eighth-grade graduation outfit.

Don't push the envelope on Casual Friday. Look crisp, clean and chaste. When you work for an organization that has to institute a "casual day" to pry people away from their ties once a week, you're working for a fairly conservative operation.

137

POWER DRESSING

Can anyone discuss this without even a hint of irony? If they can, run away, run away. The very term **power dressing** has an extremely dated, nauseating, early Reagan administration ring to it.

WE AREN'T GOING TO INSULT YOUR INTELLIGENCE AND TELL YOU WHAT TIE OR SOCK PATTERNS LOOK MORE LIKE THEY BELONG IN THE EXECUTIVE SUITE, OR URGE YOU TO HAVE YOUR COLORS DONE. We trust you can figure these things out on your own. Simply pay attention, and you'll see what senior people in your organization wear.

There is a whole cottage industry out there devoted to helping you out if you can't. Pick up any fashion magazine. They frequently publish columns devoted to polishing up your work image. Or consult a book specifically aimed at making you over into Joe or Jane Executive. GENERALLY SPEAKING, DRESS FOR THE JOB YOU WANT TO HAVE, BE CLEAN, AND COVER YOUR NAVEL.

ALWAYS REMEMBER THERE ARE FEW UNPARDONABLE SINS

Despite all the rules you have just read through in this section, keep this in mind. If you misjudge the politics of your office, spill Coke all over your boss at lunch, come to work in corduroy knickers and argyle socks or embarrass yourself in front of the president of the company, **people will nearly always forgive you.** When you are new, you make a lot of gaffes.

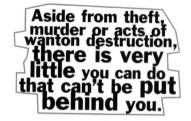

Aside from theft, murder or acts of wanton destruction, there is very little you can do that can't be put behind you.

When you screw up, say you are sorry and move on. Don't try and memorize all the guidelines in this book. The workplace is far too diverse a place for a comprehensive instruction manual. The whole idea behind these rules is to make the whole process of finding your feet less scary. You may even come to disagree with many of them. In the end, you still have to learn by trial and error.

6. MOVING ON UP —

No matter how much ink is spilled or how many motivational speakers' fortunes are made over telling people the secret to a successful career, in the end it all comes down to you. There is no guaranteed path to a four-door German sedan and a heated swimming pool, no 12-step program to catapult you into money, power and influence.

you off the dole. Maybe you'd like the freedom to travel, or an office with a window or to be challenged by greater responsibility. Most likely you want some combination of those things.

To get them, you'll obviously have to work hard. But as we have pointed out before, you'll have to do more than just what's required. Your people skills, enthusiasm and ability to set long-range goals are all critical. This chapter will give you more tips for climbing whatever mountains you think it's important to conquer.

Maybe you don't want these things. Maybe the whole idea of achieving the stereotypical American Dream makes you want to toss your cookies. Fair enough.

Don't be hemmed in by some conventional biddy's idea of what **success** means. Subscribe to your own vision of it.

But no matter what career you choose, be it poet, welder or corporate lawyer, you want to be recognized and rewarded for all your hard work. You'd like to eventually make a decent amount of money. Not necessarily stacks of cash, but enough to keep

SUCCESS IS WHAT YOU MAKE IT

"i'm always competing with other people. i'm always wondering if someone is doing better than i am."
—Giles, financial analyst

"The residents here are my family. They are the perks. i really enjoy what i do."
—Jamie, nursing home cook

Quick quiz. Who above seems more successful?

One last time with feeling. Before we go any further. Success is what you make it. This is your life, and you have to decide for yourself what it is you want out of it. Your job is hopefully but one part of a full and interesting existence on this funky green-blue orb we call home.

Frankly, it's very hard in America not to define your success in purely financial terms. Intellectually we know that's a crock. But there is that anxious feeling in the pit of our stomachs that tells us we all have to be captains of industry or be forever branded a **LOSER** (very American term, that), and this can really mess with your mind.

It takes time to "make it" to a big white house in Connecticut, complete with a kid in French baby clothes named Emma and a pair of golden retrievers. You can't have all this junk at once, and if you get it without much of a struggle, you are going to be one shallow and insufferable person.

If success to you means kayaking through Micronesia, making the cover of *Thrasher*, publishing your own underground 'zine, being surrounded by good friends and family or being the best waitress you can be, work toward accomplishing those goals and you are truly successful.

"How very *Free to Be You and Me*," you might say. Maybe so. And it's true. Career anxiety is part of life. No matter how well you do, or how directed you are, you will feel it. No matter how strongly you reject conventional ideas about getting ahead,

if you are the slightest bit introspective you will have the occasional heart flutter over whether you are doing the right thing, or whether you are ruining your life forever. We can tell you that aside from committing a capital offense, there are very few things you can do to ruin your life, and no career decision you make is necessarily for ETERNITY. You'll still worry. Welcome to the human race.

Your idea of what success means changes with your experiences. What

you want out of life at 18 is not the same as what you want at 25 or 40, and so on. Be flexible. Roll with the punches. Don't kill yourself if you aren't on the cover of *Time* or a billionaire by the time your thirtieth birthday rolls around.

Concentrate on making the most of the here and now.

THROW YOURSELF INTO THE ARENA

You may sit back and think of all the things you want from your new job, but be afraid to really commit to getting them. In grade school, some people were excellent at team sports. Some of us weren't nearly so gifted.

Coping with Stress

There is no such thing as totally stress-free living, unless you are in a coma. The key is to keep stress from transforming you into a quivering, chain-smoking, ticking time bomb. Here are just a few weapons you can enlist in the fight to stay glued together:

Get Regular Exercise
Making time during your week to work out or simply walk around the block is a good way to blow off steam and make you feel less squirrely. Break a sweat and get the stink blown off you. Spandex is totally optional.

Sleep
Is the greatest thing ever. You need it, and you probably don't get enough of it. Try and get your eight hours. An irregular pattern of all-nighters with the occasional 12-hour Saturday snooze tossed in is going to screw with both your body and your head.

Eat a Healthy Diet
A diet of candy bars and diet soda is the expressway direct to stress hell, kid, and you may not be coming back. Rediscover the four food groups. Some experts recommend you supplement your diet with vitamins B and C when you are feeling especially wigged out. Of course, before you start popping pills of any kind, check with your doctor.

Don't Bottle up Your Feelings
Remember that old song, *"Don't Cry Out Loud?"* Worst advice ever. If you are in a stressful situation, talk to someone you trust about it. Attempt to ignore the anxiety you're feeling and it doesn't go away. It just sits there and eats away at you.

Live Your Life
No matter how busy you get, don't retreat form the world outside. Rediscover your friends, family and hobbies. Go to a movie, go camping, knit a muumuu. Even a little time away from the hurly-burly can help you blow off critical steam.

Take a Personal Day
Use your vacation days. That's what they are for. This country is stingy as all get-out when it comes to paid holidays—take advantage of the few you do get.

Laugh
Have a sense of humor about yourself and what you do. Keep things in perspective. You are working at a stupid job, for God's sake, not fighting the Spanish Civil War.

Know Your Limits
You do not hail from Krypton. You can't take every task on and execute each one perfectly. It's good to push yourself, but set reasonable goals. Learn to say no when you are stretched too thin, and pay attention to what your body tells you. Otherwise you'll push yourself right over the edge.

Get Organized
You know the drill—you've been ignoring advice like this for years. But there's no doubt about it, the better organized you are, the less out-of-control you feel. When you feel powerless you get stressed out. If you feel you never have enough time, start budgeting it better. Use an organizer or daybook. Keep yourself on your schedule. Write things down. Clean up your desk. Lay your clothes out the night before so you don't have to scramble in the morning. Take a Saturday to knock out a few unfinished chores that have been hanging over your head for months.

Friends of Mr. Stress

These things may sound like just the ticket when you are feeling tense, but in the end they may only increase your anxiety level:

Dancing with Demon Caffeine
Here's an idea. You are feeling all jittery and angst-ridden. Why not swill a few pots full of black java? Mmm. Now you are really cooking with gas, Mr. Neurotico.

Hitting the Pub Like a Mack Truck
Nothing like a slobbering, sloppy, stressed-out drunk. Throw back the beers and you may forget about your problems for a couple hours, or maybe you'll just start sobbing. Or better yet, maybe you'll pick a fight.

Becoming a Human Chimney
Not since Bette Davis wheezed her last has anybody been able to look anything less than completely vile chain-smoking. You will feel even worse than you look. Nothing like a good 15 minutes of your morning spent hacking up brown goop. Yummy.

Bingeing on Junk Food
Stress kindling.
Or anxiety plus zits.

Blowing Like Vesuvius
Rage is not cathartic. Rage makes your knees feel all wobbly and your ears buzz and leaves a horrible dryness in the back of your throat. Screaming and yelling at mostly innocent people will not make you less tense. You'll only wind up wound more tightly.

The natural athletes couldn't wait to slam a tether ball around or be the first to take a swing at a baseball. Maybe you were one of them, or maybe you hung back because you were afraid you sucked and that you'd mess up and look silly. Instead of risking humiliation, you opted out. Maybe your *bête noire* wasn't sports, but math, ballroom dancing, or finger painting. Whatever it was, you decided not to join in for fear of being made a laughingstock.

Time to step up to the plate. It may be the most wretched cliché in the book, but it rings true. If you are too timid, you aren't going to get noticed. Stick your neck out a bit. Some of us are too afraid of failing to even verbalize what it is we want out of our careers.

You'll feel worse if you wait for someone to come to you and hand you the things you desire. The world is in the midst of a profound fairy-godmother shortage. When you start a new job, you should have a whole new list of aspirations to go along with it and set out to get them without the aid of someone else's magic wand.

ASK YOURSELF MORE QUESTIONS

Begin by mapping out a new set of priorities now that you are employed. It's easy to put the big picture out of your mind for a while now that you are collecting a paycheck, but don't get too comfortable.

Think about how long you want to be doing your current job. Are you being realistic? When do people usually get promoted? When can you expect a salary review? Be sensible. You cannot expect to make vice president in a year. But don't start cutting yourself down either— "I'll never be a marketing associate in three years. . . "

Call a halt to the pity parade. Stop telling yourself what you can't do.

Take the time to map out even the haziest career strategy, such as "In six months I would like to be doing_____." Give yourself little mileposts to whiz by. They could include an assignment you'd like to take on or a performance quota you'd like to pass. You decide. If you have some idea of where you'd like to be headed, you'll feel less conflicted about what you're doing in the here and now.

There's something more scary about thinking beyond what kind of granola you want for breakfast. What if you don't meet your goals? Life is unpredictable. But you'll never reach any goal, no matter how small, until you commit to setting a few.

ACQUIRING NEW SKILLS

Make the extra effort to learn new skills that will broaden your portfolio and make you more marketable. For example, many companies offer specialized management training programs, or workshops aimed at bringing you up to snuff on new technology. Take advantage of them, even if it means staying late or giving up the odd Saturday. What you learn may prove invaluable. You'll also be demonstrating your commitment to "THE ORGANIZATION," as managers like to say, which can never hurt your chances of being tapped for new responsibility.

Take classes at a local college or university. Spend your Wednesday evenings learning Spanish, a new computer program or accounting. If the course is relevant to your job, your employer may pay for it. Some companies are very generous in this department. And languages and computer skills can be extremely helpful down the line.

Yeah, yeah. You're tired. Work takes a lot out of you. You hate the stinking "organization." Nevertheless, take the time to make a wise investment in *yourself.* The best part about taking classes is that you may actually enjoy them, meet new people and keep

yourself involved in the world outside your cubicle. Consider taking a class for purely selfish reasons. Because you've always wanted to learn mime, for example, or are interested in Hawaiian culture, Greek folk music or Australian wildlife. Whatever. If you can afford it, it may just keep you from becoming a boring, stiff old coot.

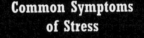

Common Symptoms of Stress

143

When stress is getting out of hand, lots of little alarms start to go off. Pay attention to your body and nip it in the bud. Here are a few possible warning signs:

• headaches

• neck or back tension

• moodiness

• chest pains or palpitations

• dizziness

• shortness or breath

• trouble sleeping or constant fatigue

• stomach pains

• trembling

• dry mouth

• sweatiness

• hyperactive behavior

• depression

• panic attacks

"if there's one thing i could tell people it's to get their education. Because there isn't much out there with just high school."

—Doug, warehouse laborer

Believe it or not, education is still highly valued in this country. If you haven't finished high school, don't be seduced by easy money now—increase your chances of a better future by studying for and passing a high school equivalency test (the GED).

If you never went to college or didn't finish your degree, you can work toward an associate's or bachelor's degree while you are working. Find out if your employer will help you with tuition. Many do. You'll be opening many more doors with your diploma, and you'll feel more confident about your ability to succeed. (Okay, you'll have to give up a lot of free nights.)

GRADUATE SCHOOL

Is graduate school for you? Ultimately, only you can answer the question. Of course the best reasons to go back to school are to improve your skills and deepen your knowledge. The worst—a belief that you will have an easy ticket to prestige and the good life.

Know why you are going to graduate school. If you are going because you want a bigger income, make sure that the program you choose will help you accomplish that. Graduate work is a major commitment of your time and funds, so the program you choose matters, and your ability to find a job after you gain the credential matters. A lot.

Investigate your options thoroughly. You want to be able to find work that will help you pay the bills for a very expensive education when you are done. You probably don't expect to make the same salary with a master's degree as someone with just a bachelor's, but in a great many instances, you will.

Look at the profession you have chosen. Is an advanced degree necessary for advancement, or just window dressing? If you want to be a social worker, a master's degree in social work is pretty critical. If you want a master's in business administration, go for it. But not all MBAs are created equal, and there are plenty of successful business people who do not have them. Much depends on the industry, and the company you work for. It's good to know what the deal is before you throw money down.

You *may* be able to get your graduate work paid for, at least in part, by your employer, while you are still working. That may make the whole process more affordable. Or you may want to quit your job and devote yourself to being a full-time student again. It's easier, and usually quicker, than juggling classes and work. **In either case, grad school is nothing like college.** For one thing, it's never as laid-back or fun. For another, at the prices you'll probably have to pay, you'd be a fool to blow things off.

You've probably heard this from time to time in the media: there are too many doctors, lawyers, MBAs, etc., etc. That doesn't mean you shouldn't

144

want to be any of these things. Good people will always be in demand. And by all means, get a master's of fine arts in poetry if that's what rocks your world. You'll spend a couple of years devoted to your craft. You may not make more money, but you may make useful contacts and be a better poet for the effort.

Don't let anybody tell you your graduate work is useless or a waste of money. It's only a waste if you let it be. But there's no question that you need to thoroughly examine what your expectations of graduate work are before you shuffle back into the classroom.

PERFORMANCE REVIEWS, RAISES, AND PROMOTIONS

Unless you really have problems, you are passed from one grade at school to another with relative ease; promotion is more or less automatic. Not so at work. No matter what anybody says, there are no guarantees when it comes to getting a raise or a promotion. You have to earn these things, every time.

GETTING YOUR REPORT CARD: PERFORMANCE REVIEWS

Just because you don't sit in a classroom all day doesn't mean you don't get a report card. It's generally called a "performance review." In one way or another, your employer expects you to produce results. Larger organizations schedule regular reviews of their employees. You sit down with your boss, go over your various pluses and minuses and get a copy of your report card for your records. Performance reviews often go hand in hand with getting a raise (more on that later).

Smaller organizations are often much less formal. As we mentioned in the previous chapter, you may have to hound your boss a bit to find out what he thinks of your work. Do it. You never want to be in the dark about how you are doing.

Sometimes it all boils down to cold hard numbers. Didn't sell enough bibles over the phone last quarter? You are going to get seriously dinged for not meeting your quota. In other cases, you are graded in a more general way. Are you part of the team? Do you take a creative approach to problem solving? Are you an all-around good egg? As usual, a lot depends on what your particular organization values. But rest assured that a cheerful, cooperative, punctual person is going to get higher marks practically anywhere outside of the furnace room in Hades.

Reviews are for your benefit. When you meet with a supervisor to go over your performance, don't be defensive. Very few individuals get extremely negative reviews. Like failing students, people in trouble know what's coming long before the ax falls. Again, the more feedback you get, the better off you are.

It is your responsibility to keep track of when you will be reviewed. If you are meant to get a six-month review, don't let

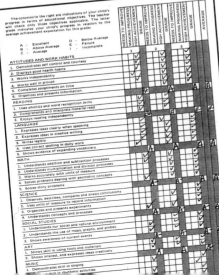

nine months slide by without being evaluated just because your boss is snowed under with work. Take it upon yourself to make sure you aren't cheated out of feedback. You should have some kind of professional checkup at least once a year.

Don't be passive about your review. When your boss calls you into his office, bring a pad of paper to write down any suggestions he might have. If you have an important accomplishment you want to make sure he notices, or a beef to discuss, now is the absolute perfect time.

Just like school, people suddenly clean up their acts around report-card time. That's why it's so important to know when you can expect a formal evaluation. You can pull the nose up on a plane in a tailspin and work toward changing someone's opinion of you before it's too late. Naturally, if you wait too long, your boss is going to see right through this.

SLACKING OFF

We have all heard of sophomore slump. None of us can keep up a fever pitch of work every day of the year. Sooner or later, you will get comfortable in your job, start to oversleep once in a while, write personal letters on your computer, sneak in after long lunches. How much you can get away with depends entirely on your situation. If you are given a great deal of freedom, try valiantly not to abuse it.

It's so easy to get lazy. Resist the urge to sit back on your laurels, put things off and dither away the day. Before you know it, you can get into a whole mess of trouble, complete with unhealthy portions of stress and panic. Slackers (and we are all slackers at least part of the time) are among the most stressed-out people around.

When you feel yourself getting all soft and squishy, you've probably **lost sight of what you want** out of your job. Feeling fuzzy and out of it all day may signal a time to make up a whole **new list of goals** for yourself. Or it may be a red flag signaling it's time to **start looking for a new job.** Dump a bucket of ice water over your head, zap yourself with a cattle prod or **slap yourself in the face a couple of times.** In short, do whatever it takes to get yourself focused again. **Nobody** has the luxury of lounging around in a custom-built fog for too long.

GETTING A RAISE

Everybody wants a raise, and most people more than deserve them. Just how you get your hands on more money depends on where you are working. At some point in your interview process, the company policy on pay increases was probably discussed. If it wasn't, ask your boss to explain it to you. This is not an issue you want to be hazy about. You may be in line for more money when you meet a performance goal, pass through a probationary period at the beginning of your job or get a favorable performance review.

Whatever the case, remember that no raise is truly guaranteed. You will need to work for, and frequently ask for, pay increases of any size. Naturally you can't expect a big raise straight off the bat. Very few people pull down huge bonuses or get their paycheck sizably beefed up when they are just beginning their careers. Banish those fantasies from your mind. They'll only make you miserable when you realize just how stingy many employers truly are.

BONUSES

A bonus is a pretty cut-and-dried little organism. It is usually a lump sum, tied to a specific accomplishment. Just how you get a bonus, if you can get one at all, depends on where you work. Your boss may give you a bonus after you complete a big assignment. People in sales frequently get bonuses when they surpass a given target.

With quota-based bonuses, make sure you grasp exactly how many pairs of galoshes you have to sell in order to win your prize. A few less-than-scrupulous employers have been known to dangle juicy bonuses or commissions in front of employees that are virtually impossible to achieve.

Then there are annual bonuses, usually given around Christmas time, generously given by the boss man as presents to all the little people. **Never** count on a holiday bonus to pay off your credit-card debt from all

the shopping you did in December. They are usually pretty modest. In fact, it's a good idea to factor in a bonus as just that something extra, something not guaranteed, gravy, icing.

RAISES

Unlike a bonus, a raise is a salary increase spread throughout an entire year. While you may be getting another thousand dollars or so added to your annual salary, you won't usually feel much of a change in your everyday life because you are only earning a few bucks more on your weekly paycheck. And that's before the IRS takes its cut.

One of the most common kinds of raise is a **cost of living increase**. That's just what it sounds—your employer is tossing a handful of pennies at you in order to nudge your salary ahead of inflation. You really aren't making more money, it's just that things cost more than they did when you were first hired. If your salary stayed the same, you'd actually be poorer. Forget about putting a downpayment on a condo with this largesse.

A favorable evaluation is frequently an occasion for a raise, but once again, don't expect a large infusion of greenbacks. A supervisor is frequently given strict parameters she must follow when awarding raises—her ceiling for top-notch work may be very low. She can argue with her superiors to give you more than that, but don't expect her to tap a mother lode.

Sometimes, raises come your way when you tell your boss you have another job offer or are considering leaving your position. If she values you, she may do whatever she can to keep you with her—including throw money at you.

Take Margaret, a dental assistant in Philadelphia. After a year at her job, she decided she wanted away from rinse and spit, rinse and spit all day long. A friend told her about a job teaching children to swim at a local recreation center. The pay was about $18,000 a year, two thousand dollars less than she was currently earning.

Margaret didn't mind taking a pay cut. She was fed up with infected mouths and interested in getting into coaching young people. Her boss begged her to stay, but she would not be swayed. As her last day approached, the desperate dentist offered her nearly *twice* her salary. "In the end he came to me and said I could name my price," she remembers. "But I just wasn't happy there."

Had Margaret decided to stay, she could have struck a very hard bargain indeed. She had become indispensable at her job, and her boss dreaded having to find a replacement. There was no predicting her particular situation—her boss may have let her go with his blessing and not have tried so hard to sweeten his pot. **Rarely** are entry-level people so zealously courted. However, if you have a serious offer on the table or are considering leaving your job for financial reasons, inform your supervisor. He may very well try and get you a raise.

Don't engage in any serious negotiations if you aren't seriously interested in staying on, though. And don't try and bluff your way into big bucks. You are not in any position to make outrageous salary demands, and in any case, no one wants an extortionist working under them. The whole thing can explode in your face quite easily.

MONEY TALK

Some people are better at money talk than others, but most of us have been brought up to feel at least vaguely nauseated by the very idea.

Asking for more money from a supervisor is an uncomfortable situation. You don't want to be an ungrateful

wretch or anything, or put him in an awkward position, so frequently you circle around what it is you really want to say and hope he'll end your misery by guessing.

This is misguided, and you know it.

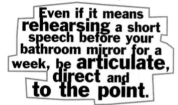
Even if it means **rehearsing** a short speech before your bathroom mirror for a week, be **articulate, direct** and **to the point.**

Your supervisor can only say no to your request. And if it is a sensible request, there's no harm in asking it. You are not asking for an advance on your allowance, don't get cutesy. This is a serious discussion, perhaps best broached during your performance review.

When you ask for more money, come armed with solid reasons for why it should be given to you. Having it on good authority that every other person with your job description makes more than you is an abysmal reason for a raise. It's extremely unprofessional to tell your boss you want extra dough because Sally in the next cubicle makes $2,000 more than you. Whine like an infant and you're liable to get a patronizing response from your boss, like, "Life isn't fair, kid."

Your reasons for why you deserve more money should always be linked tightly to your job performance. Be equipped with good, cogently thought-out arguments—the added responsibilities you took on when a co-worker left, for example, or the three new projects you are developing for the firm. Get specific. Blow that horn. Bring in visual aids if you have to. Demonstrate your worth to the company.

Careful of verging on arrogance here. Don't exaggerate your importance or make wild claims you can't back up. On the flip side, begging is not an option. Don't bring in a photo of your dog, your fiancée or the car you can't make payments on because you don't make enough money. Stress what you have done and can do for the organization, not how it can help you. You aren't a charity, but a valuable employee. Maybe your boss has forgotten that. Remember, it's part of your job to remind him from time to time.

SALARIES ARE SECRET

You know this one, right? It's probably the oldest workplace rule of them all, not that anybody pays attention to it. Still, it's a good rule—try your best to adhere to it. Avoid talking about your salary with co-workers. Even if you are certain you are all making the same money. You can never be sure, and if it turns out that your friend is making a little less than you for the same job, it can really hurt your relationship.

Inevitably you will figure out what the people around you take home. Don't start tossing figures around. Wonderful people can get very jealous and competitive about money. Your exact salary is between you and your boss. It's doubtful that two people doing the same job are going to have wildly different incomes, but even so, it's not information that you want to spread around.

PROMOTIONS

There's no magic ticket to promotion-land, of course. The better you know your organization and the bigger your accomplishments, the better your shot. Much depends on the industry you are working in, and the company you work for. Some fields are notorious for their glacial rates of promotion. Others jettison spunky newcomers forward at warp speed.

For the most part, young and fast-growing companies offer more opportunities to take risks and move up rapidly than large corporations. On the downside, they may not be able to offer you the kind of security a more established firm can offer (though in this day and age, there really aren't any "secure" jobs). If your industry has a lot of turnover, you might have more shots at job openings. Then again, working in such a volatile environment can be highly stressful.

Increasingly, younger people must leave their organization when they want a better job. There simply aren't enough entry-level positions in many companies for all the people who want them, and not enough people leaving at the top of the ladder to make room for those below. This is frequently true in media and the arts, where people often must leapfrog from employer to employer every couple of years in order to gain experience and move up.

If you knew what you were getting into from the start, you can't really be surprised by the fact that you aren't conquering the world after a few months. Even meteoric rises to the top take more time than that.

DON'T BEGRUDGE OTHER PEOPLE THEIR SUCCESS

If a peer gets a coveted promotion, warmly congratulate her. Don't curse her name. Remember way back to this book's first chapter. **This is not a race.**

You **will** get there.

Wasting precious time worrying about someone else's success is counterproductive.

Sometimes you just can't help yourself. But when you start muttering about how unfair it is that someone beat you to a raise or a great new position, remember that person is still your friend. They have not betrayed you by doing well, and that there are infinite pieces of the success pie out there for all of us.

BACKBITING

On the same note, be humble when you get rewarded, and generous to those who may have wanted to have basked in that same feeling of triumph. It only takes a few seconds to realize who those people might be. **When you move up, never forget the people who remain behind. Your friends are your friends, no matter what their income or job description.**

Envy often prompts others to bite you on the butt when they feel you are getting too big for your britches. Realize where negative comments are coming from when you get a coveted laurel. As your mother always said after a gang of kids spent all recess rubbing your face in the tan bark, "They are just jealous." If you are a nice person, that kind of nastiness is going to make you feel bad. But you can't fail just to make someone else feel better. Write off envious people. They need to work on their own careers, instead of fretting over yours.

LOOK BEYOND TITLES

There are those of us who are not at all interested in moving up the ladder—we don't want the added headache or the responsibility of telling others what to do. But let's assume you'd prefer not to be fetching other people's coffee for the rest of your days. Hopefully, getting kicked upstairs signals added responsibility, prestige and money. That's the best-case scenario. Unfortunately, a change in title may be only that.

A flashy new title can sound very sexy, and signify absolutely nothing. Call a nag destined for the glue factory a race horse and it's still a nag. People fret a lot about their titles. Nobody likes being called "peon," after all. Hence the proliferation of job titles that feature words like **associate**, **specialist**, **manager**, and **executive** in them. To look at some corporate rosters, you might think only senior people worked there.

If you get a highfalutin new title like **junior executive administrative specialist** and you are still answering the same telephones and making the same money you made when you were merely a *receptionist*; you have not really been promoted. Employers sometimes bestow fancy-schmancy titles on people when they cannot give them more money or responsibility. Don't get hung up on what you are called. It's what you do that matters.

FINDING OUT ABOUT JOBS IN-HOUSE

Many companies post job openings on bulletin boards in-house that you never hear about when you are on the outside. Keep track of what's on offer. You also have the office grapevine at your disposal—you'll know when vacancies are going to pop up. The longer you work in a place, the more extensive your network there is going to be. Your friends will be able to help you out. If you have your sights set on a particular position, talk to your supervisor about it. He may be in a position to put you in the running.

One major caveat here. **People expect you to pay your dues and put in your time on the shop floor. That means no matter how much you hate it,**

you can't do a half-assed job in the position you have and be expected to be tapped for a promotion.

When you start your job, don't look like you are itching to get a new one from day one. No one is holding a stopwatch, timing your rapid ascent up the ranks. Master each position you are given before attempting to move on. Just how long it takes to do that depends on you, and the job.

When you do a bang-up job, people notice. But promotions are not simply based on merit. There usually has to be an opening for you to move into. Sometimes it is possible to **create** your own position, by taking on more responsibilities, spotting what the organization needs and doing a fair amount of politicking.

Hopefully, when your title changes, so does your salary, and you aren't stuck doing *both* your old job and the one you just invented. In some organizations, you may have the opportunity to transfer to another division to learn a whole new set of skills instead of waiting a blue moon for a more senior position to become available in your old department. The bad news—you are moving sideways, not upward.

HASTA LA VISTA, BABY

If your gut tells you there is nowhere to go in your company, it's probably right. As we said from the outset, the days of permanent employment with one benevolent employer are as finished as pterodactyls. It may be scary to start looking elsewhere, but it's far better than stagnating right where you are.

KNOWING WHEN IT'S TIME TO GO

You will know better than anyone when you have hit a wall at your job: if **every day is a bad day,** if you constantly have to force yourself to get out of bed and **dread** looking at the faces of your colleagues every morning, if everyone else seems to be streaking ahead and you feel like your legs are encased in cinder blocks, when you feel like **you are on autopilot** all day long, when you cannot even fake caring about what you do. **Pay attention** to the **red flags** that you are frantically waving at yourself.

You may leave a job you love because you see no future in your organization, or you may just discover that what seemed so right a year ago is not at all what you want to be doing with your life. There's no shame in changing gears and chalking it all up to experience. Very few people strike pay dirt their first few times out prospecting.

Throughout college, Peter thought he wanted to be in publishing. When he graduated, he found a job at a very prestigious New York publisher, in the publicity department. At first, he thought he'd found his dream job, but after only a few months, he became disillusioned. He found his position dull and undemanding, and looking around the office, he could see that his future held more of the same, at very low pay. In the end, he decided to leave for a faster-paced job at a small financial services company.

Peter's new position was considerably more nerve-racking than his last, but he found it meshed better with what he wanted out of life. He found his day-to-day work demanded more creativity than his first job in a so-called creative industry, and that he was frequently given a chance to take on new challenges. The fit was better, and he was happier. He would not have known that if he hadn't tried the first job on for size.

Everyone sinks into the doldrums at work now and again. Give yourself time at a new job before you take off. If you've only been there a couple of months, you probably haven't given it a chance. But when you can't snap out of it—or worse, you don't even particularly want to snap out of it—it's time to start hunting for a new job. Don't wait around until someone gives you the shove.

LOOK WHILE YOU ARE STILL WORKING

Bite into this moldy slice of conventional wisdom—it happens to be good advice. You are a more attractive candidate when you are already working. Employers can feel better about taking a risk with you. Heck, you haven't sliced and diced the people you are currently working with, right? You'll also have less time between getting your last old paycheck and your first new one if you lock on to a job in advance and avoid creating a resume riddled with gaps that need explaining.

Sure, having loads of free time after quitting your old job would be great. But once you find a new job you can always plan to take a couple of weeks between jobs to sleep in and goof off.

That said, it's hard looking for a new position when you are still working at your old one. In fact, it's like working two jobs. It can be easy to put your job search on the back burner. Just because you have limited time doesn't mean it can't be anything less than fully committed.

Be organized; try to devote a small portion of each day to a particular aspect of your hunt. Maybe you spend Monday evening revamping your resume. Tuesday is for discreetly making phone calls from your desk. Wednesdays are for answering want ads and so forth. Don't let things slide.

In most cases, you'll have to be a little sneaky when you are looking for a new job from an old one. Until you decide to take an offer, keep it secret. When you have to leave work for interviews, don't be too obvious. Try and use the odd sick day to meet with a couple of potential employers. If you come to work in your best interview outfit and say you have to leave for a doctor's appointment, people are going to catch on. Some of us can get away with more than others at work. If you are left alone in an isolated cubicle, you can write cover letters on your computer, call contacts and beef up your resume. Be very careful, though. Getting caught redesigning your resume by a supervisor is a dreadful experience.

If you work in an office where you can use great stationery (though never write any personal correspondence on company letterhead), a swanky computer, laser printer, photocopier and tons of other goodies for free, don't feel too guilty about staying late one night to take advantage of these things. Okay, Saint Francis of

Assisi would probably *not* do this. Most everybody else would, and does. You have to put in your time—now use a few office supplies, damn it.

One last warning. Many a clever cuss has been dumb enough to leave a copy of her resume in the photocopier, fax or on the laser printer. Whoops. When you print a resume out in the dark of night, always make sure the printer spits out **every** copy. It always seems that whenever you want to be clandestine, the evil printer god makes sure that the machine takes long pauses, or prints two of everything, so that after you walk away another resume plops out for general consumption.

You *must* always give at least two weeks' notice when you leave a job. A month is better. This was handed down to Moses or somebody equally sage and bearded in the misty, murky past. No matter how much you hated your job, do your boss this courtesy. She is going to need some time to replace you.

Set aside time to sit down with your boss and explain why you are leaving. Pick a quiet moment when the two of you can talk. You'll probably feel apprehensive about telling your supervisor. Don't worry about whether she'll be disappointed or upset. You are expected to move on eventually, after all. Sad as someone may be to see you go, she can and will find another sucker to take your place.

Your boss should be the first person in the organization to hear your news. If you were a blurt and spilled the beans to a co-worker first, you must hold that person at knifepoint, swear them to secrecy and then immediately inform your supervisor. It is truly appalling to allow her to find out second- or third-hand.

Ordinarily when you give notice, you should follow up with a formal letter of resignation. Many companies

require you to do this. It doesn't have to be an opus. Just a couple of sentences expressing your gratitude to your supervisor, a few pleasant throwaway lines about how you enjoyed working for the company, and a short explanation of why you are leaving. Don't say you are leaving because your job was a dead end and the money was lousy. Imagine the recommendations you'll get. Just tell them you have been offered a wonderful opportunity by your new employer.

After you give notice, don't fall apart. Your last few weeks at a company should not be viewed as your kick-back, lame-duck period. Nor should you spend your final days bitching about how much you hated the job. Think about how you wish to be remembered. In many cases, you will have an opportunity to train your replacement. Don't be a schmuck—help this person to glide into your position effortlessly and avoid some of the pitfalls you faced when you were green.

YOU'RE FIRED!

Here's hoping your exit is voluntary, but if it isn't, buck up. No matter how awful you feel, **losing a job does not brand you a failure as a human being**. That can be hard to believe when you are **terminated**, as it is now charmingly called, but it's true. Terminated, vaporized, squashed like a June bug on the highway of life. Whatever you call getting sacked, it bites.

People lose their jobs for all kinds of reasons, most of which are beyond their control. You may be part of the so-called fat shed in an employer's effort to compete in a leaner, meaner marketplace, there might be a change of management, you might work for a Nazi. It's horrible, but it happens.

Anybody can get a pink slip. Even if you feel you could have done something to prevent being fired, it's too late now. **Don't beat yourself up** over what you did or didn't do. **Focus on** what you have control over— **your future.**

When you are fired, try very hard not to go berserk. You may want to argue, throw a punch or beg for your job. Rein it in. Ask for the reason why you are being terminated in writing. When you get home, you can throw a chair through a window or cry your eyes out. With your supervisor, be cool.

When you are called into a supervisor's office to be fired, bring a pen and paper. You want an accurate record of everything that was said to you. If you are being laid off, ask how the decision to lay you off in particular was made, and if there is a grievance procedure you can avail yourself of in case you wish to protest the decision.

An employer is pretty free to dismiss you at any time, and for just about any reason. You can sue her, but to win you will have to prove she disregarded your legal rights. Being mean or unfair is not a violation of those rights. But remember, certain kinds of discrimination are illegal—she can't dismiss you because you are Bulgarian, a Hindu, or a white male. If you suspect your rights have been violated, **consult a lawyer**.

When you leave a job, you are entitled to extend your employee health insurance for 18 months under a law known as the Comprehensive Omnibus Budget Reconciliation Act, or COBRA, as it is commonly known. We'll touch on COBRA again later, but for now, know that being terminated does not necessarily mean you will lose your insurance (though you will have to pick up the entire cost of your premiums).

Depending on your employer, you may also receive **severance pay**— an amount of money designed to ease the hardship of being laid off. The amount of severance pay you are entitled to, if any, is usually discussed in your employee benefits material. In some circumstances, you may be offered extra severance pay in exchange for a promise not to sue your employer for firing you— be very careful about what you sign when you are terminated. **And again, if you are unsure of what rights you may be giving up in exchange for money, talk to a lawyer.**

No matter how hard you try not to let the situation get you down, it probably will. This is a devastating, frightening experience for most people. Few of us walk away from a car wreck as if nothing happened. Don't be a tough guy, and try to go it all alone. Find someone to talk to. If you can get counseling, it's not a bad idea.

TAKE THIS JOB AND SHOVE IT

A terrible song whose enduring popularity shows that we are probably on the brink of bloody class war, and a sentiment you should keep to your-

If you lose your job, you may be eligible to collect unemployment benefits. Eligibility requirements and compensation programs vary from state to state.

How long you have worked at a job, and how much you earned while working there, are used to determine whether you get money, and how much. Work at your job for less than four months in some places, and you won't qualify for compensation. In most states, you can receive payments for up to twenty-six weeks. Your payments may also be extended if you are in an area of high unemployment. These rules generally apply across the board:

• You cannot receive unemployment when you voluntarily quit your job

• You cannot receive unemployment if you were paid under the table

• You cannot receive unemployment if you were fired for "misconduct," such as theft or insubordination

• You cannot collect unemployment over extended vacation periods while you are still employed

• You must demonstrate to your state unemployment agency that you are looking for another job to collect unemployment

Listen up: You will never get rich on unemployment. If you get laid off, Uncle Sam is not going to bail you out. The most you can expect to get is a couple of hundred dollars a week for a few months. That's why it's so important to start saving for a really, really bad day— just in case it happens.

Acting it out seldom makes you feel anything but foolish. Exit with dignity, and impress your other colleagues who will remember you with a positive impression.

7. STRIKING OUT ON YOUR OWN— STARTING YOUR OWN BUSINESS

With corporate America being buffeted by destabilizing trends like downsizing, it's no wonder that many people are interested in starting their own businesses. But don't think becoming an entrepreneur will shelter you from the stress and rejection of a job search.

self. You may think that leaving is a great excuse to give everybody who made your life miserable an earful. Curb yourself.

Even if you were fired, or are ordered to clean out your desk immediately, don't ever burn bridges. You are extinguishing still-useful relationships in a single, self-destructive act. A revenge fantasy should stay a fantasy.

Successful self-employed people must place themselves under tremendous pressure to meet the bottom line. A small businessperson may not have any supervisor kicking her around, but she still must meet the demands of the people who help keep her solvent—her clients. To do well, she has to have a lot of them. In many cases, there are also creditors to keep mollified.

Before you decide to strike out on your own, remember this: **Self-employment means a never-ending job hunt.** If you hate looking for a job, don't even think about it. To make it as a small businessperson, independent contractor or freelancer (whatever term for lone wolf you prefer), you are going to have to be up to continually selling yourself, pound on a lot of doors and accept getting quite a few slammed in your face. A few people become so successful on their own that they don't have to scrounge quite so hard for business, but in most cases, flying solo means a career full of

hustle, hustle, hustle.

Then again, there's really nothing so satisfying as setting up your own shop, creating something uniquely your own and getting other people to pay you for it. So if your heart's desire is to build a business for yourself, go for it. Before you dive in, however, keep these things in mind.

LAY A STRONG FOUNDATION

If you are committed to self-employ-ment, don't leap into it unprepared. Many people think they can work from their homes and end up memorizing the entire daytime television schedule. You can't get any kind of work by staring out your bedroom window. Striking out on your own involves taking risks, but the best strategy is to minimize your risk as much as possible through thorough preparation.

If you are in college, check to see if your school offers an **entrepreneur-ship program**—several hundred universities do. These programs will familiarize you with the various elements needed to run a successful business. You'll learn how to set up a business plan, keep out of the red,

brainstorm business ideas and market your services to customers. If you aren't in school, you may be able to take classes on starting your own business at a local university or community college. These courses are very common and popular—shop around and find one that both suits your needs and pocketbook. On the other hand, be careful of putting your money down for lectures given by a motivational speaker or get-rich-quick dude. Some of these people are sincere and on the level, but you may end up shelling out beaucoup bucks to hear something you already know.

Networking and research are critically important to anyone launching their own business. Talking to other self-employed people is key—if you want to start your own auto-body shop, seek out people who are doing the same thing. Ask how they got started, what problems plagued them at the beginning, what still runs them ragged and what they most enjoy. Ask how they surmounted any difficulties they had, and what knowledge and experiences they think are most important to be successful at what they do. In short, ask them everything.

You must conduct an exhaustive round of informational interviews. Don't just talk to people involved in the business you are interested in—anyone who's his own boss is a valuable resource. One great resource is your local Chamber of Commerce, which can usually help you find entrepreneurs in your chosen field. Really pound the pavement. When you launch your startup, you want to know exactly what to expect.

At the same time, hit the library with a vengeance. You can't just hang out a shingle and expect people to come running. If you know exactly what it is you want to do—say interior decorating, screenwriting, jewelry making, sheep farming or opening a boutique—seek out reference guides about the subject. If you are planning to manufacture feather boas, you must know everything there is to know about feather boas. You need to learn which feathers make for the best boas, what laws effect feather-boa manufacturers, how long it takes to make one, where the best boas are created, what stores carry them and who on earth boa buyers are.

Before you set up shop, you need to **know** your product's every nuance and your industry **like** the back of your hand.

All the skills used in starting a job search come into play here—it just happens to be that you are creating your own job, not looking for a company to work for. Dig up industry magazines and associations, and make contacts wherever you can find them, even if you have nothing to start with but the Yellow Pages. Beyond that, look for resources that deal with starting your own business. Libraries and bookstores are crammed full of them.

EXPLORE YOUR OPTIONS

If you don't know exactly what it is you'd like to do, but know you want to be in business for yourself, research can help you narrow down your search and identify areas of opportunity.

Get out your crystal ball and dare to dream a little (and again, seek advice from old hands). You don't have to think up a fabulous new invention to start your own business.

Be a detective—look around your community. Ask yourself what services seem needed, and try and spot important trends. It's a very old saw, but successful entrepreneurs identify a need and fill it. The exercise craze helped the manufacturers of all those

abdomen flattening machines earn untold riches. On a smaller scale, remember all the tasks that people don't have time to do themselves, from child care to dog walking to hanging dry wall to car repair to landscaping to interior decorating.

The magazine, film and music worlds are filled with people who contract out their services—these businesses have tons of freelance professionals working in them.

Don't get suckered by shysters on television who say you can make billions selling used retainers through the mail. If you are interested in starting a mail-order business or operating a franchise (buying into a business, say, opening a branch of a fast-food chain—often a very expensive thing to do), investigate the opportunity very carefully. There are plenty of shady operations out there.

No matter what type of independent work you are drawn to, whether it's manufacturing your own bolo ties, selling your artistic talent or selling plastic wear, there is no excuse for not doing your homework.

BELIEVE IN THE PRODUCT, AND YOURSELF

As important as homework is in starting a business, you must have passion to make it work. No matter what product you are pitching, believing in it is essential. Whether it's a revolutionary new water filter or your ability to transform garden hedges into lawn statuary, you have to get out there and flog your wares shamelessly. You'll have to stay true to yourself when others think your idea doesn't hold water. When rejections pour in or your parents tell you you're nuts for devoting your days to weaving your own handbags, you'll feel pressure to give up and find some nice cushy job with a benefits package. Then there will be those annoying pangs of jealousy when friends who work for other people have more money to spend on clothes or vacations. If you stick with it you'll most likely be richly rewarded, but you have to be prepared to wait a while.

Again, the more you believe in what you do, the easier it will be to convince others to give it a chance. Any advertising, sales or marketing experience you have will be valuable — a large part of making it on your own is convincing others to buy. If you aren't comfortable selling, you'll have an uphill battle. Shyness won't win you business. Some people are naturally gifted hucksters, but practice can transform the most withdrawn individual into a confident salesperson.

CREATE YOUR OWN OFFICE

You might think working from home means avoiding an office altogether. It doesn't. One of the hardest things about starting any kind of home business, be it freelance writing or selling plush toys over the phone, is that you have to carve out a space in your house in which to do it. It's critically important to separate your home life from your work life, even when your commute means walking five feet from your bed to your desk. When the business day starts, you must consider yourself at work, away from the distractions that make home such a fun place to be.

The best-case scenario is when you can use an empty room as a home office or study. Then you can shut the door on television, squabbling roommates and your comfy couch. If that isn't the case, think critically about how you will get business done. Be disciplined. You aren't playing hooky here—you'll need to create your own structure and stick by it. No one is going to make you crawl out of bed in the morning (unless you have a partner). Even if it's mostly

imaginary, your home office is sacrosanct—make sure your friends who punch a clock every day understand that during the day you, too, are at work, and cannot goof off.

Depending on what kind of business you start, you may have to invest in a range of home office equipment. A home fax, separate telephone line, high-quality printer, cellular phone and a computer equipped with a modem are often essential for many home businesses. Business cards—which can be created at many stationery stores for a pittance—can be very useful as well.

If your business demands a special workshop, studio or garage space, you may have to do considerable research and dig to find a cheap place you can rent for the purpose (remember, when you start a business you won't be earning money right away).

You may have to consider relocating if you want your dream business to work. Be flexible—obviously, if you live in Chicago and are looking to become a guava farmer, you are going to have to consider moving to where the opportunity is.

You may also need to invest in some kind of business wear. Just because you aren't working in an office doesn't give you an excuse to look sloppy or unprofessional. In fact, appearance is probably more important for many entrepreneurs—after all, every time you meet a prospective client you are being interviewed for a job. If you look shifty, you may lose their business.

BE AWARE OF THE COSTS

When you start any business, you'll have startup costs. All the gear for your home office, tools, the goods you intend to sell door-to-door— these things add up. You won't have a paycheck rolling in every week or two to cushion the blow to your bank account, either. Your rent, gas and food expenses will still have to be taken care of, and then there's the niggling problem of **insurance**. You will need to find a way to cover your health care costs, as well as protect vital equipment needed for your business.

Taxes can be a nightmare for independent contractors. If you become one, you must file with the IRS on a quarterly basis—that's right, four times a year (we'll touch on this again in the tax section). Depending on your business and the type of equipment you use, you can claim various deductions on your return. Some startup costs, travel and entertainment expenses, and the use of a home office and its equipment can be written off under certain circumstances. The best source for what you can and cannot claim as a legitimate business expense is the IRS itself. For that reason, *it's highly important that you stay organized and on top of all your expenditures*.

Complicated taxes aside, it will take time to build the kinds of contacts and client base you'll need to make ends meet. A freelance writer cannot make it on one or two big magazine articles a year, nor can a designer of children's clothes expect a few individual sales to keep him in the black. Even when money starts rolling in, there are no guarantees that it will remain constant. Business can be gangbusters one year, and collapse utterly the next.

Remember, entrepreneurship means constantly beating the bushes for new business. There is no whistle blowing at the end of the day—an infant business demands constant, often around-the-clock, care. If you are squeamish about long

hours or zealous about not working on the weekend, this may not be the route for you.

MORE THAN HALF OF ALL NEW BUSINESSES FAIL IN THEIR FIRST FIVE YEARS— NOT EXACTLY A SUNNY STATISTIC. IN ORDER TO ENSURE YOURS DOESN'T, YOU'LL HAVE TO SACRIFICE MUCH OF YOUR TIME AND PERSONAL LIFE. BUT WITH GRIT, FORTITUDE AND LUCK, YOUR BUSINESS WILL MAKE IT THROUGH ITS SHAKY START-UP PERIOD, AND THEN IT MAY PAY OFF IN A BIG WAY. JUST ASK THE MAKERS OF INLINE SKATES, OR SPAM, OR X-RAY GLASSES. WE'RE TALKING TRUE FINANCIAL FREEDOM AND INDEPENDENCE HERE— IN OTHER WORDS, THE AMERICAN DREAM.

LIVING LARGE
ON A SMALL BUDGET

"Basically I live from month to month. I have no money to put away. it makes me afraid for the future."

—Jillian, office temp

If life were perfect, we'd all hop out of school and into a lifestyle much like the one shared by the characters on *Friends*. That is, we'd have stunning New York loft apartments, great wardrobes and superbly coifed hair.

Choke down a big cup of this bitter reality java—young people are paid far too *horribly* for that to be the case for most of us. If *Friends* were in any way a reality-based TV show, the characters in it would all have to move to some miserable bombed-out walk-up studio apartment far from Manhattan, sleep in bunk beds and fight over who got to lick the macaroni-and-cheese bowl.

Poverty rots.

No two ways about it. Barring revolution, there isn't a thing anybody can do to change the fact that entry-level salaries are pitifully low. You can, however, stretch your cash so that you live comfortably and, yes, even manage to put a little aside.

1. SAVING YOUR

PENNIES
(AND A FEW DOLLARS, TOO)

Don't think of invest-
ing in purely tycoon
terms. It is far more
than a businessman on
the phone yelling at
his broker to buy all
the pork belly shares
that he can lay his
hands on, then throw-
ing himself off a tall
building when the
market takes a plunge.
You couldn't afford
to do that kind of
investing, even if
you wanted to.

As we mentioned earlier, acquiring
new skills, taking classes, going back
to school and even taking a break
are good investments in your long-
term health and well-being. One
huge investment you must make is to
start saving some of your earnings.

**This is very,
very important.**

In fact, it's probably **never** been more
important. Take the Sonny Bono
Generation, for example. Most of our
parents grew up in a time of seemingly
endless bounty. You've had all that
diabolical Baby Boomer nostalgia
crammed down your throat for years.
Moon landings, *Beach Blanket Bingo*,
The Fab Four at Shea Stadium, white
vinyl go-go boots and Walter Cronkite.
It isn't whiny to acknowledge that for
the most part our future doesn't look
quite so groovy and sunshiny as theirs
must have.

Certainly things are not all grim. At
least today we have access to natural
fibers, are free of Southeast Asian
entanglements, and listen to music
mercifully bereft of endless choruses
of "yeah, yeah" or "sha-la-la-la."

But ours are highly uncertain times.
For one thing, there won't be much
of a government safety net left to
catch us when we are ready to fall
down and break our hips, not that it's
anything to write home about now.
And we've already discussed how
uncertain the job market has become.

Investing for the future, which has
always been important (and by the
way, most studies show that Baby
Boomers haven't saved nearly as much
as they should by this point—they

probably blew it all on Monkees Reunion Concerts and Acapulco Gold) has an added urgency. Unless you are inheriting a fortune or have a massive trust fund, you need to look out for yourself and start putting some of your newly made cash toward a nest egg.

Many financial experts say that you should work toward putting a whopping six months of your salary away in case you are hit by a truck or get fired. That sounds like an enormous amount of money, and it is. But there is nothing wrong with trying to shoot for it. It's worth the added peace of mind.

You *can* start saving a few pennies. Right now. Here's the gold-medal method of doing it. When you get your

paycheck, deduct a small amount of it for a savings account. It need only be a few dollars. If your employer has **direct deposit**, this is best of all, because your paycheck goes straight into the bank. You never see the money, so you won't miss the percentage you can have earmarked for savings.

If you don't have direct deposit, you can bill yourself. Why not? You get bills from far less reputable characters. Pay yourself a specific amount every week or month—you decide how much. If you can't afford the whole amount once in a while, put just a portion in your savings account. After all, you can't sic a collections agency on yourself. But try not to skip.

The most important thing is to make saving second nature, part of the routine. The more you do it, the easier it will become.

When you have a decent amount of money tucked away, you can begin to invest it in other ways.

Then there's all the loose change you carry. At the end of the day, put most of it aside for your savings account. Okay, you may need the quarters for laundry or the bus, but think about all the bloody pennies alone. You may hate them, but they are still money. Every so often, when you have a coffee can filled up, get those paper penny rolls from the bank, fill them up and take them down to your branch. Oh sure, you can see the teller's face now— you'll feel like a geek. But you'll have tossed a little more money toward your savings.

You must make a pact with yourself never to touch this savings income except in a **dire emergency**. You will be tempted, around the first of the month, or when you step up to the ATM and your checking account is

Living in a Material World

An MTV poll asked young people what they felt they had enough money to do. Here are the results:

- **Thought they had enough cash to pay off their loans: 67 percent**

- **Felt there was enough dough to put some away in savings: 65 percent**

- **Said they could afford to go on a vacation: 51 percent**

- **Thought they could scrape enough together to move out of town: 50 percent**

- **Felt they could buy a car: 46 percent**

- **Were sure their funds would allow them to get married: 35 percent**

- **Saw enough in the kitty to buy a home: 21 percent**

lower than you thought. But don't undo what you have begun to create and give in to short-term fixes. Leave it alone. When you reach a point where you feel you have enough savings to cover you in emergencies and then some, you can put some of your savings into other investments.

SAVINGS ACCOUNTS

Hopefully you realized this when your father took you down to First National to deposit your allowance. When you plunk your money into a savings account it doesn't just sit there, collecting dust. The bank pays you interest so it can use it to give someone else a loan on a car or house, at a much higher rate of interest. The interest you earn on a savings account varies from institution to institution, but it will be criminally low. If you are looking for a way to double your money, this certainly isn't it.

Unlike some accounts that earn you more interest, there is no penalty when you withdraw money from your savings. If you have both a checking and savings accounts, leave that savings account alone unless you *really* need to use it. Find out if your bank pays a higher amount of interest if you keep your money above a certain balance.

One alternative to opening a traditional savings account is a **Money Market Deposit Account (MMDA)**. They generally offer better rates of interest and also allow you limited checking privileges (although some brokerage firms offer MMDAs with unlimited checking). Just how much interest you earn goes up and down with current rates. If you write more checks than your limit allows, you will get socked with a penalty fee, and there is usually a minimum balance requirement. *All* bank accounts come with fees of one kind or another. (We'll discuss that in more detail in the banking section.)

CERTIFICATES OF DEPOSIT (CDS)

Because savings accounts earn such low interest, people with a little more money to play with look for other options. There are a variety of them, but one of the most popular is called a Certificate of Deposit, or CD. If you have earned stacks of cash from cleaning Alaskan fish all summer and can afford not to use a portion of your money for a while, this is a good way to go.

A CD is a **timed** bank deposit. Basically, it works like this—you agree to deposit a sum of money and not touch it for a set period of time, and in exchange the bank pays you a much higher amount of interest than for a traditional savings account. Credit unions and savings and loans offer CDs as well.

The term of a CD can range from a few months to 10 years. If you take your money out of the account before it expires **(matures)**, you are punished by the bank with a penalty fee. Just how much the penalty is, and how much interest you earn, depends on the CD. So if you are considering putting a chunk of cash into one, shop around before stowing it away.

INDIVIDUAL RETIREMENT ACCOUNTS (IRAS)

Investing in an IRA does not mean sending money to cousin Seamus in Belfast to use for a bombing campaign on the London Underground. It's an Individual Retirement Account. If your employer doesn't offer you a 401(k)-type investment program, you might consider setting one up. Banks, brokerage firms, insurance companies, mutual fund companies and credit unions offer these special accounts. You can invest a proscribed amount of your pre-tax income in an IRA account. If you are self-employed, you can set up what is known as a SEP account (SEP stands for "simplified employee pension"), which allows you to invest a higher percentage of your pre-tax income. These accounts are worth looking into, if you are concerned about whether you are going to spend your sunset years sitting on a beach chair in Florida or scrounging for dog food.

2. DOING BATTLE WITH THE BUDGET MONSTER

All this talk about savings is just peachy, you say. But save *what*? When you are scraping by on $18,000 a year, *and* you have student loans and credit-card debt, there's not necessarily

copious wealth to squirrel away. When you do have a little extra money, why not buy yourself some new underwear or a spoon to eat your cereal with?

LOOK, NOBODY SAID YOU HAD TO **WEAR BURLAP** AND **LIVE OFF BOILED POTATOES.**

But if you are feeling stretched, you can give yourself more breathing room just by taking the time to map out a budget. Money gets eaten by hundreds of tiny things we never think about and can often do just as well without. Things like nightly take-out food, "sale" clothes you didn't even want once you got them home, that Mac Davis CD anthology. By simply planning, you have more disposable income—not just to put away, but to enjoy right now.

COMMIT

Here is one ugly fact you are going to have to accept. **You have to know where your money goes.** There's no use fighting it or putting it all out of your mind. You need to put yourself on a budget. Nobody likes it, certainly not the president, or your parents, or Ivana Trump. Even Ivana needs to know how many hot pink cocktail suits she sells on TV on a daily basis, and how much of that money gets scarfed up in beluga. If she didn't, one day she might find herself trying to cram a Burger King visor over her bulbous blond head.

Now here's the corollary to that ugly fact: **The hardest part about managing your finances is committing to doing it.** It really is all downhill from there, no matter how scary your financial situation. It can take a while to find the courage to do this. The idea of sitting down and mapping out just what we spend on ourselves each month is anathema to most people.

It seems so stressful, writing down figures on a yellow legal pad with a number-2 pencil and figuring out just how much money we spend, owe or need on a monthly basis. Well, it is a little stressful. And there are a lot more interesting and enjoyable things to do. Most of us would rather not think about money at all. We'd just like to have copious amounts of it around to spend. So as they say, we fiddle while Rome (or Wall Street) burns all around us.

The thing is, when you don't control your finances, they inevitably control your life. You find yourself stressed out at the beginning of the month, lodging frantic calls to your parents in the middle of the night and living from paycheck to paycheck. Unfortunately, until this becomes so unbearable that you do something about it, you may just not be disciplined enough to go on a budget. But if you can, chomp on a piece of rawhide and force yourself to take a few minutes to think about what you bring home and spend on a daily basis. You may be buying yourself some critical breathing room.

WRITE IT DOWN

When you are good and ready, get to work tracking down where all your money flew off to. Get out that old, maligned legal pad and start writing down your expenses. Not just the obvious things like telephone bills and car payments, but **everything**. Once you get started, it won't seem quite so dreadful.

Divide your list into categories—you might start with **transportation, food, rent, entertainment, clothing, household items, utilities, debts, taxes, health care and insurance,** for example. Create and subdivide categories as you need to.

Ideally, after doing this, you'd set about thoroughly documenting spending in these various categories for a couple of months. Then you'd look over all the receipts you saved, and based on your results you'd come up with a fairly accurate estimate for your expenses in each category. By adding them up and comparing them with your monthly income, you'd know if you were over budget or not.

But guess what? Chances are you aren't that dedicated, and you've lost half of your receipts. If we're wrong, more power to you. But if we're right, don't worry. And don't shy away from budgeting forever. The mere act of making a list and estimating what you spend on various items is an excellent first step. You'll be able to see where some of the biggest flab is and begin to cut back.

Chances are you already have a sense of where some of it is without even doing that much. If you find you are going out for Hunan beef every third night, that is major flab. Nobody needs that much Hunan beef. Not even Mao needed that much Hunan beef.

Draw yourself some lines in the sand—"I will eat out *only* once a week." "I will go to *one* movie a month," and so on. You decide your limit. Unless you have a creditor breathing hard down your neck. Then cut back as drastically as possible, across the board, to get them off.

Look for items you can cut out **forever**. If you are lucky enough to have some cash stowed away to pay off a student loan or credit-card debt and not wipe yourself totally out, get rid of the monster forever. Goodbye, *adios*, *sayonara*, gone. **Debt is a horrendous monkey on the back of young America. And credit-card debt is worst of all.** (We'll discuss ridding yourself of that particular monkey in the last section of this chapter.)

KNOW WHAT YOU OWE

Even if the very thought makes you cringe, you must tally up your debts and know exactly how much you owe. If you have student loans, you know how important it is to keep track of your financial-aid debts, or should, after the mandatory orientation given to all students who take this money from the government. Know the exact amount you owe each lender, and keep good records on all your loans and debts. One of the cornerstones of your financial life should be to eliminate your debts as fast as you possibly can. Even if as fast as possible still means years.

Of course you can't wash away your debts overnight. You have too many other expenditures, and a life to enjoy. But the more you can reduce expenditures in other areas of your life, the more money you'll have to fill in the hole, and the more holes you fill, the more cash you can put toward other things.

Once you start the budgeting process, keep at it. Start saving your receipts, copying every bill you pay and storing the information in files. The more exact you become in your estimates—yes, that means figuring out exactly where your money goes on a daily basis—the better you'll be able to save for your future, and the more control you'll have over your life.

PAY YOUR BILLS ON TIME

Listen Up. When you have no order in your financial house, you may frequently find yourself paying your bills late. Avoid this at all costs. When you pay late, you not only incur late fees and charges, but you can damage your credit rating. Pick one set time every month—the full moon, the last Saturday—and make that bill-paying day. We'll discuss credit histories later, but for now keep in mind that a bad credit rating can cause you all kinds of blinding, eyeball-stabbing, power-drill-through-your-temple type headaches. If you are going to have to make a late payment, it's sometimes worth calling the billing agency to inform them. You may be able to work something out.

REDISCOVER THE DOLLAR

One way to start bringing debt down is to pay in cash. Remember good old cash? Greenbacks. Simoleons. Dead presidents. Smackers. Kopeks. Try cash for eating out, buying food, getting gas, buying clothes—in fact, for everything except your bills and big-ticket items. There will invariably be times when you violate this cash-only policy. But by instituting it, you'll resist spending money that you don't have.

FLAB CUTTING— AREAS WHERE YOU CAN SAVE MONEY

Here are just a few places in nearly everyone's life that stand trimming:

Food—Yes, food. This is a major drag on expenses. Cut back on the number of nights a month you eat out, or order in. Get yourself a pan and some spaghetti and start cooking. Bring your lunch to work with you. All those burritos you're eating are smelling up the office, anyway. And

those health salads aren't healthy, or economical. Do not deny yourself the pleasure of eating out entirely, of course. Remember that many restaurants offer cheaper luncheon menus.

Plan your trips to the grocery store. **Piggly Wiggly is the Devil's Triangle.** You go in looking for a carton of milk and come out with everything Hostess ever made. **Keep yourself superglued to a shopping list, and don't go to the store just before dinner.** Hungry people buy more food than they need. Rummage through the aisles for bargains—food shelved in the most convenient location is often more expensive than a competing brand on a lower shelf. Clip coupons, compare prices (generic brands, while they are certainly kitschy and cool-looking, are not always cheaper), be a regular Happy Homemaker when it comes to hitting the Safeway.

And one more thing about food: **never buy groceries with your credit card**. You may be paying for your pawpaws long after they have been eaten, with interest to boot.

Clothing—especially if you have to dress up for work, you can spend a king's ransom on togs. Hit the department stores in January and August, when they have end-of-season

Oh, telephone line

Those phone companies, they go to awesome lengths to win your long-distance telephone business. Before you investigate any savings to be had by going with Candice Bergen's or Whoopi Goldberg's or anybody else's plan, consider this.

Write a letter.

Ye gods, we know that sounds like something your grandfather would say, but he's got a point, and anyway, letters are wonderful to get. A letter is a little present in the mailbox just for you. Without letters, one is left with only magazines, junk mail and bills. What a sad mailbox that is. If you have Internet access you can avoid both glacial posts and exorbitant bills and communicate quickly and cheaply. Best of both worlds. However, a lot depends on having someone to write to who also has e-mail. And frankly, sometimes nothing beats talking on the telephone.

Still, try and cut back on the number of long-distance calls you make. School friends in particular don't need to be rung too regularly and can stand getting the odd letter. Unfortunately, family, no matter how hard we try, is usually too bloody hard to brush off this way.

Look over old phone bills with an eye on when you call, and for how long, and to whom. When you decipher your calling pattern, you'll be able to see if there are any calls you can make less frequently and talk for shorter time on. Most of us can be more strict about how much time we spend on the telephone, but it's very hard to cut back. It's best to call at night and on weekends, of course—that's the cheapest time.

170

Knowing your calling pattern can help you shop for a discount calling plan. Dialing long distance the old-fashioned way—the old "dial-1" option—is nearly always more expensive. But beware of plans that place too many restrictions on when you call and how much you spend during the month. And ditch your plan whenever you feel they aren't meeting your needs. Flat-rate calling plans, which charge you just three different rates—one each for weekdays, weeknights and weekends—are often the best deal.

A fantastic resource for long-distance consumers is the Telecommunications Research and Action Center (TRAC), which publishes heaps of information comparing long-distance telephone rates. You can get hold of it by sending $3 and a self-addressed stamped envelope to the following address:

> **TRAC**
> PO Box 27279
> Washington, DC 20005

Long distance or local, beware of bells and whistles—most of us have become addicted to call waiting, but try to avoid buying too many extras from both your long-distance and local phone companies. You'll get charged up the yin-yang for services you never use.

sales. Warehouse stores, outlets, charity shops and thrift stores can all be good places to look for very nice turnouts at reasonable prices. But be sure that prices are truly cheaper than retail before you buy.

Never buy cheaply made clothing just because it's cheap. It looks terrible and it won't last. Invest in well-made items you can wear for a long time. **Don't go shopping for clothes when you are lonely or depressed.** You'll binge. Wait for a great outfit to go on sale. And avoid buying sale items on credit.

If you are dependent on coin-operated launderettes, don't put off doing your laundry for weeks. Not only do you have to lug all your clothes down there, wait for free machines and spend the whole day watching rinse and spin cycles, you have to scramble around to spend a megaton of quarters. Consider hand washing some frequently worn items to save on silver. Save your laundry quarters throughout the week and don't wash darks every time you wear them. And (admittedly this has nothing to do with budgeting) don't leave your clothes hanging around in coin-operated washers and dryers for a blue moon after the cycle is done. It's evil.

Watch your dry cleaning costs, too. Dry-cleaning coats, jackets and suits is expensive, so spread out the cleaning of these big items throughout the year. Don't bring in a bunch of coats all at once. Women should be aware that they are often gouged at dry cleaners. A "blouse" often costs more to clean than a "shirt," even if they are much the same garment. A miniskirt can cost as much to clean as a full-length skirt.

Save money by learning to sew and iron. Don't scoff. A lot of people don't know how to do these elementary tasks properly. You know who you are.

Hair—gets its own fabulous category. People are taken for a ride on their hair. Many hair-styling schools give cheap, completely inoffensive haircuts

for chump change. You may be styled by the future Vidal Sassoon.

Barbers are usually a good bargain. In case you didn't know, barbers are very happening cats. The pole is cool. The blue stuff he slaps on your neck is cool. The steel combs are cool. The blue smocks and the pictures of men's haircuts from 1973 are cool. Don't fork over a small fortune for some cheesy guy named Yves to fluff your head while New Age music plays in the background—check the barber out.

Furniture—you can blow a fortune on it, and chances are you'll hate most of it in a few years. So get it free whenever you can. Take dead people's furniture, your parent's old furniture, furniture you find left out on the street if it looks nice and isn't smelly. People often leave some great furniture on the street. You don't need a house full of brand-new Ikea furniture. Buy what items you need selectively, and try to inherit all the rest.

Transportation—we shouldn't have to tell you how much you can spend on driving to and from work alone. If you are lucky to

Buying a Car—Factors to Consider

If you are about to buy a car for the first time, it can be a pretty intimidating experience. Car shopping usually means *haggling*, and if you didn't grow up in Istanbul or Brooklyn, you may be worried about being ripped off. Before you walk into a showroom, make like Rocky Balboa and train to fight for a good deal.

Do Extensive Research

Before you ever go shopping for something as big as this, you should know everything about what you are about to buy. Scour car-buying guides, consumer magazines, obtain information from automobile clubs and consider purchasing data from a car-buying service. There are a plethora of sources out there aimed at helping you make this purchase. *Consumer Reports* publishes reams of useful information on car buying, and you should try to consult the NADA Blue Book on your car model if you are considering trading an old car in or buying a used car.

When you buy a new car, you need to try and figure out what price the car dealers paid for an automobile when they bought it from the manufacturer. Research from car-buying guides and services will give you the "invoice price," which should give you a pretty good idea of what the dealer paid before you set foot on a lot. Without this information, you'll get taken big time when you start to haggle, because you won't know how much the dealer has whacked on to the price. Of course, you can always come straight out and ask him.

Used cars can be bought from franchised and independent dealerships, rental car dealers and private individuals. Be careful about buying a car from an independent dealer—the stereotypical guy in the loud plaid jacket who talks a mile a minute in his ads. Check out the dealership with the Better Business Bureau, and ask if the dealership is part of the Independent Automobile Dealer's Association. No matter who you buy a used car from, you should know exactly why it is being sold.

Pick Your Moment

You may make a better deal on a new car at the end of the month, when dealers are under the gun to meet their monthly sales quotas. December can be another good time, because they are often scrambling to meet year-end quotas. You might also try at the end of your car's model year, usually around September, when it may be taking up space on the showroom floor needed for the new model. "As cars get older in their life cycle, dealers are more willing to negotiate," says Mike Morrissey, a spokesman for the American Automobile Association.

Shop Around
This can't be stressed enough. With new cars, always see several car dealers and get price quotes from each one. One hardball tactic that can work is to let a dealer know you are doing this, but don't tell him what another dealer has quoted you. You may put pressure on the seller to give you a good deal. For used cars, check used-car-buying guides and the *want ads* for prices on models you are interested in, whether you are buying from a dealer or a private owner.

Comfort in Numbers
Don't fly solo when you are considering buying any car. Bring along a friend to rein you in when you are beginning to foam at the mouth——it's good to have a trusted second opinion handy. And you'll be far less likely to be bamboozled by a slick operator.

Appear Prepared to Buy
When you walk onto a car lot, be ready to buy if the price is right. If a seller doesn't think you are serious, he's not going to be interested in bargaining with you. Let him know you are there to buy a car, and he'll try harder to make the sale.

Resist Pressure Tactics
That said, nobody needs to buy a car on the spot. Never allow yourself to be cornered into making a deal right away. If a dealer says you must make a decision that second, *get out of there.* There are other fish in the sea.

Don't Fall in Love
Put on a poker face. No matter how much you love a car, don't betray your feelings to someone selling a car. If you sigh when you get into the front seat, keep massaging the fine Corinthian leather or drool all over the hood, a car salesman will smell blood. Always be prepared to walk away from the car.

Test Drives
According to the AAA, 75 percent of new car buyers do not test drive their cars. If you fail to take a car for a test drive, you are just plain crazy. If you are ordering a car from a lot, don't hop into another model for your test—you need to drive the model you are buying. Again, take along a friend to help spot any signs of trouble as you drive. Check all the bells and whistles on your automobile during your test.

With used cars, keep a sharp lookout for strange engine noises, *any* rust, smoke, mysterious knocks and pings, burning smells, worn tires, signs of repair and dripping fluid. Check the car's alignment, spare tire, lights, doors, transmission, brakes, shocks, gear-shifting, air conditioning and radio. Inspect that clunker with the finest of fine-tooth combs. If the seller of a used car promises to make repairs before you take ownership, get it in writing.

Get an Expert's Opinion
No used-car buying trip is complete without the intervention of a trusted mechanic or inspection service. *Never* buy a car from someone who refuses to let a mechanic check it out. No matter how many times you kick the tires, keep your money in your pocket until the car gets a clean bill of health from a professional. Professional car-inspection services are listed in the Yellow Pages.

Used Car Danger Signs
The last thing you want to do is buy a hot car, so check identification numbers on auto parts to make sure they aren't obliterated or mismatched. If they are, the car could be stolen. And from your research, you should know whether or not your car has been *recalled*—taken back by the manufacturer for problems. The U.S. Department of Transportation's *Auto Safety Hotline* can supply you with information about recalled automobiles. Their number is 1-(800)-424-9393.

Know Your Warranty
As with any purchase, you should know what is included in your car's warranty when you buy it. Sometimes the manufacturer's warranty can be transferred to the new owner when a used car is sold.

Get Insurance
You cannot drive any heap, new or used, without insurance. We'll touch on auto insurance in more detail later. For now realize that you will probably be required to carry at least some insurance. For new cars, you may want to have both collision and comprehensive insurance—which protects your car if it is involved in most accidents and damage. Depending on the condition of your used car, you may choose to simply take liability insurance, a bare-bones insurance policy that will pay for at least some of the damage you wreak when you smash into some poor soul.

live in a city with a decent **public transport** network, use it. Like going to barbers, riding public transport is underrated, and quite copacetic. Trains, even the grimiest subway train, are romantic. You'll never know who you'll meet. Some poor character in Boston recently was so smitten by the woman he was sitting next to on the subway that he put fliers all over the place in an effort to track her down. He was featured in *People* Magazine. Hey, if you took public transport it could have been you. Buses are admittedly less romantic, but still filled with *interesting* characters.

Best of all, in most cases you can take a nap on public transport and not get killed. Many transit systems give regular commuters reduced fares. You will also save on gas, parking and aggravation. And you'll also be a good citizen by doing your bit to use an expensive city service and better the environment.

However, if, like most Americans, you live in a sprawling, post-modern megalopolis, try and put together a **car pool**. Never buy premium gasoline unless your car specifically requires it. You aren't giving the engine a treat, you're just spending more money. Make an exhaustive search for a very good, very honest mechanic. **Get out and walk** once in a while. This country would be better off if more of us walked.

Cheap Entertainment, and we don't mean television, comes in many forms. Half the fun is in rooting it out. You haven't gotten this far in life without knowing where a good deal of it can be found. Here's just one example. Make going to see first-run movies in the evening a treat again—the price of a ticket is usually horrendous.

Matinees are often much cheaper. Or you can rent a video, go to a dollar movie theater that shows films after they have been out in mainstream houses, check out a local art film house

or university film society. The last two places may offer memberships that discount your ticket price. Beyond films, there are a wide variety of free and cheap activities you can do in most larger communities. Start scanning the newspaper and local weeklies for ideas.

Little bills—we are stuck with many bills, but some can be quickly gotten rid of. Lots of little bills arriving at odd times can really mess you up. Until you exert firmer control over your affairs, consider ditching CD clubs, magazine subscriptions (read it on the stand or go to the library), book clubs and the like. You can check out music (not always the latest, to be sure) and videos from some libraries. You don't have to get rid of everything you enjoy, but you can cut back. If you have a store charge card that you don't need or seldom use, lose it. It's bringing you down.

I WANT IT NOW

Everybody has a little Veruca Salt in them. Not the band, but the little girl from *Charlie and the Chocolate Factory*. If you've read the book or saw the film version (and you absolutely must see it), you know all about Veruca. She was one nasty piece of work. A bratty spoiled girl who constantly demanded material things with an ear-splitting **"I WANT IT NOW."** She was a bad egg, and she came to a bad end. Don't be like her. Resist the temptation to buy on impulse.

There are loads of yummy things out there to purchase in this consumer culture of ours, but when you feel your heart beating faster and yourself getting all giddy, step back. Get out of the store, and think about it. You don't have to have every toy right away, or buy six different versions of the same tartan kilt. Resist your Veruca Salt urges. (By the way, to the British, "verucas" are disgusting boils. Think of your constant urges for material things that way, and you may not be so tempted to spend, spend, spend.)

Naturally, you should be putting all your newly saved money in a bank. Not all banks are created equal. You need to be an informed consumer when looking for a place to stow your loot.

Always remember that banks are in the business of making money off you, not charities especially designed to keep your funds secure.

3. STASHING YOUR LOOT

When you bank, you should expect that nearly everything—except the complimentary toaster you got for signing up—has a price tag. It's critical to discover just what fees the bank will charge before opening an account.

Sure, it's easier to just run straight into the waiting arms of the institution that's nearest your apartment or the one that uses cute little kids and puppy dogs in its commercials. But think about how important your earnings are to you. You work very hard for them. So don't consign your funds to a money dungeon, with surly staff that won't help you when you need it, high fees for basic services, and inconvenient hours.

One constructive way to begin shopping for a financial institution is simply by talking to friends and colleagues about where they bank. When people are unhappy with a bank's service, you will hear about it, in gory detail. That kind of feedback is important. Ideally, you want to find an institution that not only makes its customers happy but also makes a positive contribution to your community and the world. Hopefully that model bank also has convenient automatic teller locations and branches close to your home and work.

Find out about a bank's hours. There's nothing more frustrating than dealing with a bank that opens two hours after you get to work and closes by the time you reach for your peanut butter and jelly. Even if you bank exclusively by ATM, your bank should have hours that allow you to get to a human face when you need one.

On the same note, see what telephone, mail and electronic banking services the institution offers. Explore whether or not it has direct deposit, a huge time-saver that allows you to have paychecks fly straight into a bank account. How long does it take to clear checks? Does the bank credit your account immediately with a portion of the check's amount, or will an emergency loan from your mother take a week to clear while you hide from the landlord?

Also make sure that your money will be insured by the **Federal Deposit Insurance Corporation (FDIC)**. That way, if the bank goes down the toilet, your money won't go with it. An established institution should be FDIC-insured, but ask just the same. Banks often mention the FDIC in their advertising and post signs in their branches to let you know. Deposits of up to $100,000 are insured by the FDIC.

Besides the Bank

When you think of a safe place to put your money, you think bank, right? You know essentially what a bank does—it takes deposits, issues checking accounts, loans money to businesses and individuals, and exploits starving people in poor, hot, dirty countries. But the purpose of these two institutions may have confounded you:

Savings & Loans, *or thrifts, specialize in making home loans, but also offer savings accounts. They have had a bit of an image problem since the government had to bail out troubled S&Ls in the late 1980s. In fact, some are even ashamed to come out and call themselves S&Ls nowadays. As with banks, make sure any savings & loan you put your money in is FDIC-insured.*

Credit Unions *are nonprofit institutions that offer financial services to their members. Labor unions, corporations, neighborhood associations and a variety of other groups form them. A credit union can provide you with much the same things as a bank can, such as different types of accounts, loans, checks, credit and ATM cards, but your costs are usually lower because it is not out to make a buck. On the downside, you probably won't find branches of your credit union conveniently tucked all over town. Most credit unions are insured by the National Credit Union Share Insurance Fund (NCUSIF) which protects deposits of up to $100,000 if the institution fails.*

Then take a cold hard look at the different kinds of savings and checking accounts offered. You want to find an account that best fits with your own quirks—if you are truly good at saving money, then you can take an account with a high minimum balance. But don't kid yourself into getting that account because you think it will force you to turn over a new leaf. Chances are it won't, and you'll be penalized for taking out too much cash.

Every savings or checking account is going to have service charges and fees attached to it, and it's your job to know what they are. This is especially important with your workhorse account— checking. Before you sign on the dotted line, make sure you know what it is you're getting into.

CHECKING ACCOUNTS

Your checking account is your bread and butter, or pita and hummus account. So when you choose a bank, it's where you should be at your sharpest. Not that banks make it easy—you'll get eyestrain and headaches trying to figure out what all the fine print explaining their checking accounts means. But since you use your checking account nearly every day, you should nail them down on the fees they charge for common transactions. Ask a lot of questions.

Generally speaking, you earn no interest (or very low interest) and get charged for every piddling thing when you use your checking account. That's just the way it is, unfortunately. Every time you withdraw money from your account, think of the little sound a cash register makes—it's the bank scrounging yet another penny. Stop payment on a check—ca-ching! Bounce a check—ca-ching! Order checks decorated with rainbows and unicorns— ca-ching! Ask to have your canceled checks returned with your statement— ca-ching!

You get the picture. It isn't that you shouldn't do these things (except bounce a check, of course). Just be aware of what they cost you. The mere act of writing a check can cost money. And even though some bank fees seem small, your various charges can take a significant bite out of your income if you aren't careful.

SOME THINGS TO CONSIDER

Before opening an account, find out what the charge is for ATM use, a bounced check, new checks, and whether or not you have to keep a **minimum balance** to avoid service charges. Discover what the bank means by "free" checking accounts if it offers them. There really isn't any such thing as totally free checking. Are you free of certain charges as long as you bank there? Or do they kick in after a period of time or under certain circumstances? Do you have a set number of checks per month you can write before incurring fees? If you have a choice between an interest-bearing checking account and one that bears no interest, check out what the differences are. Many interest-bearing accounts hit you with charge doozies and don't earn you very much in the way of interest.

USE YOUR HEAD

Whatever type of account you open, don't let it control your life. Keep on top of your affairs. Electronic conveniences are great, but in these days of banking by gadget, it's easy to lose track of where you are. Balancing a checkbook is a dying art. And bounced checks are serious business— not only do they complicate your life and bring down heavy charges, they may end up damaging your **credit rating** (more on that later).

ATMs and You

The convenience of ATM use comes with a price tag. Most banks charge you a transaction fee every time you use the machine, and some even slap an additional charge on top of that. The best policy is to withdraw a larger amount when you visit an ATM so that you don't keep coming back to get more money as frequently.

No-Fee ATMs are as rare as woolly mammoths today, but when banks were trying to hook consumers on using the infernal machines, they were the norm. If your bank charges you nothing to use its teller machines, you have lucked out. Most banks charge you about a buck for the transaction.

Walk the Extra Block when you are looking for an ATM and can't find your own bank's. Banks charge you more when you use a competitor's ATM. When you go out of town and use an ATM on the same network, you may be doubling your charges.

A few tips on ATM cards and safety:

- *Keep your ATM card in the protective little condom it came with. Avoid storing it in your wallet near other magnetized cards, laying it on top of computers, televisions and other electronic equipment and carrying it through airport security gates. All of these things can demagnetize your card, which will render it useless.*

- *Memorize your PIN number. Never write it on your card, keep it in your wallet or give it out. Report a missing ATM card immediately. Avoid choosing obvious PIN codes—like your birthday (any slug who steals your wallet will immediately try it).*

- *Always avoid unguarded ATM vestibules at odd hours; if you must use a lonely ATM, get in and out quickly and check the reflective mirror on the terminal while you are at it. Patronize busy ATMs— even if you must pay additional charges.*

- *Be prepared when you go to use an ATM—don't fumble for your card in a wallet or purse. Fill out your deposit slips in advance.*

- *Follow good ATM etiquette—stand a few feet away from the person using the machine and don't stare at his back. It makes people nervous. Always block the ATM screen with your back when you are using it.*

- *If you are entering an ATM vestibule that can only be accessed by using your card in a door slot, look out for people who rush up behind you and follow you in.*

- *Take your ATM receipt away with you when you leave the vestibule— it contains information that thieves can use. And never, ever, walk away with your money in your hand.*

- *Be very wary of strangers who accost you at doorways to ATMs or inside the bank, no matter how respectable they appear to be.*

- *If you are robbed at an ATM, report it immediately to both the bank and the police.*

Try valiantly to get a sense of your spending patterns. How often do you go to the ATM? What do you spend most of that money on? How many checks do you write a month? Do you record them? How do you pay for your groceries? Are you living from paycheck to paycheck?

Find out where the money goes. And don't be passive. If you examine your current bank and find its fees too high, its hours too short and service generally lacking compared to a friend's, **shove off**. It can be easy to forget this in your relationship with a bank, but **you** are the customer.

GET TO KNOW YOUR BANKER

ONE FINAL TIP, BEFORE WE MOVE ON. QUICK, BEFORE SHE'S REPLACED BY R2D2, GET TO KNOW THE BRANCH MANAGER OR OTHER OFFICER IN YOUR LOCAL BANK. ALL OF US WILL PROBABLY BE BANKING BY COMPUTER NEXT YEAR (AND GETTING CHARGED A PRINCELY SUM FOR IT), SO DON'T DELAY.

Okay, it isn't practical in every case. But when you have someone at your branch who knows you, you are more likely to have an ally who can help if you are having a terrible time getting your ATM card to work, when an important check is taking too long to clear, or when you are about to bounce a check. Not a miracle worker, certainly. But likely to be a hell of a lot more sympathetic to your case than a computer or a customer service operator in some far-off town.

You don't have to take her out for donuts. When you open your account, keep the card of the bank officer who helped you handy. Call him when you have a banking problem. Maybe even say hello when you come into the branch. It could pay off later.

4. INSURANCE— BECAUSE VERY BAD THINGS CAN HAPPEN TO GOOD PEOPLE

You already know that you make substantially **less money** a year than your salary figure. **Before** you get your check, the government **takes its cut** (more on taxes later), **and then comes insurance.** All told, about **a third of your income is zapped before you ever see it.**

If you are among the estimated 39.7 million uninsured Americans, you might think you are getting a windfall. As

> **According to the Employee Benefits Research Institute, about Half of All Young Adults Between the Ages of 21 and 24 Have No Health Insurance Coverage through an Employer.**

we mentioned briefly in the last chapter, you are not. You are putting yourself at grave risk and being selfish, to boot. Other people are going to have to try and pick up the tab when you get some lingering, oozing disease, or be financially crippled in the attempt.

When you are young and healthy, you may think you don't need to see a doctor. And it's true, most young people end up needing major medical care only when there's been an accident, not because they have long-term ailments. But trauma care is the most expensive medical care of all—thousands of dollars you don't have for a trip to the emergency room.

Until there's some action on health-care reform in this country, you must take it upon yourself to think of health insurance as a **TAX** that you have no option but to pay for, just like Social Security. It is not optional. If you are working without a health plan, you need to get one. Yesterday. If you wait until you are sick or need even the most minor surgery, you'll pay much more. It's known in the insurance biz as a *preexisting condition* (see inset).

Except for special programs such as medicare and medicaid, health insurance in this country is in the hands of private businesses, which offer a host of different plans and insurance rates. The world of insurance can be difficult to negotiate, but finding the best coverage for you is extremely important—after all, you want to know you won't be financially ruined if you get sick or injured, and you want to make sure your plan covers your medical needs. "More people take time to shop around for gasoline prices than insurance plans," says Richard Corsch, of the Health Insurance Association of America, an industry organization.

These private companies offer a range

of services to individuals and employers, but generally health insurance coverage is broken down into two broad categories—the more traditional, fee-for-service, or indemnity plans, and managed care plans. A fee-for-service plan usually allows you to choose your own doctor, asks you to pay some percentage of your health care costs out of pocket when you go for a medical visit (say 20 percent) and then pays for all of your health care costs once you've spent a given amount of your own money. Managed care is typified by Health Maintenance Organizations (HMOs) and other plans that often (but not always) stipulate you use the organization's doctors and charge a small fee each time you have an appointment. Many insurers offer both kinds of coverage.

Again, obtaining insurance through an employer is by far the most headache-free method of getting healthcare and peace of mind. Finding a policy on your own can be frustrating—and expensive. But if you are unemployed or working without insurance, you have a few options. College graduates should see if their student health plan covers them at least until the August after commencement. A great many plans do, but others stop right when you throw your graduation cap up in the sky.

Depending on the plan your parents have, you may be able to remain on their policy until you reach a certain age, say 23. After that, you are on your own. In *some* cases, you may be able to extend your parents' coverage for a longer period under a plan called COBRA. As you may recall from the last section, COBRA is actually designed to help people keep their old health insurance for up to 18 months after they have left a job. You cannot continue on COBRA benefits indefinitely and you (or your parents) will be paying much more for your insurance. You'll have to pick up the full cost of the premium, plus an added charge.

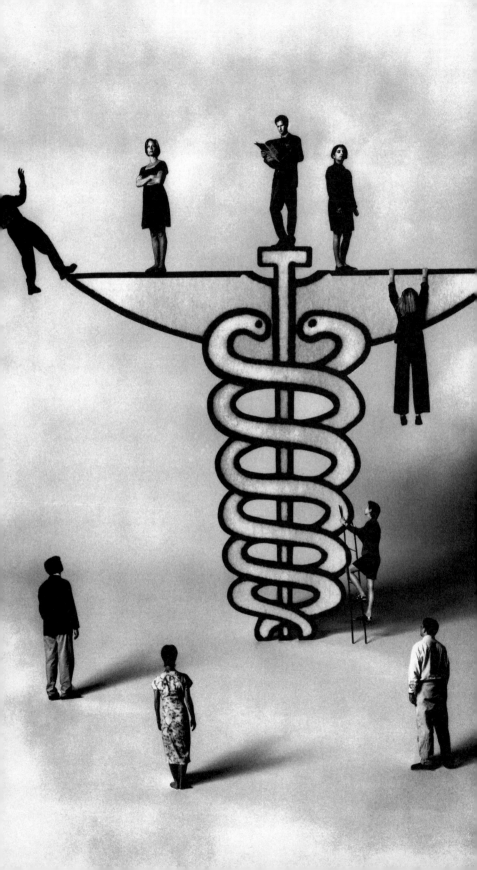

What's Covered

Know your insurance policy like the back of your hand. The last thing you want to happen is to get whacked for bills you expected to have your insurer cover. What's covered varies greatly from plan to plan. Traditionally, insurers often emphasized expensive curative medicine—that is, surgery and treatment after an illness had developed. Nowadays, HMOs in particular have led the charge to covering preventative medical treatments, including annual physical exams. Dental care remains a find in insurance policies—it's fantastic to have a plan that covers your annual checkup. But increasingly insurers are offering "cafeteria style" plans—you choose what coverage you want.

ITEMS OFTEN COVERED BY INSURERS:

- surgery
- hospitalization
- medical exams before you are admitted into the hospital
- many prescriptions
- ambulance service
- doctor's expenses
- X-rays
- nursing care

ITEMS REGULARLY EXCLUDED FROM INSURANCE PLANS:

- physicals
- eye appointments
- glasses and contact lenses
- routine dental checkups
- cosmetic surgery, wrinkle treatments and the like . . . surprised?
- certain kinds of mental health care
- alternative medicine, massage therapy, chiropractors
- use of experimental treatments or drugs
- immunizations

As we mentioned in the employment section of the book, one option is to check out if you are eligible for insurance under a group plan offered by a professional or trade organization, or a club. Actors and writers, for example, can get insurance through guilds even though they do not have regular or steady employment. Nobody just hands you access to their benefits plan, though. You have to meet their membership requirements.

Another option is to obtain a **short-term insurance plan**. These plans offer temporary insurance, usually for up to six months. You may be able to extend your plan beyond the original term of your coverage, if you are still uninsured. Some insurance companies specialize in short-term insurance, but it's not a bargain. Like standard plans, the cost of short-term insurance will vary greatly depending on individual circumstances, and what plan you choose, but you can typically expect to pay between three and five hundred dollars. Many short-term policies will not cover you if you have a preexisting condition. One more thing about buying insurance on your own—in some states insurers often group individual policy holders in pools under a system known as community rating—that means that people are grouped together and charged the same amount, no matter how sick or healthy they are. If you are quite ill, you are getting a deal, if not, well, you may be spending a great deal more than you need to.

Remember, if you leave a job or lose your job you can extend your health insurance for a limited period, under COBRA.

AN INSURANCE PRIMER

Whether you are covered by your employer or not, you should be aware of the most commonly used words in the insurance biz. If you haven't had much exposure to that arcane world, it can all sound a little like Urdu.

Premium—the amount you pay for your insurance policy. Depending on your plans, you may pay your premiums monthly, quarterly or semi-annually.

Deductible—the amount you must pay out of your own pocket before your insurance kicks in. A deductible may range from a few hundred dollars to several thousand. If your annual deductible is $250, you pay that amount for medical care before your insurance pays a cent.

It may seem initially that a low deductible is a good thing for a young person with little money. But if you are shopping for insurance on your own, a high deductible is often better because policies with high deductibles generally have lower premiums. You pay for minor medical visits on your own, and insurance will cover you when you have a major accident or disease. A healthy young person will probably not visit the doctor enough times in one year to meet his or her deductible.

Copayment—the portion of your medical bill you pay. Even after you meet your deductible, your insurance does not pay for everything. In a traditional fee-for-service arrangement, an insurer often pays between 70 and 80 percent of what is **covered** by your policy. In other words, if fillings are covered, the insurer will pick up most of the cost. The remaining amount is the copayment. And if you get your teeth cleaned as well, and the plan does not cover that procedure, you pay for the teeth cleaning on your own.

If you are a member of an HMO you may make a very low copayment every time you visit the doctor—say $10 per visit. The HMO picks up the rest of the tab, because the doctor is affiliated with the organization. Other insurers set flat limits on the amount

they will pay for different medical procedures, say $100 for a gynecological consultation, and you pay all costs after the amount is reached.

Ceiling—this is your spending limit. In traditional plans, when you spend more than a certain amount of money on covered medical care in a year (usually several thousand dollars), your insurance company steps in and picks up the **entire** cost of covered medical care for the remainder of the year.

Preexisting Condition—If you are stricken with or are treated for a medical problem before your insurance coverage begins (not before you buy insurance), you have a preexisting condition. Insurers will charge you up the wazoo, if they deign to cover you at all. The more severe the condition, the less likely you are to find insurance. For example, a pregnant woman will probably find insurance, but people who are HIV positive are frequently denied coverage.

COMMON INSURANCE PLANS

Usually, the following insurance plans are provided only to groups of customers, most commonly through your employee benefits plan. You may hear their initials bandied around a lot and wonder what the heck the difference between them is. This may help clear things up.

A **Health Maintenance Organization (HMO)**—is formed by several health-care providers. You pay a premium, and receive comprehensive health care with no or very low copayments. A visit to the doctor, for example, can be as cheap as five bucks. HMO enrollees usually choose a primary care doctor from a list of member physicians. These plans frequently operate in a clinic setting, emphasize preventative care and are generous about physical exams and other procedures pooh-poohed by traditional insurance companies. They rarely pay for visits to doctors or hospitals outside the HMO and can be stingy about medical tests and consultations with specialists.

Individual Practice Association— very much like a standard HMO, except that IPA doctors practice from their own offices and not in a clinic situation.

Preferred Provider Organizations— Unlike HMOs, people who are enrolled in a PPO pay for their medical care at reduced prices. They can see doctors outside the PPO if they choose to, but in that case they will pay more out of pocket for their care.

Blue Cross & Blue Shield—These old battle-axes are known in the insurance world simply as "the blues." They are state-regulated, usually nonprofit, and offer a range of insurance plans. In most blues, you can enroll as an individual, but you may get the blues if you do, because of **community rating**.

Whatever plan you choose, you must know how much you are spending on it, and what care will be covered before you really need it.

OTHER KINDS OF INSURANCE

Although it gets far less attention, **disability insurance** is often grouped together with health insurance in group plans. Pay attention to it. If you are stricken with sleeping sickness or are trampled by a herd of panicked gnus while walking across the savanna, your disability insurance will replace the income you would have earned while you were working. That's a good deal, especially when you are living from paycheck to paycheck. Like health insurance, it's very expensive to get disability on your own. But if you are bossless, you may be able to get it through a trade or professional association.

You probably already know this, but **car insurance** is another must-have. In fact, it's usually obligatory. Just how much and what kind you must have depends on the state where you live. Some states, for example, require you to take out insurance that protects you if you are involved in an accident with a motorist who is uninsured. All car insurance should include both property damage and bodily damage—that is, it should help you repair the other person's car, and the other person, after an accident. You may only want to take those two options now, because it will keep your costs down. But then, collision insurance is a very good thing to have, too, because under it your car repair is covered even if the accident was your fault.

When you buy a new car, you should think about getting comprehensive auto insurance that will also protect it from theft and all manner of natural disaster. If you took out a car loan to buy your DeLorean, you are probably required to by the bank.

Whether you live alone or are the high priestess of your own communal cult, you should invest in **renter's insurance** for your possessions—it usually costs about $200 annually, but much depends on where you live. Renter's insurance protects your belongings from theft, fire and other depredations likely to hit your apartment or rented house.

When you buy a renter's policy, always have your belongings insured for their **replacement cost**. Obviously the Macintosh your mother bought you in 1987 is worth about two Polish zlotys today, so if it's stolen, you need to be insured for the cost of replacing it with a new computer, not its current, or **depreciated** value. Some insurers will even replace your computer, television or stereo for you.

5. YOUR FIRST TIME—INVESTING

It will happen. If you work at it, someday you'll be able to cobble away enough money in savings for emergencies and even have a little extra to play around with. You'll have finally put yourself on a budget and made sure the money you make doesn't exceed the money you spend. Your big debts will be gone, or greatly reduced. And you'll be a happier, saner human being.

When things start coming together, you may be ready to start shopping for other kinds of investments, which will put your money to work and add to your income.

This book is not designed to tell you how to play the market or make your first trillion. And you will certainly have to turn to other resources for a truly comprehensive course in investing. But we can give you a few of the basics. It all boils down to this:

investing is taking money you earn now and making it work for you so you'll have more later, hopefully much more.

Again, you can start investing immediately by simply saving some of your money.

You may be light-years away from paying your daughter's tuition and sorority dues, and wearing ultra-suede pant suits and doing the limbo at a retirement home may be the last thing on your mind. But there are more immediate concerns worth putting money aside for. You may

find you can erase big debts faster by investing, or make money toward a future car or condominium. Investing well can give you the funds you need to travel across Africa, or cushion the blow if you lose your job. It's a critical part of the financial safety net you need to design for yourself. Nobody else is going to do it.

A FEW BASICS

The world of investing is a very complicated place. Maybe your father sat you down on his knee and went over the financial page of the newspaper with you when you were still spitting up Gerber's—if so, count yourself among the lucky ones. Most people, especially young people, tune out when they start hearing words like **Bull**, **Bear**, and **Dow Jones** industrial average. Whether you dabble in the market or not, what happens in the economy is obviously of critical importance in your life—it affects nearly every aspect of it, from what food you buy to where you work.

Start tuning into the financial news, and stop turning away from that most unloved piece of the paper, the business section. There aren't a lot of colorful pictures, and the vocabulary can be unfamiliar, but try and wade through it just the same. Business stories are filled with adventure, power struggles and even passion, though it may not be readily apparent. You don't have to understand everything right away—by simply making the effort to follow a business story in the news, you'll begin to pick things up.

If you have made a habit of ignoring newspapers, news magazines and broadcast news up until now,

snap out of it.

National newspapers and weekly news magazines are rich sources of business news that an average Joe can understand. Financial magazines and journals are out there by the dozen— many publish articles and special supplements aimed at young investors.

The personal finance section of any bookstore is also stuffed to overflowing with guides to money management and investing. We aren't talking about the book by some sleazeball who made a million bucks selling government cheese who wants to tell you his patented steps to world domination. Skip his infomercial, too. There are no shortcuts. We are talking about generalized guides to understanding the market, which define different investment strategies and explain the advantages and disadvantages of each.

In addition, you may went to enroll in a night finance class at a local college and, at some point, speak to a broker about the finer points and good investment strategies. A **broker**, in case you don't know, acts as the middleman or agent in an investment transaction, selling and buying stocks for people like yourself. He gets a commission.

Much of investing basically comes down to lending and gambling.

When you buy a government savings bond, or put your money in a CD account, you are **lending** an institution your money, usually at a fixed rate of interest. You might say they are *renting* your money from you, to build aircraft carriers or finance mortgages.

This kind of loan is known to investors as a **debt instrument**. There are a great variety of people out there who want your money, including cities, states, government agencies, private corporations and banks. Bonds, for example, are debt instruments. A municipal bond is a loan to a public authority, and a corporate bond is a loan to a private company. They pay you rent on your money in the form of interest. Think of "my word is my **bond**." A bond is an IOU from the financial institution you lent money to.

Among the loans you can make are **Treasury Bills**, or T-Bills, which help run the federal government, and plain old savings accounts. The money you put into any investment is called the **principal**, and investments differ in terms of their **liquidity**. In plain English, liquidity refers to how easily you can convert your investment into cash. Think of some villain out of James Bond—"you vill be liquidated." When you liquidate an investment, you zap it and take your money. Savings accounts are an example of an investment with very high liquidity— because you aren't penalized for closing one at any time. But most investments aren't like that.

Generally speaking, when you invest your money by loaning it to others, you take less risk than when you **gamble**, most commonly

You vill be liquidated."

give investors the best return on their investment over time, but obviously you need good counsel, patience and a little luck to make bucks this way.

The oft-referred to **Dow Jones Industrial Average** is the average of stock prices for 30 companies listed on the New York Stock Exchange. A **Bull Market** refers to the feeling that stock prices will rise, and a **Bear Market** is the exact opposite. Stocks and bonds are both referred to as **securities**, and the policing of the whole business of buying and selling them

by buying shares of stock in a corporation. The gambling side of the investment market is usually referred to as putting your money into an **equity instrument**. In such cases you are buying a piece of a business, no matter how minute. Companies sell stocks to raise money, and earnings from stock are called **dividends**. How much you earn depends on how well the business does.

While loaning money through debt instruments usually guarantees you are paid some interest on your investment, no matter what, equity instruments are where seasoned investors earn big money. But gambling doesn't necessarily equal high stakes, white knuckles and Florida swampland—the lower a roller you are, the less likely it is you will be involved in anything remotely resembling those sorts of hijinks. Few fledgling investors are ruined by their first foray into the stock market. Stocks are considered by most experts to

is handled by the Securities and Exchange Commission, or **SEC**. Every once in a while some high roller breaks the SEC's rules and, gets in a whole mess of trouble, which is about the only time many people even think about the world of high finance for a heartbeat. Securities dealers police themselves through the N.A.S.D. (National Association of Securities Dealers).

This is just the very teensiest tip of the iceberg in the world of investing. And remember, **no matter where you invest your money, you are taking some risk**. A poor grandmother with only a savings account and government savings bonds may be risking less than a Wall Street power player, but she's also not earning a great deal in interest, and taxes and inflation eat away at her investment. The Wall Street hotshot who's dabbling in all sorts of high-risk investments can be making a killing, but he could lose thousands, even

187

millions of dollars. What **you** risk ultimately comes down to your own personality and income.

GET REGULAR

If you **do** buy stocks, you probably know this from the flicks: the aim of playing the stock market is to buy stocks when the price is low and sell them when it is high. Nobody just starting out is really in a position to do this, unless they have a ton of dough and know the market like the back of their tush.

One way to get around this particular conundrum, and save yourself some stress, is to set aside a specific amount of money to buy a company's stock on a regular basis. When the price is high, your money will buy less, and when it's low, it will buy more. It's called **dollar-cost averaging**, and by doing it you will generally pay less on average for shares over time.

Starting out you probably don't need to, but somewhere along the line you may want to speak with a broker, and there are many out there. Generally your interaction with a broker is all over the phone. Be **very** careful about who you choose, and as always, try and dig up any friends, family or colleagues who have had experience with a brokerage firm before going to one. Some are very crusty and fancy, others have branches in malls. A full-service broker will advise a client on where to invest his money and help maintain and strengthen an investment **portfolio** (your combined investments), but charges all kinds of fees for services rendered (and sometimes for services not rendered, too).

When you are just starting out, **discount brokers** offer a cheaper way to fly. They cannot give advice, *per se*, but they can send you analyses of different investment possibilities

and help you set up accounts, place orders to buy and sell stock, give stock quotes and answer general questions about investing.

Any broker you choose must be insured by the Security Investors Protection Corporation, or **SIPC**. The SIPC protects you against fraud, but not against loss of your investment.

KNOW WHAT YOU ARE BUYING

No matter who you speak with, you should **never** put your money into any kind of investment program you haven't fully investigated yourself. If you are buying stock in a company, understand what the company makes, how its products work and read its prospectus. When you truly understand your investment, you greatly reduce your risk.

MUTUAL FUNDS

Many experts consider mutual funds a good way for young people with little experience or knowledge of financial markets to begin investing. In a mutual fund, your money is pooled with that of many other people and invested into a diversified portfolio of securities looked after by a professional money manager. Several mutual funds are often grouped into "families," and if you choose, you can switch your investment from one fund to another within a family, as your investment objectives change.

When you participate in a mutual fund, you share profits, losses and expenses depending on your investment. While the principal you are required to invest in a mutual fund varies, it can be very low—some funds only require an *initial* investment of around $10. You can find out about mutual funds through a broker, or you can save yourself the broker's commission and contact a mutual-fund management company yourself (funds you can invest in without paying commissions are called "no-load" funds). There are a jillion fund companies out there, and they generally have 800 numbers. Again, their investment requirements and fees vary widely, so it pays to dig around for the best deal.

You can purchase a comprehensive directory of mutual funds from the Investment Company Institute, a fund trade association, for $8.50. They also offer a mutual-fund fact book for $25 and a host of other pamphlets on investing. ICI can be reached by telephone at (202) 326-5800 or at the address below:

Investment Company Institute
1401 H Street, NW, Suite 1100
Washington, DC 20005

If you can't get your head around any of this yet, or simply don't see how you could possibly invest a cent when you haven't got enough for chocolate milk, don't worry. We are not going to depress you with stories of boy zillionaires who took 50 cents from their weekly allowance and turned it into a global empire through wise investments.

Just keep working toward making that **first investment** we mentioned—in yourself. The more **skills** you **acquire** and the more money you **save**, the **better off financially** you are likely to be.

189

6. CREDIT-CARD HELL—

> "when I was in college, some guy handed me a water bottle or something and I signed up for a credit card. it took me a little while to bail myself out of the mess I got into." –
>
> —Kyle, baker

> "It's mind-boggling the kind of debt kids get into now. kids have no idea what TRW means when they get a credit card."
>
> —Roger Witherspoon, Vice President for Student Development at John Jay College of Criminal Justice, who has campaigned to keep credit-card hawkers away from campus

Maybe when you were in college, or even high school, a **snazzy** little envelope came with your name on it. Inside was a **credit card** with your name on it, **preapproved.** All you had to do was sign it.

Jackpot.

Free money. Your passport to adulthood was stamped.

191

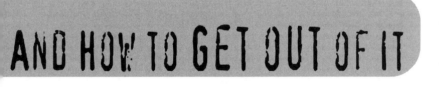

AND HOW TO GET OUT OF IT

You started charging up a blue streak, and you've been going strong ever since. More cards came in the mail, and when you couldn't pay the bills in full, you just started paying off the minimum balance each month. Now you are just a step ahead of a collection agency, with mounting bills, a total credit-card debt equal to the entire gross national product of Rwanda, and no way to pay it all back.

Welcome to Credit-Card Hell.

Americans are choking on plastic. It used to be next to impossible for people with little in the way of income or work experience to get their hands on a credit card. Now, by the time your braces are off, the mailbox is often crammed to overflowing with offers for jillions of cards. And then there are the cards you can get to shop at your favorite department store, or to fill up on gas and beef jerky treats when you hit the highway. Pretty soon you are carrying thousands of dollars of credit debt on your back, often along with thousands in student loans.

According to Gerri Detweiler, an expert on young people and plastic, creditors go after young people with such zeal for four principal reasons:

1. **The rest of the market is saturated—the average American lugs around eight to ten pieces of plastic in his wallet.**

2. **When you can't pay your bills, your parents will often come to the rescue and pay them for you.**

3. **The average credit-card holder pays more than $400 a year in interest—a regular gravy train for credit-card companies.**

4. **People usually stay loyal to their first credit card. Lenders fall over themselves sending you offers because they want you to be with them for life.**

Credit is seductive, and it's dangerous. You may have already discovered just how dangerous it can be. The irony is that even as we choke on bigger and bigger debt, good credit is increasingly important in this society. Without good credit, it becomes extremely difficult to rent or own a home, buy a car, and in some cases, get a job. Those are just the big-ticket items. There are hundreds of little everyday transactions that demand you have a major credit card.

Don't be a passive consumer when it comes to credit cards. Make educated choices about which is the best card for you. And if you get yourself into trouble, know how to bail yourself out. There are ways to do it, and the more quickly you act, the better off you—and your credit rating—will be.

Different Kinds of Plastic

There are different breeds of credit card, and they don't all behave in the same way. Know the differences before you sign on the dotted line.

Bankcards
Are what most people think of when they think credit card. **Visa and MasterCard** *enter into franchise agreements with banks and other lending institutions, which use their names and set their own rates and terms. There are Visas and MasterCards issued by everyone from your company credit union to political parties to universities. It makes no difference if your credit card is affiliated with Big Swanky Bank or Mr. Piddly's Bank—these cards can be used practically anywhere under the sun. Annual fees vary from none to some quite steep.*

Discover *is the new kid on the block. Generally speaking, it behaves like other bankcards, but it's not yet as widely accepted as Visa or MasterCard. There is no annual fee.*

American Express
As you probably know, American Express is not a credit card, but a "charge" card. You cannot carry a balance on an American Express card — you must pay your entire bill each month. Many people prefer American Express cards because they force them to charge responsibly; others hate the rigidity of having to pay up all at once.

American Express also offers the **Optima** *card, which behaves more like a regular credit card—you can carry a balance on it.*

Special Charge Cards and Gas Cards
These cards are limited to use at the retailers that issue them, be it a posh department store or a chain of filling stations. Store charge cards allow you to carry a balance on purchases, but at a high rate of interest. They show up on credit reports. A straight gas card must be paid off monthly and usually does not show up on a credit report.

Frankly, a credit card, if used wisely, is great. It is safer than money to carry, virtually essential for travel and always there when you need cash fast in an emergency. Most important, without one it will be very hard to build up a strong **credit history**, the record of how you have handled your finances over the years. Having no credit is much the same as having bad credit—institutions will not take a risk on you because they don't know if you are good for it.

Notice how we said A credit card. Not credit cards.

You may think a wallet overflowing with plastic makes you look like Aaron Spelling. You may think it equals a pocketful of glamour and good times. **Kick yourself very hard if you do.** You do not need more than one major credit card. Somebody rolling in positively sick amounts of dough can afford to have a few more lying around. You cannot.

More cards mean more bills to keep track of, more opportunities to get in trouble, more headaches. What's more, your 25 credit cards may actually *prevent* you from getting a loan you really need. That's right, even lenders don't see all that plastic and think financial prestige. They see 25 other bills you may not have the money to pay in addition to your car payment.

If you are juggling debt on several cards already, your main mission should be to pay off any outstanding balances and cancel those suckers. Keep the card that gives you the best deal on interest rates, annual fees and other charges (more on them in a bit). If you absolutely must have more than one, consider making it one with the lowest interest rate. Put your extra card in a place where you can't grab it to buy Chinese takeout, Stryper CDs, polyester active wear and other fun stuff. Swear to yourself to take it out only in a dire emergency.

SHOP AROUND

When it wasn't busy chain-sawing the rainforest and throwing old ladies out of their slum apartments, Megabank deigned to send you an application for a credit card. Or maybe you were accosted by some smiling young fellow handing out free Megabank visors near your school.

That card came with all kinds of perks. Frequent-flier-mile credit, the ability to get extra cards, a fancy water bottle, a convertible sports car, a cabin by a lake, and a big can of macadamia nuts. How can you turn them down? Heck, it's **Megabank**. Everyone knows they are the biggest hitter on Wall Street. Flash their card, and you'll be munching on caviar at the captain's table, right?

In truth, the first credit card you receive is probably sagging under high interest rates and crushing annual fees—a potential debt monster from the word go. And don't get smitten by frequent-flier miles if it means saddling yourself with stratospheric fees.

When you were a student, you may have gone with Megabank, been charged up the yin-yang for everything under the sun and not even really noticed. Start paying attention. After you have been using your card a while, paying those bills and keeping your nose clean, shop around for a card that offers you better terms.

Credit-Card Safety

Sure it's an albatross around your neck, but it's your albatross. Make sure you keep it that way. Protect your credit card by doing the following:

- *Keep your card number hush-hush. It's all people need to start charging up a storm on your tab. Never give it to people who hawk things over the phone, for example. You have no idea if the person calling is legitimate.*

- *Call the company immediately if your card is lost or stolen.*

- *Consider having your picture put on your credit card as an extra protection measure if your issuer offers that option.*

- *Read your statement carefully every month to make sure all the charges are yours and contact the card company immediately if they are not.*

- *Save all your credit-card receipts to match against the charges on your statement.*

- *Save all statements and relevant correspondence between yourself and the card issuer.*

- *Keep a record of all your credit cards in case they are stolen. You can register your cards with a card-protection service. Many credit card companies offer a service where you can register all of your credit cards with them for a fee—if your wallet is stolen the company will alert all the other creditors. You can do this on your own and avoid the fee. (The Bankcard Holders of America, a national advocacy group for credit-card holders, also offers this service to its members.)*

- *Never carry all of your credit cards around with you if you have more than one, unless you need to.*

- *Inform the issuer when you cancel your credit card. Send them a letter along with the old card cut in half.*

If you find a better deal, forget about being faithful. No matter what its brochure says, Megabank does not care about you. You are just another ant to bleed dry and squash under the cruel boot of capitalism. Save yourself some cool ones and ditch them.

The glossy ads don't say this, but **a credit card is a loan**. You are not getting anything for free. You are borrowing money from a bank. For that privilege, it is billing you for all sorts of things. And making out like a bandit.

Before you sign any credit-card agreement, get out your magnifying glass and **READ THE FINE PRINT**. Find out whether your card charges you an **annual fee**, and how much it is. This is especially important if you are a member of the mature, sane and fast-dwindling number of people who pay off their entire credit-card bill every month.

ANNUAL FEES

You may be charged a hefty yearly sum just for carrying your credit card around. Beware of card sharks who play up the fact that they charge low interest rates and then whop you with massive annual fees. You can easily shell out $50 or more a year for the honor of having a credit card, but you don't have to. There are cards out there with annual fees as low as $15, and some with no fees at all.

In addition to annual fees, banks tack on charges when you spend over your credit limit, and for late payments and getting a cash advance, among other things. It's your responsibility to wade through your contract with a bank and find out what you may be billed for. Once you use your credit card, you have entered into a legal contract and are bound to the terms of your agreement.

GRACE PERIODS

Very little about credit cards is that simple to understand, except signing your name for the next purchase. Your credit card may trumpet its generous grace period. Sounds great, but do you really understand what it is? What it *isn't* is the number of days you have to pay your credit-card bill from the time you get it in the mail.

A grace period refers to the time in which no interest is charged on purchases you made with your credit card. Frequently, banks give you 25 days from the date of your billing to make payment with no interest. Some give you no grace period at all—from the minute you buy that macramé wrap, they start heaping on charges.

Generally, when you have a zero balance on your credit card—that is, you have paid off last month's bill in **full**—you pay no interest on things you bought during the current billing period. On the other hand, if you carry a balance from the previous month, you accumulate interest on *all* your new purchases, plus everything you already owe. Thud.

The length of time you have in a grace period is not necessarily what is written on your credit-card agreement. Much depends on when in your billing cycle you pay. Pay late in your cycle, and your interest-free clock may have less days on it. Pay before it starts ticking, and you may buy yourself more grace time.

In most cases, interest collects immediately if you take out a cash advance. (See inset.) Be wary of them.

INTEREST RATES

Interest is where credit-card issuers really make the big smackers. Here's an eye-opening statistic from the Bank Card Holders of America (BHA), a national advocacy group for credit-card holders:

IN 1995, MANY LENDERS BORROWED MONEY AT AROUND A FIVE PERCENT RATE. THEY TURNED AROUND AND LENT THAT MONEY TO US POOR SLOBS CARRYING THEIR CREDIT CARDS AT RATES THAT FREQUENTLY BRUSHED UP INTO THE 20 PERCENT RANGE. THINK ABOUT IT. CAN YOU SAY "GOLD MINE"?

195

Lines of Credit

If there is one nook of credit-land that's more profitable to lenders than when you get hooked into only paying the minimum balance, it's when you ask them to extend you a line of credit or cash advance.

Cash advances sound good—you are out of cash and your credit-card company loans you a lump sum on the spot. In many cases it's as simple as stepping up to an ATM, or filling out "convenience checks" issued by your card company.

Unfortunately, when you get a cash advance from your creditor you frequently must pay it back at high rates of interest. In almost all cases, cash advances come with no grace period—that means you could be owing interest on your loan from the minute you get the money. And finally, you may be charged a cash advance fee for the transaction.

You may be better off going to the Gambino crime family for a quick infusion of dough.

If you expect to be able to pay off your balance in full every month, then interest rates are not as important as annual fees and grace periods. But if you are a sad member of the mall-addicted masses who carry a balance on their credit cards, take heed. **The rate of interest you pay on your credit-card debt is of critical importance to you.**

Your credit-card company is required by law to tell you what interest rate it is charging you. It should be listed on its glossy brochures and in your agreement. It is usually expressed as an annual percentage rate, or **APR**. Interest rates vary wildly from card to card. Some bargain-basement cards offer rates as low as 12 percent, while many others skyrocket right into the twenties. Many people consider a card with an interest rate squarely in the mid-teens to be a good deal. If you have an established credit history you *may* be able to negotiate a lower rate of interest on a card simply by calling up your creditor and asking for one.

To make matters worse, the APR stated on a credit-card application may only tell part of the story. It doesn't take into account the effect of other fees you may incur and something nasty called *compounding interest*. **In plain English, not only is your credit-card company taking you to the cleaners for paying the minimum balance, it's most likely charging you interest on the interest you've racked up.**

To find out whether your creditor compounds interest, the BHA recommends you read the portion of your credit-card agreement that discusses finance charges. When *finance charges* are included as part of the *"average daily balance,"* that's a nice way of saying they are going to give you the old double whammy.

It's easy to get yourself buried by revolving debt if you're seduced by

the idea of making minimum payments to your creditor. Interest always accrues on unpaid balances. You may only have to pay a tiny percentage of your debt each month to avoid getting into trouble with your credit-card company, but you are digging yourself a hole. Pay only the minimum, and you may barely cover the *interest* on your deficit, let alone chip away at the big amount.

Do yourself a favor. Try to **pay** your credit-card bill off **on time, in full, every month.**

DEALING WITH CREDIT DEBT

If you are in debt, don't panic. Debt is as American as good old-fashioned carjacking. You cannot expect to be able to pay for everything up front in life, it's far too expensive. Houses, automobiles and education cost a lot of money. You may be paying for these things for a long time, but they are good investments.

Credit-card debt is just bad news. For the cost of mostly short-term material fixes, you can get in way over your head and harm your chances of getting the things you want out of life. Nip it in the bud. You'll sleep better. Start by getting one of the most important documents in our society, one that few of us ever take the time to examine. Your credit report.

THIS WILL GO DOWN ON YOUR PERMANENT RECORD: CREDIT BUREAUS

Your financial history is regularly reported to at least one of the three major credit bureaus: TRW, Trans Union and Equifax. Their evil computers take note of every significant transaction you make. Whether you pay bills late, default on a loan, declare yourself bankrupt or are chased by a collections agency—all those nasty little stains on your reputation get diligently recorded.

If a landlord, employer or lender wants a detailed financial summary about you, they merely have to contact a credit bureau and they'll get one, lickety-split. A checkered credit history drives opportunities out the door. Employers are even using credit checks to evaluate people before they hire them.

To make matters worse, when you are rejected because of bad credit, the fact that you were denied is most likely going to be recorded as well. That will make a lousy report even lousier. And here's the kicker—an unsightly blemish stays on your credit history for **seven years.**

Since credit reports can play such a powerful role in your financial life, there's no excuse to be in the dark about what's on your own. **Request a copy of your report from the Big Three credit bureaus.**

Because they each operate independently of one another, you'll need to get your records from all of them. Credit bureaus are now required to send you a copy of your credit report every two years for no more than three dollars a pop, free if you're denied credit, a victim of credit fraud or on welfare.

Get a credit report even if you haven't been turned down for credit, or aren't about to buy a big-ticket item. Know the score before you get zapped, not after. Try and go over your report at least once every two years. There may be mistakes on it that could harm you, and you'll need time to straighten them out separately with each bureau. Even when your record is sterling, you'll know exactly what information has been collected about you.

Addresses for the Big Three Credit Bureaus

To obtain your record, you'll need to supply your name, Social Security number, home and work phones, date of birth and your addresses for the past five years to each of the three major credit bureaus.

If you think there's some doddering old lady thumbing through file cabinets to retrieve your records at these places, you're wrong. It's virtually impossible to talk to a human being when you contact credit bureaus. Your data is thrown together at the touch of a button by rooms full of computers. Unfortunately, they have thoroughly insulated themselves from sweet talk.

Equifax Information Service Center
PO Box 105873
Atlanta, GA 30348
(800) 685-1111

Trans Union Consumer Relations Center
25249 Country Club Blvd.
PO Box 7000
North Olmstead, OH 44070
(800) 851-2674

TRW Consumer Assistance Center*
PO Box 2350
Chatsworth, CA 91313-2350
(800) 682-7654

*TRW will send you one free credit report a year.

CREDIT DISPUTES

After college, Nick traveled across South America for five months. He arranged for his stepfather to pay any credit-card charges he made while he was away, and he had bills forwarded to that address. Unfortunately, in the middle of his extended holiday, his stepfather's employer transferred him to another state.

The post office forwarded all the family mail—except Nick's credit-card bill for $300. Because he didn't share his stepfather's last name, it was chucked back to the credit-card company, return to sender. In the rush of the move, his stepfather had forgotten all about the credit-card obligation. For his part, Nick continued to merrily trek across Patagonia, ride llamas in the Bolivian Andes and sun himself in an indecent bathing suit on Ipanema.

When Nick returned to the States, he attempted to use his credit card, and it was seized. Just one day before, the credit-card company had closed his account and sent his $300 bill to a collection agency. Thus alerted, Nick took care of the debt immediately. But that was only the beginning of his problems. Despite the fact that he'd never paid a single credit-card bill late in the past and was an all-around prince of a guy, he could not get credit bureaus to erase the blot from his record.

A credit counselor explained that the bureaus would continue to show the black mark until his credit-card company stopped confirming the information as correct, which technically it was. He had been late on his payments, after all, though through no fault of his own. Nick tried to explain his situation to the credit-card company, but no actual human beings seemed to work there. Exhausted by months of endless letters and repeated forays into the companies' vast voice-mail network, he gave up. Nick was stuck with the mark on his record for seven years.

Lenders and credit bureaus aren't easily swayed by sob stories, no matter how good a case you have. A credit-card company may have tried hard to seem warm and fuzzy before, when it was trying to win your business. Once you get into a jam, most of them mutate into a big blank wall of bureaucracy.

If you find an actual numbers *error* on your credit report—say, charges you never made—you will probably

have an easier time of it than Nick did. But even some simple disputes with creditors can turn into grueling experiences. A big credit-card company has time, money and loads of other people to torment. They expect you to curl up and die.

The credit bureau itself only collects and verifies information. If you find an error in your credit report, you must fill out the dispute form attached to it and send in evidence that supports your case. The bureau will then go back and check with your creditors, and if they back up your story, the false information will be removed. Remember, you must contact the other credit-reporting agencies to ensure that all three have the correct data.

If the disputed item is confirmed by the bureau's sources, the information stays. Period. You are, however, entitled to write a statement of 100 words or less to go along with your credit report. In it, you should be direct and businesslike. Clearly outline the nature of your dispute, or explain dispassionately the reasons why you were unable to pay your bills. No tearstains, curses or threats of divine retribution.

Writing the statement certainly can't hurt. It can make you feel a little bit vindicated when you feel you've been horribly wronged. Here's your chance to logically and eloquently take apart your creditor. But there's no guarantee people reading your credit report will pay any attention to it. In fact, many experts say the vermin probably won't.

While you are haranguing the credit bureaus, you should direct a second prong of attack toward the creditor who reported you. This is where the real power lies, and where somewhere—deep down, partially buried by a thicket of computer terminals—is a real live customer-service person who you just might be able to talk to and reason with.

Be a **pest.** Lodge a **complaint.**

If these people have screwed up, you have every right to be furious. Their error could be very costly to you. Naturally, yelling and screaming at the poor functionaries who are paid to answer complaints won't get you as far as an endless stream of polite, reasoned arguments. Write a letter detailing the problem. As with every other piece of correspondence regarding your credit, you should keep a copy for your own files.

Remember to send the creditor copies of everything you sent to the credit bureau. Start working the phone until you find someone who can help you. You just may be able to simply exhaust a credit-card company into accepting your point of view—keep after them.

Consider consulting a lawyer if you can afford it. A nice legal-sounding missive stating your case can be an effective weapon in a credit fight. Credit counseling services, and state and local consumer protection agencies can also offer good advice.

DIGGING YOURSELF OUT OF DEBT

If you incur debts you can't pay, the sooner you act to solve the problem, the better. If the creditor sends your

bill to a collection agency, you have waited too long. Whenever you think you are going to be late with a payment or cannot make a bill, **call your credit-card company**. Before they send you threatening letters or slap on penalty fees, you may be able to work out a payment schedule between the two of you. If you are surrounded on all sides by people who want money from you, consider going to a **credit counselor** (see inset on page 200).

The first thing you need to do to get yourself out of trouble is count. Tally up exactly how much you owe, and who you owe it to. Sounds easy enough, but you probably wouldn't have gotten into so much trouble if you had a clear sense of how much money you were spending, right? If you have multiple credit cards, it's time to start retiring them. Try and move your debt to a nicer neighborhood—you should be able to transfer your balance from a high-interest-rate card to one with a lower one. Talk to your creditors about it.

When you do decide to retire a card, officially end the relationship with your credit-card company with a letter stating your wish to cancel the card. As with any correspondence, keep a copy of the letter for your files. It need only be a brief statement, sent to the customer-service department at the company's billing address, with your card enclosed, cut in half. **You are under no obligation to keep a credit card you don't want—even if you still owe the issuer money.** You can keep paying your debt back after you have canceled the card, thus freeing yourself from annual fees and some other charges. If you have been in a bad-credit scrape, you'll need to start repairing your credit rating. It isn't simply a matter of

Allies in the Credit Wars

Whether you need help managing your debt, have a question about a dispute with a creditor or simply want to find a better deal on a card, you may want to ask these people for help. They know the credit world inside and out.

The Bankcard Holders of America (BHA)
524 Branch Drive
Salem, VA 24153
(540) 389-5445

The BHA is dedicated to informing the public about their credit rights and the potential perils of credit cards. They publish helpful brochures aimed at educating you about using credit wisely, and maintain lists of secured, low-interest and no-fee credit cards. They also offer a personalized debt repayment plan called DEBT ZAPPER.

Consumer Credit Counseling Services (CCCS)
*More than 500 branches nationwide
Call 1 (800) 388-2227
or check your local directory*

A nonprofit agency funded by creditors, CCCS are experts at bailing people out of serious debt. A counselor will help you work out a repayment schedule, develop a budget and, best of all, CUT UP your troublesome cards into little plastic pieces—it's the glamorous part of the job. They can also advise you if you have questions about pursuing a credit dispute.

If you have questions about your treatment at the hands of a creditor, you might also want to contact your state or local **Office of Consumer Affairs or Consumer Protection Agency.** *The people there may be able to advise you or point you in the direction of someone who can.* **Your** *bank or credit union may also be of help. One shot might be the local* **university**—*some run workshops on credit for students.*

into the background, the less damage it can do. But if it's sitting there by itself, with no recent examples of good credit to demonstrate your trustworthiness, you can have a tough time just the same.

How do you get good credit? By being scrupulous about paying your remaining bills on time, for a start. If you have lost all your credit cards because of debt, it's going to be difficult getting a new one to use occasionally and demonstrate you can pay back in full, which can be very therapeutic for an ailing credit history.

Consider applying for a **secured** credit card if you can afford to. With these cards, you deposit a couple of hundred dollars as a kind of security deposit with a bank or credit union, and you are issued a line of credit based upon it. Secured cards usually have higher rates of interest, but they operate like unsecured bankcards in most other ways. Using this kind of card every once in a while can help you build your good credit back up, so that you can apply for a standard credit card down the line without getting dinged. Some secured cards can be transformed into a regular Visa or MasterCard after a certain period. One last note on secured cards—you want one that appears on your credit history as a *regular* credit card, not the kind that is reported to credit bureaus with a notation that says "secured." The second type will do your credit record no good at all. There are a good many secured cards that do not betray your special status to the Big Three. Check the card's literature or ask before you sign up; otherwise, you may further jeopardize your credit rating.

Again, in order to keep yourself on the straight and narrow, rediscover **CASH**. Pay in greenbacks whenever you can. Whether you are in debt trouble or not, you should always try to pay cash for groceries, music, movies, sale items and going out to

waiting until your seven years is up. After all, it's possible you may want or need something that requires a credit check before then. The farther your bad-credit experience recedes eat. These things were made for cash. Use it, and hold your credit card for special purchases.

When you do use your credit card, keep tabs on your spending. It's easy to lose track of your purchases on a credit card. Try and write down every charge you make when you make it, and you won't have any surprises when your bill arrives. Last, set **yourself** a credit limit; don't just go along with the issuer's figure. If you feel that you cannot afford to charge more than $100 a month, then draw that line in the sand, even if your "official" limit is more than ten times that.

And please, do what your mother has been begging you to do since she gave you your first dollar for taking out the garbage. Put yourself on a budget. It's tiresome, boring, dullsville, soul-destroying, enough to send you spiraling into a coma. Why not just take things as they come and live life? Because, if you take the time to wrestle control over your money, you will feel more in control of your destiny, and ultimately you'll earn both more freedom and increased peace of mind.

7. JOUSTING WITH THE TAX MAN

"The hardest thing in the world to understand is income tax."
—Albert Einstein

"Only little people pay taxes." —Leona Helmsley

Taxes have been a **monkey on the back** of humankind for **ages,** and they **aren't going away** anytime soon, no matter what Rush Limbaugh says.

If you make $20,000 a year, your actual take-home pay is much lower—in the mid-teens—after income tax, FICA (The Federal Insurance Compensation Act—your Social Security and Medicare tax) and others chomp into your paycheck. All in all, 15 percent or more of your money is zapped before you ever see it. You may not like it, but you'll have to accept it. Grumble all you want—without taxes we wouldn't have efficient interstate highways, a beautiful national parks system or the Smithsonian.

WHICH FORMS TO USE

People are often needlessly bewildered and intimidated by tax forms.

You can use a 1040-EZ form if you meet these requirements:

• Your taxable income is less than $50,000 a year.

• You don't have any rug rats (you cannot claim any dependents on this form)

• You earned less than $400 in interest income (sorry, Trust Fund babies)

• You are under 65, and aren't blind.

There are a few other guidelines for using the 1040-EZ, but these are perhaps the most important. When you are just starting your career, chances are you can fill one out. Better still, many people are now eligible to complete their 1040-EZ by telephone, mercifully liberated from all paperwork (to qualify you must have filled out a 1040-EZ in the previous tax year and reside at the same address—the IRS will send you information).

If, however, you are earning loads of interest from money stashed in various accounts or are scoring *any* dividends from investments—say from stocks or a mutual fund—you will have to use form **1040A**, and fill out the schedule (IRS for *yet another form*) attached asking for information about this income.

Self-employed people have still more hoops to jump through. They must pay their *estimated* taxes quarterly. That means if you are a freelance writer or the proprietor of your own locksmith business, you have to fill out an IRS form four times a year—in April, June, September and January. Why? Because an employer is not withholding any funds from your

Before you go running off in a panic to an accountant, force yourself to read through various forms and their accompanying booklets. Scary as they look, they are generally pretty simple to understand. The best thing about struggling to make it on a frightfully low salary is that in most cases you'll be able to fill out the simplest form of all—the fabulous **1040-EZ**. It's a breeze.

paycheck, so you have to try and guess how much money you'll earn each quarter, and pay tax on it.

For the April 15th tax due date, the appropriate schedules for independent contractors are found with IRS form **1040**. Hey, nobody said being a lone wolf was easy—there's no question that going into business on your own makes filing more complicated than running with the pack. The IRS publishes a booklet, **Publication 505, Tax Withholding and Estimated Tax**, that is designed to help independent contractors negotiate the quarterly payment morass. Remember, it's *especially* important for self-employed persons to hang on to all receipts for business expenses over the year—you may quality for certain tax deductions. If you earn *capital gains*, that is when you make money by selling an investment, say by unloading stock or selling your home, you must also fill out a **1040**.

Try to get your tax forms well in advance of the month of April. February 1st is a good deadline—you will have all your documents together, even if you put off completing them to the last minute. Generally, you can expect to receive a tax packet in the mail if you filed before (and live at the same address). But you can also get tax forms and special schedules you may need from the public library, the post office and the IRS itself.

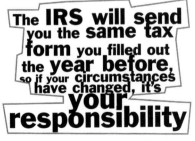
The **IRS will send** you the **same tax form** you **filled out** the **year before**, so if your circumstances have changed, it's **your responsibility**

to find out exactly what new forms you need to fill out and send in.

When you have questions about your tax status and what forms you should use, the very best source of good advice and information is the tax man himself. You can call your local IRS office, visit an agency branch that has walk-in hours, or call the Tele-Tax numbers listed in your tax packet for prerecorded answers to more than 100 questions. The IRS also offers these two national hotlines:

• 1-800-TAX-FORM
(to request specific forms)

• 1-800-TAX-1040
(for questions and advice)

There is also an IRS web site, where you can access specific tax forms from your computer:
http://www.irs.ustreas.gov

No matter what form you use, you simply have to provide the requested information in the given boxes, do some arithmetic and send it all in by April 15th.

In order to complete your taxes, you'll need a **W-2 Form** from your employer, which details the amount of taxable pay you earned over the year. Nearly every cent you get from work—from vacation pay to bonuses to severance—is taxable. By January 31st, you should receive a W-2 form from **every** employer you worked for during the previous year. Tear off the stub meant to be sent in with your tax forms and keep the remainder of the form for your records.

Naturally, you should not do your taxes in crayon or try to figure your calculations on your fingers. Fill out the forms neatly and accurately. A mistake on your tax form is going to make you wait longer for that most delicious little windfall that comes your way after tax time: the **refund.**

In most cases, the key to panic-free-tax-paying lies with this rule: **have enough money withheld from your paycheck so that when April rolls around, you don't owe the government anything, or very little.** That's right, the best tax strategy is to pay **more** than you owe.

When you fill out your W-4 form at the beginning of a new job, you are offered a host of personal allowances by the government. The *fewer* allowances you claim, the more money the government will take out of your paycheck over the course of the year.

You may think that it would be good to claim as many allowances as possible, and increase the amount of spondoolicks you get each week. But if the government withholds too little tax, you'll have to pay them the difference in April, and very few people on a tight budget can afford to shell out several hundred dollars in taxes in one go. It's far better to have the government owe *you* money, then pay you back in the form of a refund.

Read through the *Personal Allowance* section of your W-4 carefully. If you are single, working only one job and have no dependents, fill in the appropriate boxes. You should have minimal personal allowances, and a lot of money taken right out of your check. Then you'll probably only have to send in a completed tax form, and wait for Uncle Sam to toss you some change after tax time.

There's one wrinkle in the withholding game you should be aware of, though. When the government holds extra money for you, the funds earn no interest. So if a large slice is taken out of your check, you'll be getting back *exactly* what the government owes you, and not a penny more. If you are confused about what

allowances you should claim, the IRS booklet, **Publication 919**, goes into detail about withholding. It can be ordered from the agency 800 numbers or picked up at an IRS office.

One more thing. If you willfully lie to the government about your status, you can get yourself in a whole mess of trouble.

Pity the poor unloved souls who work for the IRS. They beat out meter maids, prison guards and toxic-waste-dump planners when it comes to unpopular civil servants. That's too bad, because for the most part they can be a very helpful lot. If you have a question about how to prepare your taxes, you should not hesitate to call them. After all, your taxes pay their salaries. **That said, few things make the IRS snippier than when you fail to file your return on time.**

You must file a tax return by April 15th. No excuses. If you find yourself in the unhappy position of not being able to pay all your taxes by that date, file anyway. Pay what you can. When you can't make payment in full, you may request an installment payment plan from the IRS (Form 9465). The penalty for late payment is far less stiff than the penalty for late filing— the government punishes you for tardiness in the form of interest on taxes owed—around five percent for late filers, much lower for late payers. If you know you are going to be late, file for an **extension** (Form 4868) before April 15th. That will push your deadline ahead four months. However, you will still be charged interest on unpaid taxes.

THE VERY BEST MOVE IS TO ALWAYS **FILE ON TIME,** AND **AVOID** THE ADDED **HEADACHE.**

Rapid Refund Alert

Many tax-preparation services are now offering a Rapid Refund option—a very sexy little gimmick that you should steer clear of. A service will figure out your taxes and estimated refund, and give you the cash right away, cutting short your tedious wait for a government check. Here's the problem—this isn't a refund at all, but a LOAN. When your real refund check arrives, the money goes to the tax service, with a ton of interest tacked on.

GETTING HELP

Before you break out into a cold sweat, remember that for the vast majority of people just starting out, taxes are a cinch. Simply fill out a couple of forms, send them in and wait for a refund check. As your income grows, and life gets more complicated, you may want to find someone to help prepare your taxes for you. Competent tax professionals are not hard to find, but be choosy—you will be paying them for their services, after all. For the most part, they shouldn't be necessary at this stage in the game. There are several good tax-preparation books out there, which go into great detail about various tax forms, withholdings and due dates. Among them are guides published by J.K. Lasser, Ernst & Young, and Consumer Reports.

Again, if you can't get your head around your taxes, you can always start with the IRS. One program you may want to avail yourself of is Voluntary Income Tax Assistance, or **VITA**. At tax time, volunteers, many of them retired accountants, are available to help you understand and prepare your tax forms in local community centers and other locations. And their wisdom won't cost you a penny. Some IRS branches can also help you file your return electronically (a service provided by many private tax-preparation services for a fee). Ring your local agency office for information about these and other services. No matter who helps you do your taxes, you are held responsible for turning in an accurate return.

KEEP A RECORD

Before you send off your completed tax packet, photocopy all the documents for your files. By this point you should have invested in some sort of cabinet contraption and a copious supply of Manila folders. Tax information is the most important of all your financial records and should be kept for five to seven years. You'll need to have this material handy in case you are audited, and to apply for certain student loans, among other things.

Hopefully, as you grapple with **money** matters in general, you have realized the importance of **good record-keeping.** Without it, you can kiss

any hope of **budgeting** (and long-term sanity) goodbye.

If your credit-card statement shows charges you never made, or your electric company accuses you of not paying a bill, you are in a far better position when you have hard evidence backing you up.

Always save your bank statements and canceled checks (if you choose to have your bank send them back to you), and keep the check registry in your checkbook up-to-date. Try and save bank statements for at least three years. When you receive utilities, credit-card or other important bills, file them chronologically and **write the date you paid each bill on the statements**. You may even want to go so far as to write the number of the check you paid the bill with on the statement.

Having an old bill on file says very little if you are involved in an actual dispute, though. It's a thorough checking-account record that is really compelling, because it clearly shows when money left your account and for what. Unless you find that saving bills longer helps you feel more in control of your financial affairs, you really don't need to keep most statements around for more than a year.

Information about yearly income from stocks and investments should also be kept on file for tax purposes. Keeping good financial records is a critical step in whipping your whole financial house in order. We'll turn to the actual roof over your head in the next section.

Whoops!

If you make a mistake on your taxes, don't get hysterical. If you realize you've made an error on your tax return, the IRS gives you three years from the date the return was filed or two years after the tax was paid. The form you need to fill out is called the 1040X. By filling one out you will protect yourself from possible penalty and interest charges.

Perhaps the most terrifying word in tax land is AUDIT, which is when the IRS decides to pick on some poor soul and verify that everything represented on his tax return is correct. If you are audited, don't panic—if you've played the rules and kept good records, you have nothing to fear. Plenty of honest, hardworking citizens are audited by the IRS. In most cases, you'll be asked to come down to an IRS office, or you may receive a questionnaire in the mail. Sometimes the IRS comes to you—but usually only in serious cases. In the event of an audit, look over your tax return and go through your records to double-check everything on it. Don't get defensive or angry—be as cooperative as you can be, and ask why the audit is taking place.

Again, good financial records are your strongest weapon in an audit. You must save records of investments, business or job expenses, charity donations, insurance payments and income from freelance work or tips. Whenever you make a claim on a tax form, be able to back it up.

FINDING A ROOM OF YOUR OWN

Whether you are **kicked out** or **run away screaming**, eventually you ditch the nest. Finding a new place to hang out in your underwear can, depending on **where** you live and how **prepared** you are, be as **easy** as opening the Sunday paper, **or** it can feel like a barefoot march across **Siberia.**

Before you begin the search for new digs, **ground yourself** in a little reality. If you are wandering around with a **TV-induced fantasy** about what your first apartment should look like, you **are going to be brutally disappointed.**

This is especially true in large cities. You may have to live in a closet for a while, but at least it will be **your** closet, and your mother won't be sharing it with you.

1. (PA)RENTAL AGREEMENTS— MOVING IN WITH THE FOLKS

Recently a situation comedy debuted that featured a couple in late middle age whose grown sons all moved back into the house with them. It was canceled in a millisecond. Perhaps the concept was too depressing for most Americans to spend 30 minutes watching.

Many of us dread the idea of moving home. We'd rather have our heads shaved, or one of our ears lopped off. Maybe it's because parents have that diabolical ability to suck every ounce of maturity straight out of our bodies. You could be a Mafia hit man—sit down to eat Brussels sprouts and chicken pot pie with your family, and poof, you're six years old all over again.

You may not have enough money for your own place, or maybe just want to cool your jets before plunging into the job market, but even toying with the idea of sleeping over the garage brings on nightmares. You can see it now. There you are, forty years old, in a dirty undershirt, sitting in your parent's darkened living room watching George on *Seinfeld* reruns, beer cans, candy bar wrappers and dirty ashtrays littered all around you. What's that? Why, it's your mother shrieking from the kitchen. You can hear her now.

"WHY DON'T YOU GET OFF MY COUCH AND GET A JOB?!

I KNEW YOU'D NEVER AMOUNT TO ANYTHING, YOU STINKING BUM!" THE HORROR, THE HORROR.

What on earth happened? You who were once so bright, attractive and directed. Suddenly you became marshmallow boy.

Moving to a New Town

Break out. Be a pioneer. Don't live in the same patch of suburbia you tricycled around for the rest of your life. Picking a new pool of mud to wallow in will make you a more interesting person. It can also be a little nerve-racking. Reduce your butterflies by trying the following:

• Do Research Ahead of Time.
Call the Chamber of Commerce for brochures and maps, go to the library or a good bookstore to get local magazines and newspapers, and if you are online check to see if the community has a web site.

• Know the Local Housing Market in Advance.
This is critical. Look through local publications and talk to everybody you can. Make advance apartment-hunting trips if you can afford to.

• Make Contacts.
Talk to as many people from the area as you can. Don't know anyone at your destination? Ask everyone you know if they know anyone. If you are a member of any associations, churches, synagogues or alumni clubs, you might try to see if they can hook you up with local contacts. The more people you know in advance, the less alone you feel. And your contacts may be able to help you find an apartment, job and a wealth of community resources when you arrive.

• Volunteer.
Along with joining a church, this is a very fifties, very effective, way to meet people in a new community. But there are also loads of contemporary causes you can get involved with on your Saturdays. There are more volunteer and charity organizations in most communities of any size than you can shake a tin cup at. From the junior league to Big Sisters to Amnesty International, from Habitat for Humanity to Do Something to the Audubon Society. And then there are local museums, nature centers, political parties . . .

• Roam.
When you get to your new town, start walking. Walk everywhere. (Okay, if it's L.A., drive everywhere.) Try and hit every major tourist attraction, discover its neighborhoods. Read guidebooks and local histories. A city is never more romantic than when you first get to know it.

Go home? You'd rather join the French Foreign Legion.

All right, some people don't dread moving back in with their folks quite that much. But few find it all that appetizing, either.

Sometimes moving back home can make good sense. If you have no money for an apartment, if you are just starting a job search, if you simply need to sort out what it is you want to do with your life. More and more people are moving home simply out of economic necessity. The trick is to not make it a permanent arrangement.

Living with your family can mess with your head. You can get along great, but the fact that you are still sleeping under your *Star Wars* blanket can make you feel like a failure. Take a deep breath. You aren't stuck.

Set a date by which you will be out of the house. Structure your days—this is really important when you are at home—so that you feel you are making progress toward your goals and not sleeping until one in the afternoon and lounging on the sofa.

Get up when your parents do. Get out of the house as often as you can—it will help you combat depression. If you want to be treated like an adult, check yourself when you find yourself lapsing back into your junior high personality around your parents. Try and complete all those grotty little chores they want you to do without complaint.

You'll feel better about yourself if you feel like you are moving forward and not retreating from the working world. If you truly want to be, you'll be on your way sooner than you think.

2. APARTMENT SCROUNGING FINDING ELBOW ROOM WITHOUT LOSING AN ARM AND A LEG

You may already have had experience tracking down places to live by the time you enter the job market. It isn't brain surgery. Patience is the most important ingredient in a successful apartment search. Eventually, no matter how many cockroaches you look at or how many places are snatched right out from under you, you'll find a decent place to put your futon.

infested rattraps

NEWSPAPER ADS AND OTHER RESOURCES

Newspaper classifieds are still the most popular way to find apartments.

Popular is the key word here—every other person hunting for a place to live in the area is going to be looking at the daily paper, so if you see a good deal, act quickly. Before you launch into your search, start checking out the real estate section to get a sense of what rents are like. If you are moving to a new city, get a hold of the local paper before you pack up the Mustang. You'll know what the rents are like. Currently, in Cincinnati $500 will get you a very nice one-bedroom in town. In Manhattan, the same money may not cover the rent for a small cruddy room with a giant hole in the floor.

Often better than daily newspapers are neighborhood weeklies. Some of these are incredible sources for good cheap places to live. Get these papers as early as you can to beat the mad rush for the best deals. For example, if the paper officially comes out on Thursday but copies hit the stands late on Wednesday nights, get a copy that evening so you can make calls right away.

Bulletin boards in the areas where you want to live are another good source. If you have access to a campus housing office, check it out. People frequently list apartments through them. Unfortunately, you are often required to be enrolled in order to look at their listings.

Last, word of mouth is still the champion apartment-finding method. If you have friends in the area, work that grapevine. Ask them if there are any vacancies in their buildings, or if they know of any in the neighborhood. Your contacts will be able to steer you toward great deals, and away from buildings or landlords that are bad news.

REAL ESTATE BROKERS

Some newspaper ads are placed by individuals, others by **real estate brokers**. In some cases, the landlord pays the broker a fee when an apartment is rented. In others, you must pay the fee to the broker if you take the place—an amount that is often equal to one month's rent. Usually, realtors are upfront about identifying

themselves in classifieds, but sometimes they are sneaky and you won't know until you talk to someone on the telephone. Always keep a lookout for ads that say "no fee" when you are apartment hunting. You'll save yourself some significant change.

There are advantages to finding an apartment through a realtor. So if you can afford it, there's no reason to avoid them. In the first place, you may feel safer looking at places someone else has listed with a third party. Second, real estate people often have vast listings and can phone you immediately when an apartment comes on the market—before an ad goes into the newspaper. Watch for sharks, though. Especially in areas where there is a tremendous demand for housing.

There are all manner of realtors. Some deal mostly with cheap apartments for students and young professionals. Others are exclusively on the posh side of the market. You can contact a realtor directly, either by setting up an appointment or walking into her office. If you're prowling around a neighborhood you'd like to live in and see a real estate agency, pop in and start looking at the rents they have posted. They can be a good indication of whether it's an area you can afford or not.

Never walk into a real estate agency looking like dog meat and say you are in the market for an apartment. If it looks like you might skip out on your rent or trash a place, they may not help you or show you only the Z-list stuff. **LOOK NEAT AND PRESENTABLE FOR THESE PEOPLE.** Some of them are not exactly *enlightened* characters.

214

The Best Place to Live in America—According to The Places Rated Almanac

Looking for a new place to build your love shack? One of the most engaging resources to consult is The Places Rated Almanac, which rates 343 North American communities using an exhaustive selection of criteria that includes health care, crime rates, transportation, the arts, housing, jobs, climate and recreational activities. Some of the results may surprise you:

According to the most recent edition of the almanac, the most fabulous place to live in all of North America is:

Cincinnati, Ohio?

Yes, Cincy, the Queen City, Porkopolis, home of Skyline Chili, the Big Red Machine, Procter & Gamble, the Cincinnati Pops Orchestra, the University of Cincinnati Bearcats, and gamblin' Pete Rose.

According to the almanac, Cincinnati has just the right combination of economic opportunities and quality-of-life boosters to make it an urban oasis. So if you can take the muggy summers, southern Ohio just may be the place for you . . .

And out of hundreds of communities across the continent, which came in dead last? Well, that would be:

Yuba City, California.

Yuba City! Seat of Yuba County, er . . ., location of the Yuba County Airport, um . . ., not too far from Butte Sink National Wildlife Refuge, and just down the pike from Marysville . . .

Look, it's not all that bad. Really.

SCAM ARTISTS

Go to any place where there are large numbers of renters, and you'll get an equally large number of horror stories. Here is just one:

Maria was a young artist who had lived in a big East Coast city for two years—she thought she was the last person who could get taken for a ride. Searching frantically for new digs, she came across an ad that seemed to be a godsend. A large, cheap place in an elegant neighborhood. She called the owner, a grandmotherly type who said she wanted to rent her apartment to a nice young lady while she went on an extended holiday.

Maria arranged to see the woman's flat, and fell in love with its hardwood floors and high ceilings. She was also charmed by the sweet old landlady. The two agreed that Maria would move into the apartment the next month. As an act of good faith, the woman asked for a $300 security deposit up front. The night before Maria was to move in, she called the woman to find when a good time would be to come by. The woman wasn't home. Maria frantically tried the woman again and again over the next few days, and got no answer. With nowhere else to go, she was forced to put all of her things into storage and move in with a friend.

Finally the woman called to say she was sick, and unable to leave when she had planned. Could Maria wait another week to move in? She had no choice but to agree. Once again, Maria's move-in date came and went. The woman continued to dodge telephone calls.

It became obvious that the hag had no intention of moving out, or giving back the deposit. Maria went by the apartment to confront her. The woman didn't answer the bell, but a helpful neighbor broke the bad news. Maria had been had, and she wasn't the first.

Relocating—Won't You Take Me to Crunchytown?

You've heard of Crunchytown, right? Oh, maybe you know it as Granolaburg. There's a big university there, and a lot of people who haven't washed their clothes since 1968. The underground music scene was just written up in Details Magazine. It's a nuclear-free zone and its sister city is Managua, Nicaragua. There are a lot of great coffee bars around, a few shops specializing in Third World jewelry and vegetarian whole foods and a great bookstore run by a lesbian separatist collective. Never been? You'll love it.

Here are some hip little burgs with large numbers of young residents, some extra crunchola, some much less so:

- *Burlington, VT*
- *Amherst-Northampton, MA*
- *Chapel Hill-Durham, NC*
- *Santa Cruz, CA*
- *Cambridge-Somerville, MA*
- *Ann Arbor, MI*
- *Madison, WI*
- *Bloomington, IN*
- *Berkeley, CA*
- *Woodstock, NY*
- *Ithaca, NY*
- *New Paltz, NY*
- *Austin, TX*

and a few of the larger communities where you are sure to find many floppy-haired garage bands kicking around:

- *Minneapolis-St. Paul, MN*
- *Portland, OR*
- *Providence, RI*
- *That aging wellspring of much crunchitude, San Francisco, CA*
- *And the perennial fave . . . Seattle, WA*

This crone had pulled the same scam on a number of young women over the years. What's more, she was being evicted from the apartment she said she owned, for not paying rent. Maria was lucky. Eventually she got her money back.

BIG DISCLAIMER TIME, BEFORE WE HEAR FROM THE LANDLORDS' UNION.
The vast majority of people in the business of renting apartments are decent and honorable.

STILL AND ALL, BEWARE OF UNSCRUPULOUS REALTORS AND LANDLORDS.

Never give someone money up front. No matter how much you love the apartment, no matter how nice someone seems.
Nobody sees a penny until you have your mitts on a lease. Realtors are regulated by different agencies depending on the state. If you have a questions about the way you have been treated by one, go to the appropriate licensing authority.

Do not let yourself get sweet talked into an apartment. You are plopping down some serious money here. Before you talk to a landlord or realtor, have a sense of what the average rents are in the area. If what he has as an offer for the apartment you desperately covet seems wildly out of whack, he may be trying to snow you.

FOLLOWING UP ON A LISTING

If you see a listing you like, remember to call as soon as possible. A great apartment may be gone by the time you finish your morning coffee. Naturally you should only call when civilized human beings expect to receive phone calls—not at four in the morning.

When you call someone up to ask about an apartment listing, you are interviewing that person. If the landlord sounds crazy, she's probably crazy. If the person sounds like a con man, he may very well be.

Go with your gut.

Confirm the listed rent over the phone. Ask the person to describe the apartment, building and neighborhood in **detail**. Ask if there is a fee, a security deposit, and if utilities are paid by the landlord or yourself. If you still like the sound of things, set up a time to look at the flat.

INSPECTION TIME

When you go to check out an apartment, it's good to bring a friend along. Some landlords and realtors are slick high-pressure salesmen. They'll have you signing away your life for a rattrap before you can bat an eye. It's good to have someone there to run interference just in case. Even if you love an apartment, if you see it by yourself, come back with a trusted companion to look it over again. (Also, you might feel safer with someone accompanying you.)

When you are looking with roommates, never let one person find the apartment all by himself. Everyone must look the flat over, and discuss whether or not

they want to live there before they sign on. Try to see the place as a group if you can. And resist any pressure tactics to say "yes" on the spot.

Sometimes you have no choice but to rely on someone else's judgment. When a friend is looking for you both in a distant city, ask her to tell you about each apartment she sees over the telephone, and make sure she brings up any concerns you have with landlords and gets satisfactory answers. Be unpopular and veto her dream squat if you feel you must. It's better to fight with her now than get stuck in a place you hate.

To make an informed decision, test out everything in the apartment when you visit. Don't worry about appearing nosy or rude. Check all the lights and every tap in the house. Flush the toilet. Turn on the shower. Try all locks and latches. Look inside every nook and cranny. Open and close everything. Take note of how many stairs you'll have to walk up, and if your apartment faces the street, take note if it is on the first floor or it is near a laundry room or any other potentially noisy area. Is it near the garbage deposit, does it look safe?

If something is broken, get a commitment from the landlord to fix it **before** you move in. You may be charged for any damage to the apartment when you move out— make sure that you note every scratch and ding. Ask that the apartment be cleaned before you move in, and if it needs it, repainted.

Crime is everywhere, but moving to a big strange city can feel especially threatening. Don't take chances with your personal safety no matter where you live. Here are just a few ideas that can help you feel more at ease. As you grow more comfortable in your environment, you may decide some of them are a bit prissy.

Here is one rule that is a perennial: **keep your wits about you.**

Everything we do involves some element of risk, from getting a haircut to running naked at 3:00 A.M. through the worst part of town. You shouldn't be held hostage by fear, but your life and property are too important to take silly chances with.

- Check all the latches and locks in your apartment. Report any broken ones to your landlord ASAP.

- Ask your landlord or building manager exactly who, if anyone, may have access to your apartment.

- Always change the locks on your front door when you move into a new place. You don't know who's wandering around with the old key.

- If you live alone, make a copy of your keys to keep with a trusted friend or neighbor. Make it a policy to check in frequently with people. No matter what your living situation, do not hand out extra copies of your keys right and left.

- If you lose your keys outside your apartment, change the locks immediately.

- Be wary of ground-floor apartments. If you rent one, ask if window bars can be installed if there are none.

- Protect your belongings by investing in renter's insurance. It can cost around a couple of hundred bucks a year, and for that price, you protect your great CD collection, your television, stereo and designer wardrobe from theft, fire and other depredations.

- In multi-unit buildings, check the lighting in both the interior and exterior of the building. Take special note of elevators and stairwells.

- Avoid letting people you don't know into your apartment building. Watch out for people who come up behind you when you are at the door, and don't buzz strangers inside.

- If you leave your home for long periods at a time, consider installing a timer on your lights, and suspending any newspaper delivery. Have a friend house-sit and pick up your mail.

- Don't tell callers you are away from your apartment on your answering machine. If you live alone, consider saying "we" instead of "I" on your machine. The Queen does it, why can't you?

- Always carry your apartment keys where you can easily retrieve them. Don't throw them loose into a purse or backpack where you may have to shuffle for them late at night. Haven't you ever seen **any** TV cop shows?

- Avoid walking alone late at night. Stay off public transport at odd hours, but if you must take it, then ride near the engineer in an occupied car on the train or close to the driver on the bus, and wait for your ride in a well-lit area.

- If you go running, stay off isolated paths in quiet hours, try and run when there is ample light, keep to busy thoroughfares and wear reflectors on your clothing.

- In highly crowded situations where pickpockets may prowl, put your wallet in your front pocket where you can feel it. If you carry a purse or satchel, put your hand on it and wear the strap so that it crosses your torso. Wear your backpack backwards—so that it juts out from your chest, South American-style. You'll look like a dork, but if you're worried about losing something you are carrying, you'll be able to keep an eye on it.

- Ask local people where the safe and unsafe areas are. Believe them, even when they seem fine to you. After you truly get your bearings, you can make your own judgment.

- When you are lost, ask for directions. Don't be a macho jerk . . .

- . . .but even when you are in a totally unfamiliar neighborhood, look like you know where you are going. Go into stores to ask directions or to consult your map.

- If you leave a friend's house late at night, arrange to phone them as soon as you get home.

- If you are mugged, cooperate. Never fight for your possessions. Your life is worth more.

- Take self-defense classes, carry a whistle, do whatever it takes to feel more confident. But no matter what the NRA says, we still think it's plumb foolish to lug around a lethal weapon. You may hurt someone. And it could get turned on you. Check the facts— where there are guns, tragedy follows. (Didn't you see David Schwimmer as 4B in "N.Y.P.D. Blue"?)

. . . And in your Car

- Never park your car in poorly lit, isolated locations. Ensure that you have a safe, convenient place to park it.

- If you are rear-ended on an isolated stretch of road, do not pull over. Drive to a well-lit area with people around before you consider stopping the car.

- Car alarms get ignored. Look into other anti-theft devices. Nice tape players that can't be removed from your dashboard when you park may get removed anyway.

219

The Safest and Most Dangerous Cities in America— More Stats from <u>The Places Rated Almanac</u>

The Places Rated Almanac uses FBI statistics to get a picture of how safe or dangerous a community is. Here are the winner, and loser, according to the most recent edition:

And the safest city in America is:

Johnstown, Pennsylvania

Nestled between the metropolises of Pittsburgh and Altoona in the verdant hills of the Quaker state, Johnstown boasts a positively Swedish rate of 0.9 Johnstownians iced per 100,000 people.

Perhaps most famous for a great big messy flood, this community's 28,134 citizens can sleep easy knowing that their chances of being burgled, raped, robbed, beaten to a pulp or having their car window smashed in are far lower than the beleaguered inhabitants of:

Miami, Florida

Ah, pity poor sun-splashed, blood-spattered Miami. Where are Crockett and Tubbs when you need them? Sure, on the surface you might think it's a tad bit warmer and more glitzy than Johnstown, and, yes, Madonna and Sly Stallone live there, and, okay, there's all that beautiful art deco architecture. But is it worth a murder rate of 15.6? Yikes. Chew on that while you are rubbing in your tanning butter. And watch your back . . .

"One tip I give tenants is to take a photograph of any damage with the front page of a newspaper in the frame so that the date is clearly shown. That way the landlord can't pin the damage on you later."

—Bill Rowen, Board Member,
Met Council on Housing, New York

When you bump into one of your prospective neighbors, ask them how they like living in the building or neighborhood. Try and do this when the landlord or realtor isn't around. You'll get the honest poop. If you run into someone from the building while you're together and the landlord seems agitated or uncomfortable about you talking with this person, it could mean trouble. Maybe there's a side to living under his roof he doesn't want you to hear about.

CHECK OUT THE NEIGHBORHOOD

Here's a trick many people forget to pull in their rush to find a new place. Always see an apartment at night as well as in the day time. Many beautiful neighborhoods have a Jekyll-and-Hyde complex. When the sun is shining, things are great. When the sun goes down, all manner of freaker comes out of the woodwork.

Walk around your prospective neighborhood. How far is a grocery store and bank from your house? If there are no laundry facilities in your building, where is the nearest Laundromat? Is the area well lit? Is it close to public transport or a convenient, secure and cheap place to park your car? Ask local people if they feel safe in the neighborhood. Trust your instincts. If it feels dangerous to you, forget about it. You don't have to be an urban pioneer if you don't want to be. You should feel comfortable in your home.

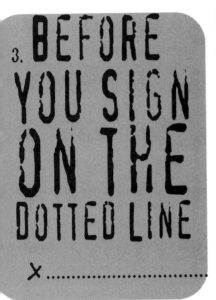

3. BEFORE YOU SIGN ON THE DOTTED LINE

X ....

When you agree to let an apartment, *you must have a lease for your own protection.* Some people think leases are **evil devices** employed by landlords **to rip you off. They are not.**

A lease is your contract with the landlord, outlining how much rent you will pay, how long you can stay, how many people are living in the apartment and any other special

agreements you make. Never move in without one, no matter how tempted you are. You'll be virtually defenseless against any action your landlord may take against you—including getting unceremoniously shoved out.

WHAT YOU MAY BE ASKED FOR

You often have to jump through an annoying number of hoops to rent an apartment, especially if you are young and have never rented before. This is especially true in large cities, but even in small towns, landlords are asking for some pretty thorough documentation from renters these days.

Make sure you have a couple of references handy in case a landlord asks for them. In most cases, this is just a formality, but there are paranoids out there who probably have your fingerprints sent to the FBI. Employers and previous landlords are ideal. Your landlord may also ask for the dates of your previous employment and contact numbers.

Unfortunately, the insidious credit report has thoroughly infected this whole business. Everybody is asking for these nowadays, so if you have a checkered history, come prepared to explain it. The landlord may even have the cheek to ask you to pay to have your credit checked.

Your age may also be a factor in whether a landlord will rent to you or not. In some cases, you may be asked to get a **guarantor** for your lease. This is always the case with minors, but it might also be required if you have a limited work history, bad credit, no credit, or just because you are young. Landlords ask for guarantors when they are unsure of your ability to pay the rent and want someone to promise to pay it in case you can't. Many successful, hard-working and cleannosed people are asked to supply guarantors, so don't get offended.

Landlords usually want parents to act as guarantors. But because of the nature of the agreement—"if my kid screws up, I cover everything"—many are naturally a little wary. If you can't get a guarantor, and the landlord won't waive the requirement, you'll have to kiss the apartment goodbye.

able to supply you with information about your landlord and reams of pamphlets detailing local laws that protect you from getting the shaft.

Unfortunately, whether you have access to the services of a tenant's association typically depends on if you live in an area with a high percentage of renters. People in rural areas or areas of high home ownership are at a distinct disadvantage. If you have a problem with your landlord, you may have to consult an attorney. Expensive, yes, but it's cheaper to consult one for an hour before a problem snowballs than to be dragged through small-claims court later.

> "The worst apartment-hunting experience i ever had was in Manhattan. i had to live in three different states before i found a place. when we did find a place we had to pay six months' cash in advance so the landlord wouldn't rent it to someone who earned eight times more than my roommate and i did. we were constantly turned down because we had no economic power."
>
> —Jen, 24, junior account executive

222

In areas where there is rent regulation—usually large cities, and woolly, Earth-shoe–wearing socialist college towns—you theoretically have more protection, and certainly more offices to wait in, during a dispute with a landlord. In other cases, you may have to sort out what local codes he may have violated on your own, or with a lawyer's help.

KNOW YOUR RIGHTS

If you are feeling overwhelmed by the whole process of renting an apartment, or are worried that your landlord may be taking advantage of you, check to see if your community has a **tenant's association** or other housing advocacy group. These people are devoted to protecting the rights or renters and will be able to explain what your legal options are.

In many cases, good advice is only a phone call away. They may also be

In any case, it's never a fair fight. Your landlord holds the ultimate trump card—the roof over your head. Know what your options are before you get into a tussle.

UNDERSTANDING YOUR LEASE

Leases are very frightening-looking documents, scripted in often impenetrable legalese. You may have difficulty understanding your lease the first time you read it. Despite that, you should understand the whole shebang before you sign.

Never skim over a lease. Your signature binds you to everything in the agreement.

Scary as that sounds, most leases are not chock full of sneaky clauses. They vary from place to place, but their terms are usually pretty standard. If you are confused about a point, ask for an explanation from your landlord. If you are not satisfied with an answer, you may want to have someone else look it over. Perhaps a representative of a tenant's association, or a lawyer.

Before signing your lease, make sure of the following:

- THE RENT AND OCCUPANCY DATES ARE WHAT YOU AGREED TO.

- IT IS CLEAR YOU ARE RENTING THE APARTMENT YOU HAVE SEEN—ITS ADDRESS SHOULD BE PRINTED ON THE LEASE.

- THE LANDLORD'S OBLIGATIONS ARE CLEAR—DOES HE TAKE CARE OF MAINTENANCE AND REPAIRS, OR DO YOU?

- YOU UNDERSTAND ANY SPECIAL POLICIES YOU ARE AGREEING TO ABIDE BY, SUCH AS A "NO PETS" RULE OR RESTRICTIONS ON NOISE OR CHANGES YOU CAN MAKE TO THE PROPERTY.

- YOU KNOW EXACTLY WHEN YOUR RENT IS DUE, IF THERE IS A GRACE PERIOD BEFORE IT IS OFFICIALLY CONSIDERED LATE, AND IF YOU MUST PAY ANY LATE FEES WHEN YOUR CHECK IS TARDY.

Try and get the landlord to send the lease to your work or old apartment; you can feel pressured to sign it too quickly at a landlord's office, while he's breathing heavily down your neck and rubbing his palms together. This way you'll have plenty of time to read through everything completely and ask for outside advice if you need it.

SECURITY DEPOSITS

When you hand over your lease, you will be forking over a lot of money. You will almost certainly have to pay your first month's rent on the spot, plus a security deposit. You may also have to pay your last month's rent as well. Get receipts for all funds that change hands.

A security deposit is usually meant to ensure that you don't skip out before your lease runs out, and to pay for any damage you do to the apartment. Typically, you get the deposit back in full when you move out, barring any wholesale destruction on your part. Know exactly what your security is meant to cover, and ask if the money will be put into an interest-bearing bank account. Some states require that it be held this way.

Your landlord cannot put your security deposit in his bank account or mingle it with other funds. If you are concerned that your landlord is fiddling around with your money, the best place to turn is the state agency that polices the world of security deposits, usually the Attorney General's office.

Just how much you pay in security varies from place to place. Frequently the deposit is one and a half month's rent; it all depends on where you live. If the security deposit seems outrageous to you, see if you can work something out. If you can't you might want to check and see if the landlord can legally ask for so much money up front, but it might be easier just to walk. You can't be asked to put up several months' rent at this point in your life.

Tacked on to your security deposit may be special nonrefundable recreation, maintenance and cleaning fees. You may also have to cover any possible havoc your mongrel may wreak with a pet security deposit. Ask for a thorough explanation of these or any other charges, if they are optional and, as *always*, get a receipt.

ROOMMATES ON YOUR LEASE

With very few exceptions, any adult who lives in your apartment should be on the lease. If you sneak another person in, and your landlord catches wind of it, he may try to throw you out. Getting evicted isn't funny. Always tell your landlord when a new person moves into the apartment.

It usually isn't a problem for someone moving into an apartment to inherit the remainder of the lease signed by a person moving out. When you leave a group apartment before a lease expires, make sure that your name is removed from all agreements and that all your deposits are returned to you.

SPECIAL CLAUSES

Pay attention to the special clauses in your lease. Many apartment buildings are quite strict about what kind of changes you can make to your apartment. Ask permission before you repaint the porch, sand the floorboards or knock out a wall. Your landlord has a right to know about any renovations that will drastically alter the way your living space looks.

There may also be restrictions on noise or pets. Don't try to get around a "no pets" rule by smuggling in your tabby. Go to the landlord and try and work something out. If you get caught with a contraband kitty, you could lose your home.

Make sure you understand when the landlord or building staff can enter your apartment, and if they have to give you any notice at all when they barge in to replace the toilet seat or rip out the ceiling. Most communities require that a landlord inspect the apartment to make sure it is fire safe and structurally sound before you take up residence. In emergencies, your landlord can bust right in without knocking.

BREAKING OR RENEWING YOUR LEASE

Some landlords are very nice about broken leases, others are downright Satanic. If you decide to leave before your lease is up, you must give your landlord plenty of notice. The exact length of time is generally spelled out in your lease.

Find out what legal ways there are to break a lease in your community.

In many situations, breaking a lease is no big deal if you come up with a substitute renter to fill out the terms of your agreement. Then the landlord isn't out any money, and you get your deposit back. In New York City, for example, a landlord cannot keep your security deposit if you provide a suitable replacement and he rejects that person. But if your guy is insolvent, or loopy, he can.

However, you may not be so lucky. Read the termination clause of your lease *very* carefully before you sign it. If you break your lease before it expires, not only do you risk forfeiting your security deposit, but also you may be taken to court for the balance of your rent, and in some areas charged a penalty known as a "reletting fee." You may also get collection agencies and lawyers sent down on you like a swarm of killer bees.

Check to see if your lease protects you from all manner of horrendous retaliation if you terminate it in certain cases. Examples might be a job transfer or a move into another building owned by the same landlord.

You may be able to renew your lease simply by staying put after it expires, or your lease may give your landlord the power to stop you from re-signing without explanation. You may be allowed a generous amount of time to gather your things and go, or you might be expected to be gone at the crack of dawn the day your agreement ends. In many cases, your rent will go up when you sign on for another year. Understand what the conditions are from the outset. Procedures for renewal depend on the agreement.

KEEPING IN TOUCH WITH YOUR LANDLORD

BEFORE YOU ARE **FRIGHTENED** OUT OF EVER ENTERING INTO ANY RENTAL AGREEMENT, REMEMBER THAT DESPITE A **HANDFUL** OF **PSYCHOS** AND **SCUMBAGS** OUT THERE, <u>MOST</u> LANDLORDS ARE **DECENT**, UNDERSTANDING FOLK. THE **BEST WAY** TO CLEAR UP **ANY** MISUNDERSTANDING IS TO **KEEP** THE LINES OF COMMUNICATION **OPEN** THROUGHOUT YOUR OCCUPANCY.

When you need something fixed in your apartment, need to break your lease or are going to be late with the rent, call the landlord immediately to let him know. If you are intending to have a platoon of Buddhist monks camp on the living room floor for six weeks, don't try and hide it, inform the landlord. Chances are he won't put you in a hammer-lock if you simply keep him posted.

Make Nice-Nice to Your Neighbors

If you thought not stepping on your roomie's toes was important, remember that enemies next door can make your life miserable. The last thing you want is to have some Gladys Kravitz-type in the neighboring apartment calling the cops on you every five minutes. Treat your neighbors well, and you'll have an extra pair of eyes watching out for you and your property. Here are a few tips that will keep border skirmishes to a minimum:

1. Be courteous—always greet your neighbors when you see them in the hallway of your building or on the street, never pretend like you don't see them (unless they are trying just as hard to pretend not to see you). If you borrow somebody's wrench, dish, milk, washing liquid or nail polish, return or replace it.

2. Do your neighbor favors—offer to carry groceries, hold doors, watch their property, baby-sit, water plants or feed pets while they are away. Remember, when you go away on your dream vacation you'll need someone to get your mail and water your plants, too.

3. Curb your mongrel—if your mutt poops on your neighbor's lawn, chases his cat, barks all night long or mauls his children, take measures to put him on the straight and narrow. Don't let your pooch roam loose, and consider a military obedience school.

4. No frat house hijinks—inform your neighbor when you are having a party, and break it up after midnight. Do not have more than two big parties a year, and spread your parties apart—no weeklong bacchanalian orgies. Parties stay inside the house or apartment, and do not flow onto lawns or into corridors. Respond immediately to any complaints made by your neighbors. And if your neighbor calls the police, don't firebomb her house. End the party right away and apologize to her. If it's the kind of party where your neighbors would feel comfortable, you can squash a lot of potential sour grapes by inviting them.

5. Silence is golden—you do not need to blast your stereo, especially after nine o'clock at night. If you are doing noisy household work, limit it to daylight hours, and only for a few hours a day. If you are working on an ear-splitting project, inform your neighbor in advance. In apartment buildings, vacuuming or other floor thumping can disturb your neighbors, as can loud televisions or slamming doors. When the sun goes down, be extrasensitive to others' ears. Keep your voice down — don't yodel or scream at the top of your lungs. And if your car has one of those rumbly good-ol'-boy mufflers, take steps to make it respectable again.

6. Be a model musician—some noises are so diabolical they get their own category. There is a special place reserved in Bad Neighbor Hell for players of trumpets, electric guitars, synthesizers, drums and other musical instruments. Mute yourself. Invest in noise-reducing technology. If you have to turn the volume up for any reason, do it for no more than an hour, in the daytime, after consulting with your neighbor. People can forgive almost anything, but not hours and hours of scales, or some wretch stumbling though his 700th stab at "Stairway to Heaven."

7. Keep up appearances— do the inside of your home in early dungeon if you want, keep the outside sparkling. No Black Sabbath posters on the front door, rusted Chevys and old refrigerators on the front lawn or chin-high grass. If you are renting a house and it's your responsibility to keep up the lawn and exterior, do it. If it's your landlord's, ask him to.

8. Watch your smells—stinky carries, especially in apartment buildings. Tobacco, pot, pungent food and incense can waft throughout your complex, assaulting sensitive nostrils far and wide. Open a window, blow a fan, keep things aired out. Take loads of dirty laundry, spoiled food and a musty-smelling dog, and you have an apartment that's a deadly weapon.

9. Invite a neighbor over—nothing charms most people faster than a little
hospitality. When you are the young kid who's just moved into a respectable bl
the neighbors will be impressed and reassured by your maturity and outstret
hand. You might want to ask them in for coffee, or send them a holiday card, ba
a whole mess of fudge. Martha Stewart would weep tears of joy. But use your
and don't make these kinds of overtures to creepy, scary neighbors.

10. Be a good neighbor to your neighborhood—get involved and become a p
of your community. Find a volunteer project in your area that you believe in
it might be an environmental or political group, reading to house-bound sen
tutoring children at a local school, helping someone with AIDS manage his sho
Check local community centers for more options, as well as churches, synago
local government agencies and charities.

11. "I'm sorry"—it does the trick. If you piss off your neighbor for the
or any other reasons, you can forestall a lot of aggro by using it.

One last thing. Hold your neighbor to equally high standards. When you ha
nuisance next door, don't be a doormat. Politely tell the person to turn the n
down if it bothers you, or ask them to keep their kid chained if he's peeing on
rhododendrons. Don't start screaming at neighbors, though—be calm when y
upstairs to tell someone they flooded your living room. If your neighbor i
thug or lunatic, consider informing the building management, the bloc
association or the cops.

4. PUCK-FREE COMMUNAL LIVING

The irony. You want to be out on your own, but in order to accomplish it you have to ask some other slob to move in with you. Roommates are a fact of life when you don't make enough money to comfortably pay the whole rent. If you snag a crackerjack housemate, your existence will be richer for it.

For one thing, living alone is isolating. You probably don't want to become some bizarre old character, holed up in an apartment with 17 cats and yellowed stacks of newspapers, playing lint hockey by yourself and scraping tuna out of old tins.

Sometimes flying solo can make you feel like you're on the way to becoming such a hermit. You find yourself not answering the telephone, or pretending you aren't home when the doorbell rings. A roommate can keep you in the loop, and force you to interact with the world around you.

The downside is you'll squabble over who ate all the Fiddle-Faddle, endure someone else's drunken friends coming over at three in the morning and clean a stranger's biological stains off the toilet seat. When you live with someone you hate, you can feel under siege in your own home. A tense living situation engulfs you in a sea of vexation.

In college, people are often thrown together with little or no concern for whether they are compatible or not. Almost everyone has a roommate-from-hell story in their past. Try and assert better judgment now that you are paying your own way. Avoid turning your hair white at an early age, and be extremely careful when you select a roommate.

This includes friends you have known since your Sit-and-Spin days. Some great friendships are completely wrecked by a decision to split the rent. If you adore your friend Shaniqua, but her obsessive love of Metallica drives you up a wall, don't ignore your fears and move in together to spare her feelings. Do you want Shaniqua's blood and brains splattered all over your hands? Of course not. You should be just as cautious about living with friends as with strangers. Maybe more so. You want them to be in your life for a while.

Successful group living demands a Gandhi-like attitude toward violence and the ability to compromise, compromise, compromise.

You don't have to become Bert and Ernie, but you and your roommate can learn to successfully coexist without eye-scratching and hair-pulling. However, if you can easily picture waking up one night with your future flatmate standing over you swathed in witchy robes, meat cleaver in hand, run.

FINDING A ROOMMATE

When friends fail you and you are forced to join forces with a stranger to find lodging, one place to start is a newspaper. Hopefully, you have seen enough horror movies to know placing and answering classified advertisements for roommates demands **caution**.

That said, thousands of people find shares this way and live to tell the tale. Most people out there seeking someone to share with are just as nice, clean-living and nervous about the process as you.

Community newspapers are the richest trawling grounds for roommates, but you can often find notices pinned to neighborhood bulletin boards, especially in student areas. Again, if you are taking college courses, check to see if you have a housing office at your disposal. They may have a screened list of people looking for bunkmates. If you are looking for someone to share your apartment, it's usually not a problem to place your listing with a local university even if you are not enrolled.

When you are the one with the empty room, finding a flatmate can be as easy as copying a few fliers with your number on strips at the bottom and hitting cafes, bus shelters and campuses in your neck of the woods. It's cheaper than placing an advertisement.

In both cases, you have no idea who you may be dragging in. You may not want every Tom, Dick and Ted Bundy calling you up at all hours, looking for a place to sack out. When placing an advertisement for a roommate, be vague about your address. Give the neighborhood, or a major street or landmark, but don't let anybody know exactly where you live until you are ready. If you are especially nervous about inviting a stranger to your place after only one telephone call, get the stranger's home/work phone number *first*, then arrange your first meeting at a neutral place, like a coffee shop.

You still have to **make your ad reasonably sexy**, though. "Bay Windows," "Close to Golden Gate Park," or "Three Blocks to DuPont Circle Metro Stop" are clearly going to get you more action than something that gives no details except the number of rooms, rent and everything you **don't** want in a roommate. You want to have people to choose from, not be stuck taking the only loony tune desperate enough to answer your plea.

ROOMMATE MATCHING SERVICES

Maybe you feel uncomfortable wading into the murky waters of roommate finding all by yourself. If so, you may want to use a service that links people with empty rooms to people hunting for a place to stow their pillow.

Such agencies stress safety and usually trumpet their thorough screening procedures. For example, one company in New York City gives an extensive compatibility quiz to clients and even maintains a rogue's gallery of people who have been blacklisted from ever using their service.

Roommate matching firms generally conduct preliminary interviews with both parties and then try and match people based on their interests and personalities. They usually ask for personal references. Still, it's not an exact science. No one can guarantee you a wonderful roommate.

The services aren't exactly cheap, either. It probably won't cost anything to list your apartment with a matching service, but if you are looking for a place to live, you can be out hundreds of dollars. Your peace of mind may be worth a steep fee. **But never hand a roommate service money unless they guarantee they'll find you an apartment within a set period of time, or grant you a refund if you are not satisfied.**

MEETING WITH A PROSPECTIVE ROOMMATE

Always talk for a little while with a prospective roommate on the phone before meeting face to face. Of course you want to know if the person smokes or owns a cat, and also what they do for a living. But more important, you are trying to get a sense of their character. Don't try to give someone the third degree, though. Nobody will want to live with you. You can find out a great deal simply by chatting casually for a few minutes.

When you visit a stranger's apartment, you might feel more comfortable dragging a good friend along. Your friend can give you an opinion of the place and your prospective roomie, and you can always use them to shield you from power saws, machine-gun fire and butcher knives.

All joking aside, trust your instincts. If you start for the door of a place, and you feel creeped out, turn around, walk back down the walk, and get in your car and drive. Even if you clicked with the person on the phone. Even if you think you are being ridiculous. **DON'T GET HUNG UP ON LOGIC WHEN INTUITION KICKS YOU IN THE KEESTER. BETTER SAFE THAN EMBALMED.**

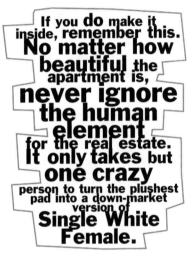

If you **do make it inside, remember this. No matter how beautiful** the apartment is, **never ignore the human element** for the real estate. **It only takes but one crazy** person to turn the plushest pad into a down-market version of **Single White Female.**

When you actually sit down together, you will really be able to check the other person out. If she's a pig, a nut or anal retentive, you'll probably hear little alarms going off. Once more, pay attention to them. Don't disregard a red flag because the skylight is tremendous or you can walk to work. Here are some famous last words: "Sure, she's a little kooky, but we don't have to hang out together all the time." Next thing you know, it's moving time all over again.

You may be paying the same rent, but the person who has lived in a flat longer may have pretty set ideas about the way the apartment should look and how tasks get done. If you feel you are going to have to wage a long struggle to overthrow her hegemony over every inch of public space, pass. Fighting constantly about fluffy pink throw pillows on the living-room couch or religious poems tacked up on the kitchen wall is exhausting business.

During your conversation with a prospective roommate, be frank about what you're looking for, any quirks you have, how you feel about visitors and the hours you keep. We are conditioned to be agreeable in uncomfortable situations. But if you love staying up at night and your roommate goes to bed at eight, you may rue the day you glossed over your differences in order to keep a roof over your head.

You are not initiating someone into the Tri-Deltas, however. Don't ask flaky questions like "If you were a tree, what kind of tree would you be?" or grill someone about their religion, politics or sex life. Nobody gave you license to be impolite.

That said, some sex matters should be up for general discussion. If you expect that your boyfriend will stay overnight frequently, bring it up. Still, the most important thing you should do is just shoot the breeze and get a sense of each other. It may be the beginning of a long friendship.

Then again, when you know immediately that the arrangement will not work out, politely say so. You'll be saving the other person a lot of precious time. Don't let someone badger or beg you into changing your mind. You will be very, very sorry you did. Refusal to take no for an answer is a good window into that person's soul—just picture the shower scene in *Psycho* and move on.

Take time to sort things over before committing to live with a stranger. Handle the situation as you would a job interview.

SET UP A TIME TO TALK OVER THE TELEPHONE IN A FEW DAYS, AND KEEP TO THAT DATE. THERE ARE FEW THINGS RUDER THAN BLOWING SOMEONE OFF. IT'S SPINELESS AND LOATHSOME. BE A STRAIGHT SHOOTER— TELL THE PERSON IF YOU'VE CHOSEN SOMEBODY ELSE.

You may have met with 17 different people. Just the same, call each one up and inform them of your decision. It doesn't matter if you were looking for a room or trying to fill one. Courtesy is a two-way street.

MOVING INTO A GROUP SHARE

If one crazy roommate isn't bad enough, a houseful of them is an excursion to Jonestown. If you are considering moving into a flat with multiple roommates or a group house, you should meet **everyone** living there before you come on board. They may have locked Puck in the attic when you came to see the place, but as soon as you unpack your things, there he'll be to annoy and torment you, rifle through your sock drawer and flick scabs into your clam chowder.

Group houses have their own particular groove, and it's often rough to be the outsider. You may not want to be the one person in the place who is not a vegetarian, ice-climbing beautician. If everyone else has been chummy since kindergarten, you may feel as if your opinions don't carry as much weight in house affairs.

Obviously, you want to avoid situations where you might be ignored or tormented by a clique of nasty roommates. If you hit it off with members of the house, group living can be tremendous fun, but forget privacy. Make sure you ask about noise, who cleans things up, when and how bills are split up between flatmates. Dirty, messy, noisy chaos all the time quickly becomes hellish.

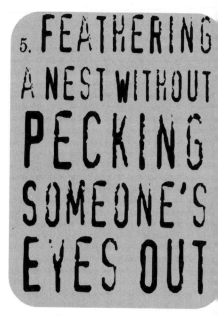

5. FEATHERING A NEST WITHOUT PECKING SOMEONE'S EYES OUT

Why can't we all just get along? Because we are all nasty, selfish, bitchy little creatures, that's why. Except maybe the Amish, but they don't get running water.

It takes serious effort to peacefully coexist with another human being. You can be sweet as a Hostess Fruit Pie at work, but your cheery facade will start to crack by the end of the day. When you come home exhausted, sometimes all you want to do is lie down on the couch and zone out for two hours.

Instead, right there, in your face, a mere two inches from it in fact, is your *roommate*, blasting his diabolical Jamie Walters CD as he polishes off your cheese doodles.

God sent this person to test you.

Outside of a few fascist dictators bent on global domination, there are few people you can't get along with if you really try. When your lease ends you can burn your roommate in effigy. In the meantime, put away all sharp objects.

Hopefully, you've picked someone to live with whose interests and tastes are at least somewhat similar to your own. Someone you maybe even like, at least a little. But you really don't have to strangle a complete opposite.

Really.

SORRY TO SOUND LIKE A SELF-HELP BOOK FROM 1978, BUT YOU WILL GET ALONG BETTER WITH YOUR ROOMMATE WHEN YOU COMMUNICATE. YOU KNOW, RAP, CARE, SHARE, HUG, INTERFACE, BROTHER MAN. FROM DAY ONE, COBBLE TOGETHER SOME HOUSE RULES. TALK OUT PROBLEMS WHEN THEY CROP UP INSTEAD OF PUTTING EX-LAX IN SOMEONE'S COFFEE.

Arguments are going to happen, but they'll be less explosive if you talk frequently and openly about your concerns. Set aside the odd evening to eat hoagies, watch a Schwarzenegger movie and talk house business. A little of that caring, sharing, feeling nonsense from the Me Decade is helpful if used in extreme moderation.

Learn to bend a little. You can't have everything just the way you want it.

You need your own place for that and you obviously don't have the money. Until you do, you are going to be living with somebody who has different ideas. Make some adjustments for the greater good. Turn the music down. Vacuum once a week. Smoke on the porch. Whatever. Don't turn your flat into the former Yugoslavia. Compromise.

Respecting personal space, another phrase coined in the feathered hairdo era, is equally important. Don't invade your roommate's privacy. Okay, you may be tempted to dress up in her Holly Hobby sweatshirt and take pictures with friends when she's out of the house, but it's definitely not on. Stay out of her stuff. Respect closed doors. Don't blast the stereo when she's sleeping. You might want to agree to give the other the entire apartment alone for an occasional weekend, or give him a quiet evening with his honey. In case you thought you were free of bothersome rules once you fled your mother's house, here are a few tips to conflict-free communal living. Think of them as a road map to communal harmony—ignore them and you are zooming down the highway to roommate hell:

1. Clean Up Your Act
Listen up you grungy little stinkberry: sloppiness is rude, rude, rude. That's right, you heard us. Get those dirty tube socks out of the living room and rinse your crusty cereal bowl before leaving it in the sink. And if you are a fella, for pity's sake, lift up the toilet seat, put it down when your business is through, and wipe away any little reminders of your visit.

2. Don't Be Catty
If you discuss your problems, they won't fester. When your roommate does something that irks you, tell him, *not your best friend*. This is a diabolical tar baby. Start complaining about him, and pretty soon everything he does is obnoxious. Next thing you know, you are working with a voodoo doll and a lock of his hair.

3. Don't Eat Her Food
We all get weak once in a while, and those mint Milanos look awfully good . . . Be strong. Go buy your own cookies. People get **very** touchy about their food. When you lose it and reach for her Doritos, go replace them. And don't drink all the milk and put the carton back in the fridge with just a tiny swallow left. You aren't fooling anyone, you know. That milk thing can get you killed.

4. Don't Borrow His Things Without Asking
Ever. Even if he is out of town. Not his chocolate velour body suit, not his pink Power Ranger doll, not even his vintage Magic Eight Ball. *Nada*. People who ask usually receive, but never grab without asking.

5. Share
People should never go rifling through your Milanos without permission, but offer your roommate some cookies, you insufferable miser. Let her use your CD player, or borrow your sweater. Buy the pizza once in a while. You certainly don't have to give up everything, but try to be generous. You'll be more popular.

6. Declare a Truce in the Great Television and Stereo War
She loves *Singled Out*, your favorite series is *X-Files*. You like to listen to Patti Smith, she thinks TLC speak to America's youth. Don't do the adolescent sneer thing and ridicule her taste, or resort to the "it's-my-television-so-I-get-to-decide-what-to-watch" thing. Grow up, and agree to disagree. If you have to, set some rules about when the stereo gets played, and who gets to watch what when.

DITCHING A NIGHTMARE ROOMMATE

"You know what I get the most calls about here? Not landlord-tenant disputes but roommates trying to get rid of each other. One roommate has locked the other out of the apartment, or the like. People who really hate one another, I mean murder is definitely on the table."

—Bill Rowan, Met Council on Housing

234

Sometimes, despite your best efforts, you get a monster. Things not only don't work out, but you have to sleep with your door locked. Ditch a scary roommate as fast as you possibly can. Go to your landlord and explain the situation. Risk losing your deposit if you have to.

When you are **working** all day like a dog, the last thing you need is to come home to **threats, screaming and terror. No apartment is worth it.**

Hopefully, your roommate won't be a pain in the keester, and you can settle snugly into your new home. And your new life, for that matter.

Register to Vote in Your New Home

When you move to a new community, you should switch your registration as soon as possible. A state will not allow you to vote in an upcoming election unless you registered a set number of days before it—sometimes ten days, but sometimes several months in advance. Contact your local board of elections or city or county clerk's office to find out where you can register. If, for in-state tuition or other reasons, you intend on keeping your old state as your residence, contact your local officials back home for an absentee ballot in advance of an important decision.

And if you are going to be a jerk and not vote at all, just remember that one day jack-booted storm troopers could rip off the door of your apartment, drag you screaming into the street and kick your face in. See if anyone helps you then. That's what you get for spitting on democracy.

YOUR PICTURE HERE

6. SETTLING IN FOR THE LONG HAUL

If you made it this far, you are definitely on your way. To where is entirely up to you.

Okay, you'll probably fall face first into a few piles of steaming muck on your ascent ever upward, but you'll be able to deal with that. There will undoubtedly be times when you'll worry that you're becoming a job slave, that life has gotten a bit crunchy and stale. You will have apartments you hate and roommates you love, bosses that take you under their wing and those that just ride you, and there will never be enough money. Embrace the good where you can find it and try and cut out the bad as quickly as you can. That's success.

Remember one of the first tips in this book, and probably the most important: **Resist the urge to** constantly **compare your-self to others.** You are on your own clock, racing against yourself. And you can stop your clock whenever you want, change directions, reevaluate, decide to join the Moonies or grab the keys to the executive suite.

Don't reduce your life to a numbers game, or a status game. It's easy to fall into, and it's an empty way to live, in case you haven't guessed. It's also not very appealing to be around. Just because you're working hard and paying rent and bills is no excuse to **CHECK OUT**. You still have hours to volunteer, write a few poems, keep in touch with old friends, plan a bicycle trip across the Himalayas, campaign for the cause of your choice, and organize the junior league charity sale.

Chances are you'll feel less weary if you keep your irons in other fires besides money and career. That's the gravy on this mortal coil. Give them up and you'll be sorry. You're opting to become a stiff, which is a choice, not an inevitability. Having your own life is essential to getting a life, if you catch our drift.

USE YOUR VACATION DAYS. PLAY HOOKY ONCE IN A WHILE— RENT A FEW MOVIES, GET UNDER THAT COMFORTER, AND

PUT IT ALL OUT OF YOUR MIND. **WAY OUT.**

One last thing. As you get your feet wet in the adult world,

keep a **sense of humor.**

Life is pretty absurd most of the time. When you run into some suspendered, slick-haired, power-tied dude in a blue suit yapping on and on about "the organization" and "networking" and "the learning curve," don't let your insides turn to mush and your heart flutter over whether or not you are making the grade. Laugh at the silliness of it all. All the empty lingo and tips don't mean anything unless at least a fraction of your heart is in what you do.

So off you go. Charge out there like the light brigade. Jump at every opportunity, pay your dues, keep laughing and keep your cool.

And you'll make it after all.

J.D. Heiman lives and writes in New York City.

CREDITS: Archive Photos: 9, 43 (Express Newspapers), 51, 52 (Darlene Hammond), 57 (Lee), 59, 65, 74, 87 (David LaChapelle), 95, 105 (Pvt. Glenda Ashley), 113, 115 right, 128, 166, 182 top, 227; **Courtesy Carol Bobolts:** 84 left, 145; **Courtesy Fredrik Broden:** 11, 17, 71, 119, 133, 139, 140, 162, 181, 208, 237; **Courtesy Adam Chiu:** 4, 5, 39, 88, 115 left, 136, 137, 141, 210, 211, 216, 223 left, 238; **Ewing Galloway:** 15, 16, 93; **FPG International:** 85 (Mark Reinstein), 102 (Telegraph Colour Library), 106 (Ron Chapple), 108 (Telegraph Colour Library), 110 (James Porto), 171 top (Kent Knudson), 172 (Jeffry Myers), 175 (Spencer Grant), 190 bottom (Jeffrey Sylvester), 213 (Bruce Byers), 214 (Dick Luria); **Graphistock:** 22 (Edward Spiro), 29 (Guy Aroch), 75 (Jose Molina), 182 bottom (Neal Brown); **International Stock:** 112 (Vincent Graziani), 143 (Patrick Ramsey), 163 (Frank Grant), 236 (Peter Langone); **Photofest:** 7, 84 right (Nels Israelson), 118 (Capital Cities/ABC Inc.), 161, 174; **Photonica:** 24 (Paul Taylor), 64 top (Kei Muto), 66 (Paul Taylor), 124 (P. McDonough), 190 top (Marc Tauss), 207 (Keyvan Behpour), 223 right (Joe Squillante); **Spots On The Spot!:** 8 (Christophe Vorlet), 18 (Bill Russell), 26 (M.E. Cohen), 41 (Alison Seiffer), 45 (John Margeson), 64 bottom (Steve Gray), 67 (Peter Hoey), 80 (John Margeson), 153 (M. E. Cohen), 199 (Robert); **Superstock:** 31, 37, 116, 129, 202, 229

For orders other than by individual consumers, Pocket Books grants a discount on the purchase of **10 or more** copies of single titles for special markets or premium use. For further details, please write to the Vice-President of Special Markets, Pocket Books, 1633 Broadway, New York, NY 10019-6785, 8th Floor.

For information on how individual consumers can place orders, please write to Mail Order Department, Simon & Schuster Inc., 200 Old Tappan Road, Old Tappan, NJ 07675.